CAMBRIDGE
UNIVERSITY PRESS

Cambridge Lower Secondary
Science

LEARNER'S BOOK 9

Mary Jones, Diane Fellowes-Freeman & Michael Smyth

CAMBRIDGE
UNIVERSITY PRESS

Shaftesbury Road, Cambridge CB2 8EA, United Kingdom

One Liberty Plaza, 20th Floor, New York, NY 10006, USA

477 Williamstown Road, Port Melbourne, VIC 3207, Australia

314–321, 3rd Floor, Plot 3, Splendor Forum, Jasola District Centre, New Delhi – 110025, India

103 Penang Road, #05–06/07, Visioncrest Commercial, Singapore 238467

Cambridge University Press is part of the University of Cambridge.

It furthers the University's mission by disseminating knowledge in the pursuit of education, learning and research at the highest international levels of excellence.

www.cambridge.org
Information on this title: www.cambridge.org/9781108742863

© Cambridge University Press & Assessment 2021

First published 2013
Second edition 2021

20 19 18 17 16 15 14 13 12 11 10

Printed in Malaysia by Vivar Printing

A catalogue record for this publication is available from the British Library

ISBN 978-1-108-74286-3 Paperback with Digital Access (1 year)
ISBN 978-1-108-74287-0 Digital Learner's Book (1 year)
ISBN 978-1-108-74288-7 eBook

〉 Introduction

Welcome to Stage 9 of Cambridge International Lower Secondary Science. We hope this book will show you how interesting and exciting science can be.

Science is everywhere. Everyone uses science every day. Can you think of examples of science that you have seen or used today?

Have you ever wondered about any of these questions?

- How do scientists plan experiments to find out if their ideas are correct?
- Why do people all look different from each other, even though we all belong to the same species?
- Why do elements react to form compounds?
- How can we increase the rate at which a reaction takes place?
- Where are stars formed?
- How can two sounds result in silence?

You will work like a scientist to find answers to these questions and more. It is good to talk about science as you investigate and learn. You will share your ideas with classmates to help them understand, and listen to them when you need reassurance. You will reflect on what you did and how you did it, and ask yourself: 'would I do things differently next time?'

You will practise new skills and techniques, check your progress, and challenge yourself to find out more. You will make connections between the different sciences, and how they link to maths, English and other subjects.

We hope you enjoy thinking and working like a scientist.

Mary Jones, Diane Fellowes-Freeman, Michael Smyth

› Contents

> How to use this book

This book contains lots of different features that will help your learning. These are explained below.

This list sets out what you will learn in each topic. You can use these points to identify the important topics for the lesson.

In this topic you will:

- discover that thermal energy always transfers from hotter places to colder places
- understand what is meant by heat dissipation.

This contains questions or activities to help find out what you know already about this topic.

Getting started

1 Thermal is an energy store. List as many other types of energy store as you can remember.

2 Choose two of your energy stores. Describe how the energy can be changed between these energy stores.

3 Describe what is meant by dissipated energy.

Important words are highlighted and explained in the text when they first appear in the book. You will also find definitions of all these words in the Glossary and index at the back of this book.

Key words

chlorophyll   light intensity   photosynthesis

You will have the opportunity to practise and develop the new skills and knowledge that you learn in each topic. Activities will involve answering questions or completing tasks.

Activity 3.1.1

Densities of some regular objects

In this activity, you will calculate the densities of some different materials, using the mass and volume of regular objects.

You will need:

- a balance, a calculator, a ruler that can measure in millimetres, some regular objects made from different materials.

Method

1 Measure the length, width and height of each object. You should measure to the nearest 0.1 cm.

2 Calculate the volume of each object in cm³.

3 Measure the mass of each object in grams. Remember to check that the balance is reading 0.0 g before you place the material on the balance.

4 Calculate the density of each material using the volumes and masses

This provides an opportunity for you to practise and develop practical skills with a partner or in groups.

Think like a scientist

Densities of irregular objects

In this investigation, you will calculate the densities of irregular objects.

You will need:

- a balance, measuring cylinders of various sizes, water, a calculator, small irregular objects that will sink in water and will fit inside the measuring cylinders

Safety

Do not drop heavy objects into glass measuring cylinders; either use a plastic measuring cylinder, or hold the glass measuring cylinder at an angle, so that the object slides down slowly.

Method

1 Use the displacement method to calculate the volumes of your objects in cm³.

2 Measure the mass of each object in grams. Remember to check that the balance is reading 0.0 g before you place the material on the balance.

3 Calculate the density of each material using the volumes and masses that

After completing an activity, this provides you with the opportunity to either assess your own work or another student's work.

Self-assessment

For each of these statements, decide on how confident you are.
Give yourself 5 if you are very confident and 1 if you are not confident at all.

- I understand how to calculate the volume of a regular object.
- I understand how to calculate the volume of an irregular object.
- I know the equation for density.
- I can use density to predict whether an object will float or sink in water.

This contains questions that ask you to look back at what you have covered and encourages you to think about your learning.

The carbon cycle is a complicated diagram. What can you do to help you to remember it?

This list summarises the important ideas that you have learned in the topic.

Summary checklist

- ☐ I can describe what is meant by density.
- ☐ I know the equation for density.
- ☐ I can use the equation for density and can calculate density, mass or volume.
- ☐ I know how to use density to predict whether an object will float or sink in water.

At the end of each unit, there is a group project that you can carry out with other learners. This will involve using some of the knowledge that you developed during the unit. Your project might involve creating or producing something, or you might all solve a problem together.

Project: Load lines

Background

Load lines, sometimes called Plimsoll lines, are painted on the sides of many ships. The picture shows an example of load lines.

The load lines are on the side of a ship, half way between the front and the back.

When cargo or passengers go onto a ship, the ship goes further down into the water. The load lines show how far down a ship can be in water and still be safe. The letters stand for different types of water and different conditions.

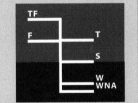

Your task

Find out what the letters on the load lines stand for.

Use a block of wood to model a ship. You will prepare different water conditions and test how your model floats in each. Your water conditions will model those

These questions look back at some of the content you learnt in each lesson in this unit. If you can answer these, you are ready to move on to the next unit

Check your progress

3.1 Which of these is the correct equation to calculate density?

Give **one** letter. [1]

A density = weight × volume

B density = $\dfrac{\text{mass}}{\text{volume}}$

C density = $\dfrac{\text{volume}}{\text{mass}}$

D density = $\dfrac{\text{weight}}{\text{volume}}$

3.2 Which statements are true about the density of air?

1 Photosynthesis and the carbon cycle

> 1.1 Photosynthesis

In this topic you will:

- practise using the word equation for photosynthesis
- learn what photosynthesis is, how it happens and why it is important.

Getting started

Look at the pictures of the young maize (corn) plants. The plants on the left have been given light, but the ones on the right have not had light.

You may also be able to look at some actual plants that have been grown in the light and in the dark.

With a partner, make a list of the differences you can see between the two sets of plants.

Suggest what has caused these differences.

Key words

chlorophyll   light intensity   photosynthesis

How plants make food

Plants make food by **photosynthesis**. 'Photo' means 'light'. 'Synthesis' means 'making'. So photosynthesis means 'making with light'.

Activity 1.1.1

Words beginning with photo-

Work in a team.

In two minutes, write down as many words as you can think of that start with 'photo'.

The winning team is the one which has thought of the most words – but only if they are all real words, and are spelt correctly.

What does each word have to do with light?

In photosynthesis, plants use:

- water, which they get from the soil

- carbon dioxide, which they get from the air

- energy, which they get from sunlight.

The energy in sunlight is captured by a green pigment, called **chlorophyll**, which is inside some of the cells in the leaves of plants.

The plants use the energy to make the water and carbon dioxide combine together in a chemical reaction.

Two new substances are made in the reaction. These are glucose and oxygen.

You can write the word equation for photosynthesis like this:

water + carbon dioxide → glucose + oxygen

Photosynthesis happens in the leaves of a plant. You will find out more about this in the next topic.

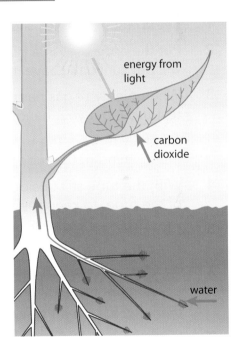

Questions

1 What are the reactants in photosynthesis?

2 What are the products in photosynthesis?

Think like a scientist

Collecting the gas produced in photosynthesis

You are going to use a plant that grows in water for this experiment.
This makes it easy to collect the gas that it releases.

You will need:

- the apparatus shown in the diagram.

If you do not have any pond water, you can use ordinary tap water.

You can use any plant that grows under water. You can often buy water plants in pet shops, because people like to put them into tanks with their pet fish.

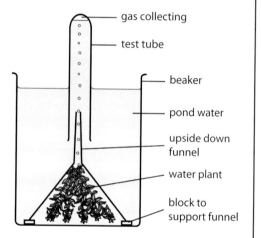

gas collecting
test tube
beaker
pond water
upside down funnel
water plant
block to support funnel

Method

1   Set up the apparatus shown in the diagram.

2   Put the apparatus in a place where the water plant will get sunlight. Leave it for at least one day.

3   When plenty of gas has collected in the top of the test tube, put your hand into the beaker of water.

   Carefully remove the tube from the top of the funnel. Keep the opening of the tube under the water, or the gas will escape!

4   With the tube still upside down, put your thumb over the end of the tube, to keep the water and gas inside.

5   Take the tube out of the water, keeping your thumb over the end. Keep the tube upside down.

6   Very carefully, move your thumb just a little bit, so that the water runs out of the tube but the gas stays inside. Push a stopper into the tube, then place it – right way up – in a test tube rack.

7   Light a splint, and then blow it out so that it is glowing but not burning.

8   Test the gas with the glowing splint. (Try not to touch the wet sides of the test tube, or the splint will be extinguished!)
   If the gas contains a lot of oxygen, the splint will relight.

Questions

1   Explain why it was best to use a water plant in this experiment.

2   Explain why it was important to leave the apparatus where it would get plenty of sunlight.

Think like a scientist

Investigating how light intensity affects the rate of photosynthesis

Like the previous experiment, this experiment uses a water plant.
You are going to change the amount of light that falls onto the
plant and see how this affects the number of bubbles it produces
in one minute.

You will need:

- a test tube containing water, a piece of water plant, a lamp, a beaker in which you
  can stand the test tube, a ruler for measuring the distance between the lamp and
  the test tube, a timer.

Safety

It is very important to keep electrical wires, plugs and the
lamp away from the water.

Method

1. Set up your equipment. Place the lamp close to the
    test tube. Leave the equipment like that for about
    5 minutes, to give the plant time to settle down
    and start to photosynthesise.

    While you are waiting, read the rest of these
    instructions and then draw a results chart.

    When you can see bubbles coming from the cut end of the
    plant stem, you can start your experiment.

2. Measure the distance between the lamp and the test tube,
    and write it down in your results chart.

3. Start the timer. Count how many bubbles the plant produces
    in one minute, and write this down.

4. Repeat step 3 two more times.

5. Now move the lamp a little bit further away from the test tube.
    Measure the new distance.

6. Repeats steps 3 and 4.

7. Repeat steps 5 and 6 for at least two more distances of the
    lamp, further from the test tube.

Continued

Questions

1 Calculate the mean number of bubbles for each distance of the lamp from the test tube.

2 Plot a graph of your results.

   • Put distance of lamp from the test tube on the x-axis.
     Remember to include units.

   • Put mean number of bubbles per minute on the y-axis.

   • Plot your points as small, neat crosses.

   • Draw a line to show the trend in your results.

3 **Light intensity** means the amount of light. Copy and complete this sentence:

   As the distance of the lamp from the test tube increases, the light intensity ....

4 Now write a conclusion for your experiment, by copying and completing this sentence:

   As the light intensity increases, the rate of photosynthesis ....

Peer assessment

Exchange your results chart with a partner (not the person who worked with you on your experiment).

How well did they construct and complete their results chart?

Give them a mark, from 0 to 2, to show how well they did on each of the five statements below:

   0 if they did not try, or you think they could do better

   1 if you think they did quite well

   2 if you think they did it really well

• They drew a results chart using a ruler and pencil, so that it was easy for you to read.

• They wrote a heading for the distance of the lamp from the plant, including units.

• They wrote a heading for the number of bubbles per minute.

• They included a column or row for the mean number of bubbles per minute.

• Overall, it was really easy to understand everything in the results chart.

If you gave your partner two marks for everything, the best possible score would be 10. How many marks did you give them out of 10? If it was less than 10, explain to them what they could do better.

If you were asked to draw another results chart in the future, how could you do it better?

Activity 1.1.2

Photosynthesis and respiration

In Stage 8, you learnt about respiration.

Think about each of these questions on your own.
Then turn and discuss them with your partner.

- What similarities are there between photosynthesis and respiration?

- What differences are there between photosynthesis and respiration?

Now share your ideas with the rest of the class.

Why is photosynthesis important?

First, photosynthesis provides energy, in the form of chemical energy in nutrients, for most other organisms.

Plants use the energy in sunlight to make glucose and other carbohydrates. These carbohydrates contain some of the energy that was originally in the sunlight.

Think about what you have learnt about food chains. When animals eat food, they get some of the energy that was captured by plants. Most of the energy in all the food in the world comes from plants. A food chain shows us how this energy is passed along from one organism to another.

The second reason that photosynthesis is so important is that it provides oxygen for the Earth's atmosphere. Animals and plants, of course, need oxygen for respiration.

Oxygen is a waste product of photosynthesis. It is released from the leaves of plants and mixes with the other gases in the atmosphere. About 20% of the air around us is oxygen.

When the Earth was first formed, about 4.6 billion years ago, there was almost no oxygen in the Earth's atmosphere. Scientists think that oxygen first began to collect in the air when bacteria first began to photosynthesise. (There were no plants at that time – they did not appear on Earth until about 4.7 million years ago.)
If photosynthesis had never begun on Earth, then no animals would ever have been able to live here.

Questions

3   The picture shows a lizard eating a grasshopper. Grasshoppers eat grass.

Explain how the lizard relies on photosynthesis to provide it with energy.

4   Explain one other reason (apart from food) why the lizard would not be able to survive if there were no plants on Earth.

Summary checklist

☐   I can write the word equation for photosynthesis.
☐   I can explain that photosynthesis is the way that plants make carbohydrates, using energy from light.
☐   I can explain why photosynthesis is important for most life on Earth.
☐   I can collect results carefully, and record them in a chart that I design myself.
☐   I can use my results to make a conclusion.

> 1.2 More about photosynthesis

In this topic you will:

- find out where photosynthesis happens in plants
- learn why plants need magnesium and nitrate.

Getting started

Look at a complete plant – one that has stems, leaves, flowers and roots.

1 In which parts of the plant do you think photosynthesis happens?

2 Why do you think photosynthesis happens there?

3 Why do you think photosynthesis doesn't happen in other parts of the plant?

Key words

fertiliser

stomata (singular: stoma)

yield

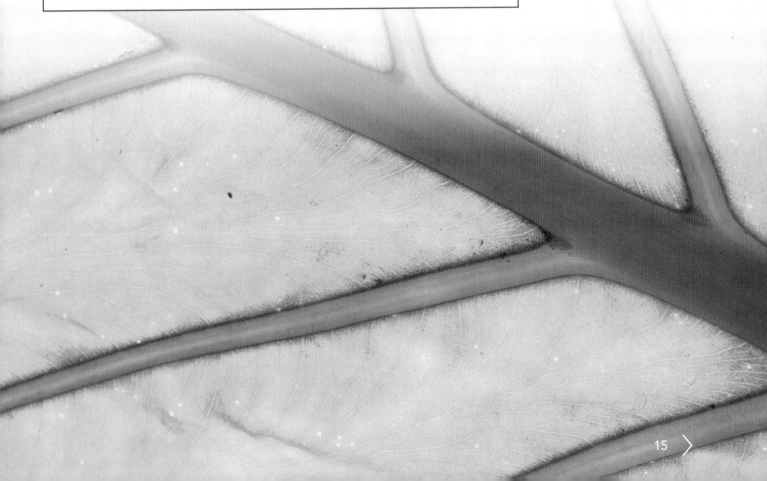

Chloroplasts and chlorophyll

In the previous topic, you saw that chlorophyll is essential for photosynthesis. Chlorophyll captures energy from sunlight. The energy helps water and carbon dioxide to react together.

Chlorophyll is kept inside chloroplasts, inside plant cells.

This means that photosynthesis happens inside chloroplasts. Not all plant cells have chloroplasts, so not all of them can photosynthesise.

In most plants, the cells in the leaves have the most chloroplasts. Inside the cells in a leaf, carbon dioxide and water are made to react, to produce carbohydrates and oxygen. We can think of the field of lettuces in the photograph as a giant carbohydrate factory.

On warm, sunny days, plants can make more carbohydrate than they need to use immediately. So they store some it for use later on – perhaps at night, or at a time of year when there is less sunlight. Plants store carbohydrates as starch. They store the starch inside the chloroplasts in their cells. One way to check whether a leaf has been photosynthesising is to test it for starch.

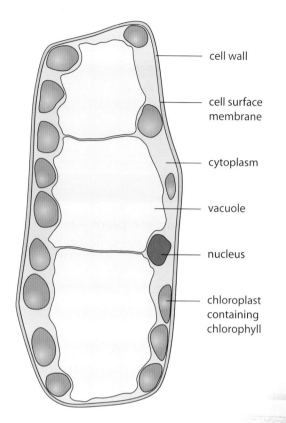

cell wall

cell surface membrane

cytoplasm

vacuole

nucleus

chloroplast containing chlorophyll

Think like a scientist

Testing a leaf for starch

You are going to use a test you may already know – the iodine test for starch – to find out if a leaf has been photosynthesising.

You will need:

- a healthy plant that has been kept where it gets plenty of sunlight (if possible, use a plant whose leaves have some green parts and some white parts), a burner (e.g. a Bunsen burner or a spirit burner), a tripod and gauze, a medium-sized beaker (e.g. 250 cm³), a large test tube that can be safely heated, some ethanol, tongs or another way of handling a hot test tube, forceps (tweezers), some iodine solution with a dropper, a tile.

Safety

- You will be using hot water, so make sure you keep safe. It is best to stand up while you work, so that if something is spilt you can easily move away.
- Be very careful to turn off the flame before you use any ethanol. Ethanol is very flammable (it catches light easily).

Method

1 Put some water into your beaker. Stand the beaker on the tripod and gauze and heat it until it starts to boil.

2 Take a healthy leaf from the plant. Carefully drop it into the boiling water.

3 After about two minutes, turn off the burner. This is really important, because you will use ethanol in the next step.

4 Collect some ethanol in the large test tube.

5 Use forceps to remove the leaf from the hot water. Carefully drop the leaf into the ethanol in the test tube.

6 Stand the test tube in the hot water. This will safely heat the ethanol. Watch what happens. You should see the green colour dissolve out of the leaf into the ethanol.

7 When you think most of the green colour has come out of the leaf, use forceps to gently take the leaf out of the tube. Be very careful – the leaf will be brittle. Dip it into the warm water to soften it.

8 Spread the leaf out onto a tile. Use the dropper to spread iodine solution over the leaf. If the leaf contains any starch, it will go blue-black.

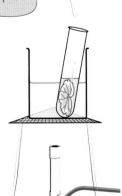
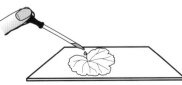

Continued

Questions

1   Iodine solution cannot get through cell membranes.
    Boiling the leaf breaks the cell membranes apart.

    a   In which part of a cell is starch stored?

    b   Explain why it was important to boil the leaf before the starch test could work.

2   Suggest why it is a good idea to remove the green colour from the leaf before you add iodine solution to it.

3   Did the leaf contain starch? If so, explain where the starch came from.

4   If your leaf had some green parts and some white parts, which parts contained starch? Can you explain why?

Inside a leaf

Photosynthesis happens inside chloroplasts, which are inside some of the cells in a leaf.

The diagram opposite shows a magnified view of the inside of a leaf.

On the diagram, you can see that chloroplasts are mostly inside the cells in the middle layers of the leaf. Leaves are very thin, so it is easy for sunlight to reach these cells.

Chloroplasts also need plenty of water and carbon dioxide, because these are used in photosynthesis. Water is brought to the cells in the leaf along the veins. You can read more about this in Unit 4.

Carbon dioxide diffuses into the leaf from the air. If you look at the diagram, you can see that there are tiny holes in the leaf, which allow gases to diffuse in and out. These holes are called **stomata** (singular: **stoma**). The gases can easily diffuse through the air spaces between the cells inside the leaf.

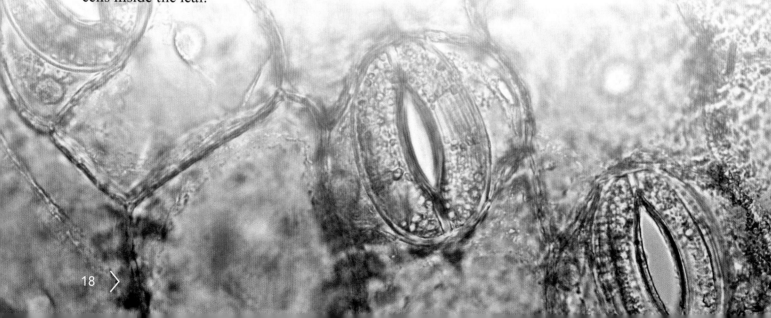

The diagram on the right shows what a leaf looks like if you cut it across, and then look at the cut edge.

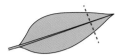

Leaves are so thin that it is difficult to imagine they contain several layers of cells. It is the cells in the middle of the leaf that carry out photosynthesis.

A **waxy layer** on the leaf surface stops the leaf cells from drying out.

The **upper epidermis** protects the cells inside the leaf.

The **palisade layer** contains cells that do most of the photosynthesis.

The **spongy layer** has lots of air spaces. The cells in the spongy layer do a small amount of photosynthesis.

A **vein** carries water to the cells in the leaf.

The **lower epidermis** protects the cells inside the leaf.

A **stoma** (plural: stomata) is a tiny hole in the lower epidermis. These holes let carbon dioxide from the air get into the leaf.

Activity 1.2.1

Which surface of a leaf has most stomata?

Work with a partner for this activity.

Put some warm (not hot) water into a beaker or glass.

Take a fresh leaf, and push it down under the water.

Can you see any bubbles coming out of the leaf? Which surface of the leaf do most of the bubbles come from?

Discuss these questions with your partner.

- What do you think the bubbles contain?

- If most bubbles came from one surface of the leaf, why do you think this happened?

- Think about what you know about the effect of increased temperature on gases. Can you suggest why the bubbles came out of the leaf when you put it into warm water?

Questions

1   The cells inside a plant leaf use up carbon dioxide when they photosynthesise. Use what you have learnt about diffusion to explain how carbon dioxide diffuses into the leaf.

2   The cells inside a plant leaf produce oxygen when they photosynthesise. Suggest what happens to this oxygen.

Minerals and plant growth

The farmer in the picture is adding **fertiliser** to a field of wheat.

Farmers add fertiliser to their fields because it makes the crops grow larger and produce a higher **yield**. Yield is the quantity of crop that the farmer harvests.

Fertilisers contain minerals. Like the minerals that we need in our diet, plants need only quite small quantities of minerals. They get these minerals from the soil, through their roots. But sometimes the soil does not contain enough of certain minerals. This stops the plants growing to their full potential.

Two important minerals for plants are magnesium and nitrate.

Magnesium is needed to make the green pigment, chlorophyll. If a plant does not have enough magnesium, its leaves look yellow instead of green. It cannot grow well, because it does not have much chlorophyll to absorb energy from sunlight, and so it cannot photosynthesise as much as it should.

Nitrate contains nitrogen atoms. These are needed so that the plant can convert carbohydrates to proteins. Proteins are essential for making new cells, so that the plant can grow well. Without enough nitrogen, leaves die and the plant stays small, like these maize (corn) plants. Nitrogen is also needed to make chlorophyll.

Farmers can test the soil in their fields to find out exactly which minerals are lacking in each part of the field. This tells the farmer where they need to add fertiliser, and where it is not needed.

Farmers who can afford the latest technology can use global positioning satellites (GPS) with their machinery.

The screen in the tractor cab shows the farmer exactly where he is in the field, as well as the results of the soil tests. The farmer can easily control how much fertiliser is added in each part of the field.

Questions

3   All organisms need protein for growth. Compare the way in which plants obtain protein with the way that you and other animals obtain protein.

4   It can be difficult, even for an expert, to tell the difference between a plant that is short of magnesium, and one that is short of protein. Suggest why.

Think like a scientist

Planning an investigation into the effect of fertilisers on plant growth

You are going to plan an experiment to find out how fertiliser affects the rate of growth of duckweed.

You may be able to do your experiment after you have planned it.

Duckweed is a tiny plant. There are lots of different species of duckweed, and they grow in most countries in the world. Some kinds of duckweed have just a single leaf, while others may have little groups of leaves. The leaves float on the water surface. All duckweed plants have roots that dangle down into the water.

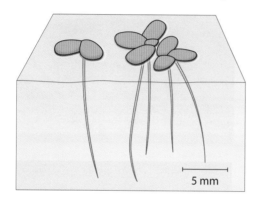 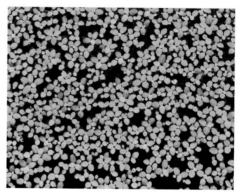

- You could investigate effects of different kinds of fertiliser, or you could use just one kind and try different quantities of it.

- You could grow your duckweed in small containers – for example, Petri dishes.

- You could measure how much the duckweed grows by counting the number of leaves.

Part 1: Planning the investigation

1 Decide on a hypothesis that you will test.

2 How will you change your independent variable?
How many different values will you use?

3 How will you measure your dependent variable?
How many times will you measure it?

4 Which variables will you try to keep the same?

5 What equipment will you need?

6 What risks might there be in your experiment? How will you control the risks?

7 Predict the results you would expect to find and explain why you think this is what will happen.

Continued

Part 2: Carrying out the investigation

Collect the equipment that you chose in your plan.

Make sure you have your step-by-step method to follow.

Questions

1   Scientists almost always find that they need to change something – even
    if it is only very small – when they carry out the experiment they have planned.
    Did you change anything in your plan? If so, explain what you changed, and why.

2   Write down a conclusion that you can make from your results.
    Do they support your hypothesis?

Summary checklist

☐ I can explain that photosynthesis happens in chloroplasts,
   because this is where chlorophyll is found.

☐ I can explain why plants need magnesium and nitrate.

☐ I can suggest a hypothesis, and plan an experiment to test it.

☐ I can make a risk assessment of my experiment, and carry out
   practical work safely.

> 1.3 The carbon cycle

In this topic you will:

- find out how carbon atoms move between the air, living organisms and fossil fuels

- bring together what you know about respiration and photosynthesis, to think about how they affect the amount of carbon dioxide in the atmosphere.

Getting started

Work with a partner.

Imagine one of you is a carbon atom. You are part of some carbon dioxide in the air.

Do you exist as an element, or are you part of a compound?

What happens to you when a plant uses you in photosynthesis? Do you change into something else, or are you still a carbon atom?

Key words

carbon cycle

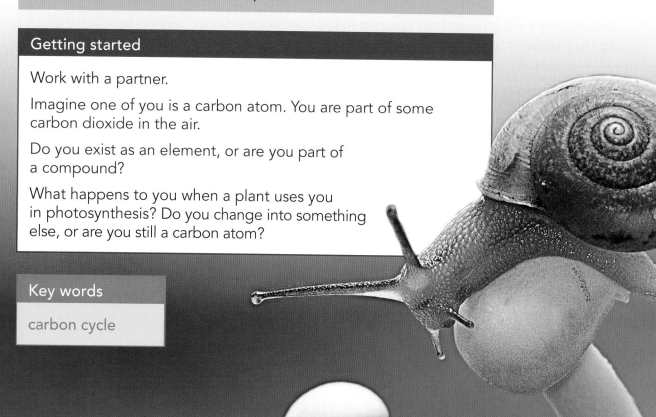

Carbon and living organisms

Carbon is an element. The symbol for carbon is C.

Carbon is a non-metal. It occurs naturally in different forms. (You will find out more about carbon in Topic 2.4.)

Diamonds are made of carbon.

The 'lead' in a pencil is not lead at all - it is another form of the element carbon, called graphite.

Living organisms do not need diamonds or pencil leads, but they do need carbon. Organisms cannot use carbon in the form of an element. They can only use it when it is part of a compound.

Carbon is part of many different compounds that make up cells. Carbohydrates, proteins and fats are all compounds that contain carbon.

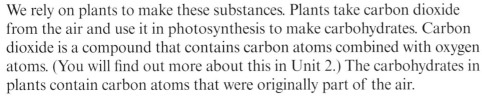

We rely on plants to make these substances. Plants take carbon dioxide from the air and use it in photosynthesis to make carbohydrates. Carbon dioxide is a compound that contains carbon atoms combined with oxygen atoms. (You will find out more about this in Unit 2.) The carbohydrates in plants contain carbon atoms that were originally part of the air.

Plants use the carbohydrates to make proteins and fats. All of these nutrients are compounds that contain carbon atoms.

We are animals, so we get all of these carbon-containing nutrients when we eat plants or other animals. Decomposers get their carbon when they break down waste products from plants and animals.

We can show how carbon gets into the bodies of animals and decomposers using a flow diagram.

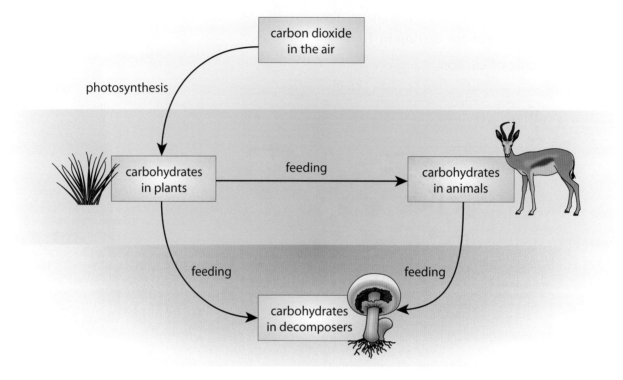

Questions

1   a   Draw a food chain with one plant and three animals in it.

    b   The arrows in your food chain represent energy passing from one organism to the next. Do they also show how carbon atoms pass from one organism to the next? Explain your answer.

2   The human body contains atoms of many different elements. Carbon is one of the most common elements. Name three different compounds in your body that contain carbon atoms.

Returning carbon dioxide to the air

A lot of the carbon dioxide that plants take from the air eventually goes back into the air again. This happens when plants and animal respire. You may remember the respiration equation:

glucose + oxygen → carbon dioxide + water

When you breathe out, carbon dioxide that was produced in your cells, by respiration, goes into the air around you.

All organisms respire. Plants respire all the time. At night, when they cannot photosynthesise, they give out carbon dioxide, just as we do.

Decomposers respire, too. As they break down waste products from plants and animals, they release carbon dioxide into the air.

We can add this information to the flow diagram.

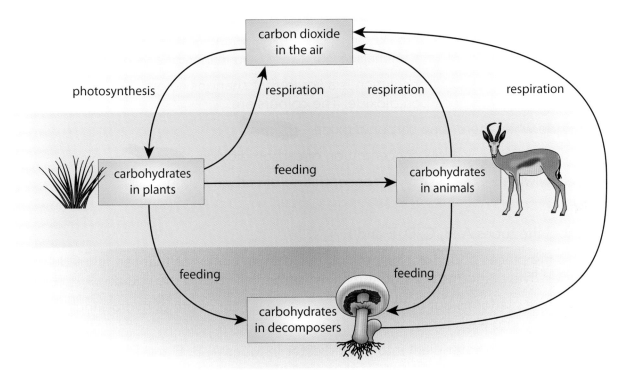

Think like a scientist

How do plants and animals affect carbon dioxide concentration?

In this investigation, you are going to think about two processes that you have learnt about – respiration and photosynthesis – and how they affect the concentration of carbon dioxide.

You will need:

- six clean test tubes, and a beaker or rack to stand them in, rubber bungs to fit the test tubes, small pieces of perforated metal (e.g. zinc gauze) to make platforms inside the tubes (see the diagram), some small pieces of water plant, some small animals such as maggots (fly larvae) or woodlice, blunt forceps (tweezers) for handling the plants and small animals, some black paper and sticky tape, some hydrogencarbonate indicator solution.

Note

The animals did not volunteer to be part of your experiment. Treat them with care. After the experiment is finished, put the animals back into their container, or a safe place outside.

Hydrogencarbonate indicator solution is a liquid that changes colour depending on the concentration of carbon dioxide. The colours are:

- purple when there is no carbon dioxide
- red when there is a low concentration of carbon dioxide
- yellow when there is a higher concentration of carbon dioxide

Method

1   Label the tubes A, B, C, D, E and F.

2   Use the pieces of perforated metal to make small platforms that can fit inside the tubes. The platforms will stop the animals from falling into the liquid.

3   Take the platforms out of the tubes. Pour about 3 cm depth of hydrogencarbonate indicator into each tube.

4   Put a piece of water plant into the indicator in tubes A, B, E and F.

5   Put the platforms back into the tubes. Try to make them level, with each one at approximately the same position in each tube.

Continued

6   Carefully place animals on the platforms in tubes C, D, E and F and fit the bungs.

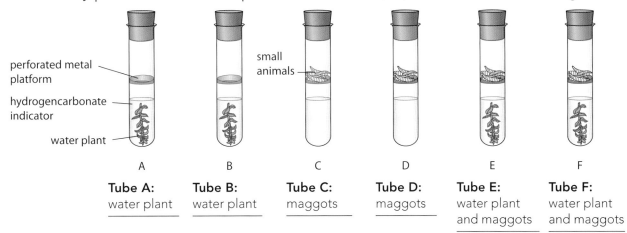

perforated metal platform

small animals

hydrogencarbonate indicator

water plant

A   B   C   D   E   F

Tube A:
water plant

Tube B:
water plant

Tube C:
maggots

Tube D:
maggots

Tube E:
water plant and maggots

Tube F:
water plant and maggots

7   Record the colour of the hydrogencarbonate indicator in each tube.

8   Now wrap black paper around tubes A, C and E, so that no light can get in.

9   Leave all the tubes in the same place for at least 30 minutes. (It is even better if you can set your experiment up in the morning, and then check it in the afternoon.) While you are waiting:

•   write down your prediction of the results you expect to find.

•   draw a results chart, ready to fill in.

10 Return to your tubes and take off the black paper. Record the colour of the indicator in each tube.

Questions

1   Use the colours of the indicator to record how much carbon dioxide is present in each of the six tubes.

2   All organisms respire all the time. In which tubes were organisms respiring?

3   Plants also photosynthesise when they have light. In which tubes were plants photosynthesising?

4   In the light, plants photosynthesise faster than they respire.

   a   In which tubes would you expect carbon dioxide to be used?

   b   In which tubes would you expect carbon dioxide to be given out?

5   Use your answers to the questions above to explain your results. (If your results do not match what you expect, try to suggest why they do not.)

6   Suggest why you were asked to put a little platform into each tube, even if there were no animals to put onto it.

Continued

Self-assessment

The instructions for this experiment are quite long.

How carefully did you follow the instructions?

How fully do you feel you understand why the indicator changed to different colours in the different tubes?

Fossil fuels and combustion

There is one more very important set of processes to add to the diagram showing how carbon moves from the air, through organisms, and back to the air again.

When organisms die, they are not always broken down quickly by decomposers. Sometimes, their bodies fall into places where there is no oxygen, such as deep in the ocean. In these places, the decomposers cannot respire, because there is not enough oxygen for them. Instead, the organisms' bodies get gradually buried, as more and more sediment builds up on top of them. High pressure and heat change their remains into fossil fuels, including coal, oil or natural gas.

Changing dead organisms to fossil fuels takes a very long time. Most of the fossil fuels that we use on Earth today were formed hundreds of millions of years ago.

Oil and natural gas formed when tiny marine organisms died and fell to the sea bed. This oil rig, in the sea off West Africa, has pipes that go deep into the sea bed where deposits of liquid oil are present. The oil is brought up through the pipes, and taken ashore to be used as fuel.

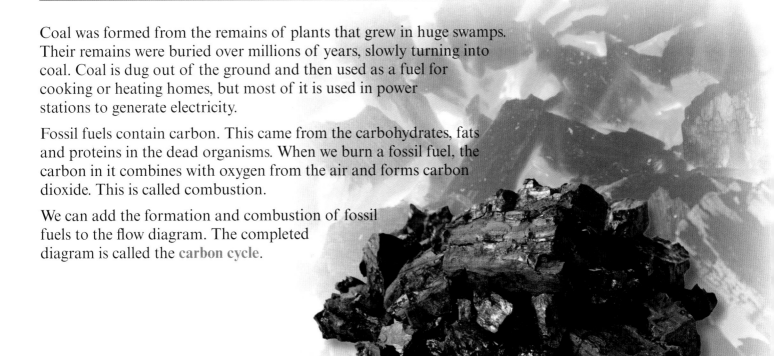

Coal was formed from the remains of plants that grew in huge swamps. Their remains were buried over millions of years, slowly turning into coal. Coal is dug out of the ground and then used as a fuel for cooking or heating homes, but most of it is used in power stations to generate electricity.

Fossil fuels contain carbon. This came from the carbohydrates, fats and proteins in the dead organisms. When we burn a fossil fuel, the carbon in it combines with oxygen from the air and forms carbon dioxide. This is called combustion.

We can add the formation and combustion of fossil fuels to the flow diagram. The completed diagram is called the **carbon cycle**.

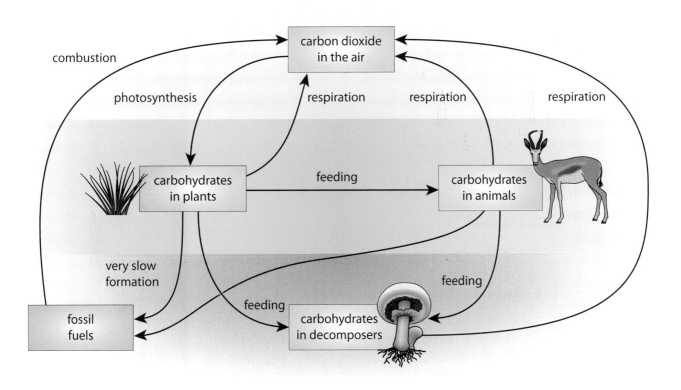

It is important to remember that fossil fuels are not the same as fossils. A fossil is the remains of an organism, or traces of it (such as its burrows) that have turned to rock. We can still see the shape of the organism in a fossil. But fossil fuels do not look like organisms at all, and oil and gas are not even rocks. Fossil fuels are given this name because – like fossils – they were formed a very long time ago and buried underground.

Activity 1.3.1

Modelling the carbon cycle

In this activity, you will play the part of a carbon atom in the carbon cycle.

First, make some big labels and stick them in five different places in the room. You only need one set of labels for the whole class.

IN THE AIR

INSIDE A PLANT

INSIDE AN ANIMAL

INSIDE A DECOMPOSER

IN A FOSSIL FUEL

Now write the following numbers and what they mean on the board, where everyone will be able to see them from every part of the room:

1 photosynthesis

2 respiration

3 feeding

4 formation of fossil fuels

5 decomposition

6 combustion.

Divide the class except one person (who could be your teacher) between the five places. Each person is a carbon atom.

The one person who is not a carbon atom now holds a die. (A die is a cube with the numbers 1 to 6 on it. The plural is dice.) They roll it, and call out the number. All the carbon atoms who are affected by the process linked to this number, move to

Continued

the correct place. For example, if the number is 1, then all the carbon atoms in the air move into a green plant, as a result of photosynthesis. If the number is 3, then all the carbon atoms in a green plant move into an animal.

You can keep a record of how many carbon atoms are in each place after each roll of the die.

Questions

1   In this model, all the carbon atoms in one place move to another place at the same time. Is that what happens in the real carbon cycle? If not, how could you modify this model to make it a better representation? If you can, try out your suggestion on your model.

2   Predict what would happen to the carbon atoms if one of the processes stopped completely – for example, combustion. If you can, try it out on your model.

The carbon cycle is a complicated diagram. What can you do to help you to remember it?

Questions

3   If you drew a carbon cycle to show what was happening before humans were present on Earth, how would it differ from the carbon cycle diagram above?

4   Explain why fossil fuels are non-renewable resources.

Summary checklist

☐   I can describe the carbon cycle, including photosynthesis, respiration, feeding, decomposition and combustion.

☐   I can explain how these processes affect the concentration of carbon dioxide in the air.

> 1.4 Climate change

In this topic you will:

- find out how the Earth's climate has changed in the past
- learn what happened when an asteroid collided with Earth
- consider how the increase in carbon dioxide in the atmosphere affects climate today and also in the future, and describe some of the predicted impacts of climate change.

Getting started

In Stage 8, you learnt how carbon dioxide concentration in the atmosphere has been steadily increasing. Carbon dioxide is a greenhouse gas, which traps heat energy in the atmosphere and keeps the Earth warm.

Look at this diagram. It is similar, but not identical, to one that you may remember.

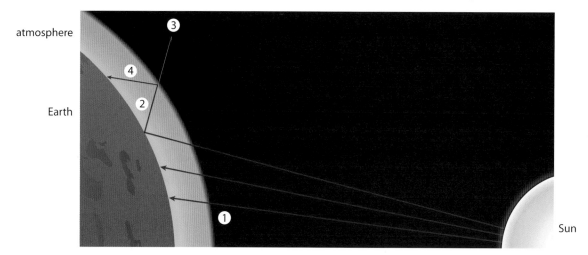

With a partner, match each of these statements to one of the numbers on the diagram.

A   Some of the reflected energy passes back out through the atmosphere and is lost to space.

B   Energy from the Sun passes through the atmosphere and warms the surface of the ground.

C   Some of the reflected energy is blocked by carbon dioxide in the atmosphere, so it stays close to the Earth.

D   Some of the energy that reaches the ground is reflected.

Key words

slush   mass extinction   meteorites   meteoroids   meteors

Greenhouse gases

Carbon dioxide and methane are 'greenhouse gases'. In Stage 8, you learnt how carbon dioxide helps to keep the Earth warm. Without any carbon dioxide in the atmosphere at all, the Earth would be a frozen place, unable to support life. But at the moment, we have too much carbon dioxide in the atmosphere.

Look back at the carbon cycle diagram in Topic 1.3. You can see that some carbon from the atmosphere ends up in fossil fuels. It takes a long time to form fossil fuels, and they can then stay buried in the ground for millions of years. But if we extract them and burn them, we release the carbon in them back into the air, in the form of carbon dioxide.

Carbon dioxide levels in the atmosphere are increasing. This is affecting the climate on Earth.

Climate change in the past

Climate is the long-term pattern of temperatures, wind and rainfall on Earth. The Earth's climate has been very different in the past compared to the climate today. Here are some examples of changes.

Ice ages

About 2 billion years ago, the Earth experienced the first ice age that we know about. Since then, the Earth has cycled between relatively warm periods and relatively cold ones. In the warm periods, there was no ice at all, even at the poles. In the colder periods, called ice ages, there was ice at the poles.

Snowball Earth

On at least one occasion, perhaps about 650 million years ago, the whole Earth was covered with ice and snow. Scientists call this 'snowball Earth', or sometimes 'slushball Earth', because they are not sure whether everything was completely frozen. (Slush is melting ice.) Scientists still do not completely understand what caused this to happen.

This is what the Earth may have looked like, 650 million years ago. At that time, the continents were not in the same positions as now.

Asteroids colliding with each other

Around 470 million years ago, scientists think that two asteroids collided with one another when they were in space, somewhere in-between Earth and Mars.

The collision produced huge quantities of dust. The dust reduced the amount of light and heat from the Sun reaching the Earth's surface. This triggered an ice age. The Earth became much colder – the ice caps spread much further from the poles and sea level fell.

Asteroids colliding with Earth

Around 67 million years ago, an asteroid collided with Earth. Researchers have identified an area on the coast of Mexico where the asteroid impact took place. There was huge devastation close to where the asteroid fell. It would have been like a massive bomb exploding, with shock waves and very high temperatures spreading out from the crater.

But the collision affected the whole planet, not just the surrounding area, because it threw huge quantities of rock and dust into the air. It would also have created a massive tsunami (a huge sea wave), which could have spread across all of the Earth's oceans.

The dust in the air meant that less light reached the Earth's surface. Plants could not photosynthesise, so animals had less food. As well as the disruption to food chains, the Earth became much colder, because less heat from the Sun could reach the surface.

Most scientists think that these changes in climate, caused by the asteroid impact, explain why dinosaurs became extinct around this time. Not only the dinosaurs, but also many other species on Earth, were destroyed as a result of the climate change following the asteroid collision. The asteroid caused a **mass extinction**. Up to three-quarters (75%) of all the species on Earth that were alive at that time are thought to have become extinct because of the asteroid collision.

There are about 175 known asteroid impact craters around the world. The crater shown in the picture is in the USA. The crater is more than 1 km wide and 170 m deep. It is estimated that the asteroid collision that formed this crater happened 50 000 years ago.

Could other objects collide with Earth?

Objects in space that are smaller than an asteroid are called **meteoroids**. When meteoroids enter Earth's atmosphere they are called **meteors**. Some people call meteors shooting stars because they appear like stars moving very fast across the sky. They usually present little risk because they burn in the atmosphere due to heat from friction. Some large ones can create shockwaves; in 2013 a meteor exploded over Russia and shattered windows. The parts of meteoroids that do collide with Earth are called **meteorites**. Around 500 of these reach Earth's surface each year.

If an object is large enough, it can cause local damage, or even damage that affects the whole planet.

In 1998, scientists started making detailed observations of objects that could possibly cause damage to Earth. When assessing the possible risk to Earth, scientists look at:

- the mass or diameter of the asteroid

- the closest possible approach to Earth.

An asteroid passing further from Earth may be a greater risk than one passing closer if its mass is greater.

The picture shows an asteroid, called 2006 DP14, that passed 2 400 000 km from Earth in 2014. This asteroid measures 200 m × 400 m so is considered a potential risk. An asteroid such as 2006 DP14 colliding with Earth would cause an explosion equivalent to about 20 million tonnes of explosives.

Questions

1 You learnt about asteroids in Stage 8. Describe what an asteroid is, and where asteroids are found.

2 Outline **three** different ways in which the asteroid collision 67 million years ago would have made it difficult for plants and animals to survive.

Climate change today and in the future

For the last 2000 years or so, our climate has been fairly stable. People living in different places have become used to having more rain at some times of year than at other times, or temperatures that change in a predictable way during one year. Knowing this helps people to choose the best crops to grow, and to know when they should sow seed and collect the harvest.

Now, however, the mean temperatures on Earth are increasing. This is caused by an increase in carbon dioxide concentration in the atmosphere. Remember that carbon dioxide is a greenhouse gas, which traps heat energy close to the Earth's surface. When carbon dioxide concentrations increase, more heat is trapped.

The graph shows how the Earth's mean temperature changed between 1880 and 2016. Notice that the *y*-axis on the graph does not show the actual temperature – it shows how much it differs from the temperature in 1880.

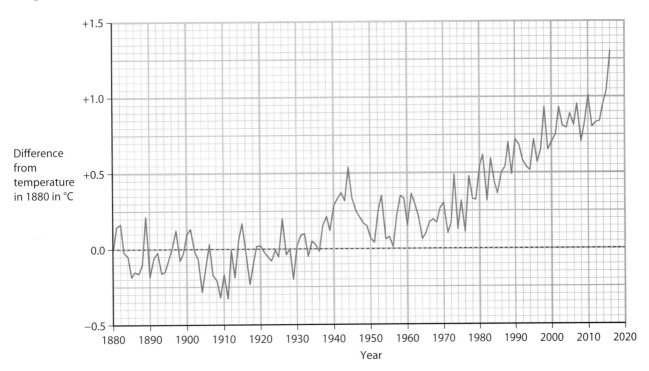

Questions

3   Look at the graph. How much higher was the mean temperature in 2016 than in 1880?

4   Describe the trend shown by the graph between:
- 1880 and 1910 and
- 1910 and 2016.

Impacts of climate change

More extreme weather events

We are already feeling the effects of this increase in temperature. The higher temperatures mean that there is more energy in the atmosphere. This increases the chance of extreme weather events, such as hurricanes and typhoons. Many scientists think that we are already seeing an increase in the number of storms, and in their severity. It is difficult to be certain, because there has always been a lot of variation each year in the number of big storms.

Tropical cyclone Idai hit the east coast of southern Africa in 2019. It was one of the worst storms ever to affect Africa and killed more than 1300 people. Severe flooding destroyed homes and fields, damaging people's livelihoods. Was this a result of climate change? We cannot say, because storms like this can happen anyway. However, there seem to be more of them now, and they are more violent.

Less predictable rainfall

The changing climate is also making it more difficult for people in some parts of the world to grow crops. Rains may come late, or might not come at all. Or rain may fall when it doesn't normally fall – or fall much more heavily, causing flooding.

Monsoon rains are usually welcomed, but not when they are so heavy that they cause severe flooding. In 2019, the monsoon rains in Pakistan, India, Nepal and Bangladesh came later and were heavier than usual. Millions of people in these countries were affected by floods.

When rains fail, people may lose their harvests. Long droughts also increase the risk of wildfires. All of these changes affect not only people, but also plants and animals.

This wildfire in Australia followed a long period of drought.

Rising sea levels

The increase in the Earth's mean temperature affects sea level. Water expands as it is heated, so if the sea temperature increases, sea level rises. Melting ice caps and glaciers add extra water to the oceans.

This glacier is getting smaller (retreating) as temperatures increase. The ice used to reach much higher up the sides of the valley.

Sea level has been rising at a rate of about 3 mm per year. Scientists estimate that more than 600 million people are at risk from flooding caused by sea-level rise by the end of this century. Many megacities are built on the coast – such as Shanghai, Mumbai and Los Angeles – and these are especially vulnerable to sea-level rise.

Questions

5   Calculate by how much sea level is predicted to rise by the end of this century.

6   Explain why sea level is predicted to rise.

Think like a scientist

How do rising temperatures affect sea level?

In this experiment, you will investigate how rising temperature can affect sea level.

Experiment 1

You will need:

- two large measuring cylinders, a funnel big enough to hold 10 ice cubes, 20 ice cubes all the same size.

Method

1   Put 10 ice cubes into one of the measuring cylinders. Add water so that the cylinder is about three quarters full. Record this level.

2   Add water to the second measuring cylinder to exactly the same level as in the first one.

3   Place the funnel in the second measuring cylinder. Put 10 ice cubes into the funnel.

4   Leave both cylinders at room temperature, until the ice melts.

5   When the ice has melted, record the new levels in both measuring cylinders.

Experiment 2

You will need:

- the apparatus shown in the diagram – make sure that the water is really cold, a lamp.

Method

1   Read the temperature on the thermometer, and the level of the water in the glass tubing. Record them in a results chart.

2   Place a lamp close to the conical flask and switch it on. The lamp will gently warm the water in the flask.

3   Approximately every five minutes (the exact timing does not matter), record the temperature and the level of the water in the glass tubing. Keep going until you have at least 10 readings.

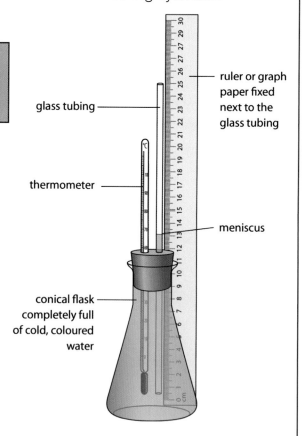

glass tubing

ruler or graph paper fixed next to the glass tubing

thermometer

meniscus

conical flask completely full of cold, coloured water

Continued

Method

4   Draw a graph to display your results. Put temperature on the x-axis and height of water in the glass tube on the y-axis. (Remember to include the units when you label the axes.)

Questions

1   Which of these changes increased the level of the 'ocean' in your experiment?
   • melting ice in the sea
   • melting ice on the land
   • increasing water temperature

2   How do your results relate to what might happen to sea level as a result of climate change?

Activity 1.4.1

The carbon cycle and climate change

Work in a group of three or four.

Look at the complete diagram of the carbon cycle in Topic 1.3.

Which activities *increase* the quantity of carbon dioxide in the atmosphere?

Which activities *decrease* the quantity of carbon dioxide in the atmosphere?

Use your answers to these two questions to suggest what we can do to help to slow climate change. Write a list.

With the other groups in your class, build up a list of suggestions. For each one:
• explain why it would help
• explain why it might be difficult to make it happen.

Summary checklist

☐ I can describe some examples of how the Earth's climate has changed in the past.

☐ I can explain how an asteroid collision is believed to have caused climate change and mass extinctions.

☐ I can explain how scientists predict climate change will affect the Earth in future, including rising sea level, more flooding, more droughts and more extreme weather events.

Project: What happened to the dinosaurs?

You are going to work in a group to contribute to a display about the extinction of the dinosaurs.

Choose one or more of these issues to research. Try to make sure that each group researches a different issue.

Issues to research

- Who first developed the idea that there was an asteroid impact that killed the dinosaurs? When did they put forward this theory, and what was their evidence?

- What do scientists think could have happened as a result of the asteroid impact? What is their evidence?

- Scientists think that other events may have contributed to the extinction of the dinosaurs. What are these events, and what is the evidence for them?

- How have the early theories changed over time? Why have they changed?

- Are dinosaurs really extinct? Some biologists think that a very familiar group of animals that live on Earth today are really dinosaurs. What are they, and why do biologists think this?

Doing your research

Use the internet to find information.

Before you begin, discuss in your group how you will choose the most trustworthy websites.

Here are some possible search terms you could try:

- dinosaur extinction event
- asteroid in the Cretaceous period
- Luis Walter Alvarez
- asteroid impact
- living dinosaurs.

Making the display

Work with the rest of the class to decide how the display will be made. For example, each group could produce a poster containing the results of their research. The posters could be displayed on the wall together. Alternatively, you could work together to create a multimedia class presentation.

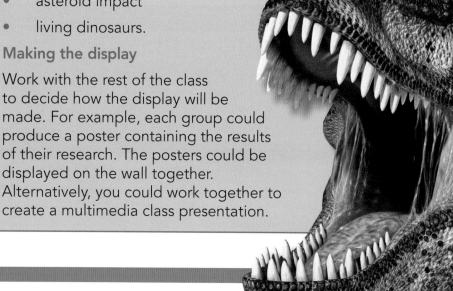

Check your progress

1.1 Choose the correct word from the list to match each description.
You can use each word once, more than once or not at all.

air   carbon dioxide   chlorophyll   chloroplast

oxygen   soil   stomata   veins

    a   This gas is used by plants in photosynthesis. [1]

    b   This gas is made by plants in photosynthesis. [1]

    c   Plants get their water for photosynthesis from here. [1]

    d   This green pigment absorbs energy from sunlight. [1]

    e   These tiny holes in a leaf allow gases to diffuse in and out. [1]

1.2 Marcus did an experiment to compare the rate of photosynthesis of two types of seaweed. Seaweeds are plant-like organisms that live in sea water.

The diagram shows the apparatus he used.

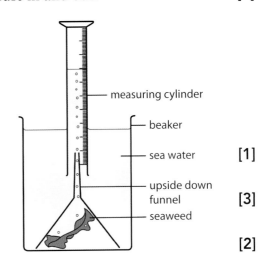

    a   What variable should Marcus change in his experiment? [1]

    b   List **three** variables that Marcus should keep the same. [3]

    c   What should Marcus measure during his experiment? [2]

1.3 A farmer carried out an experiment to find out how adding different quantities of nitrate-containing fertiliser affected the quantity of grain that she harvested from her wheat crop. The graph shows the results.

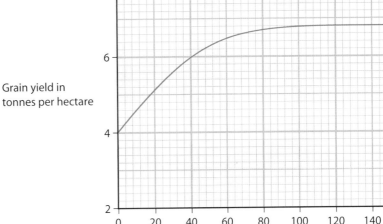

a What yield of grain did the farmer get when she did not add any fertiliser? [1]

b The farmer decided that there was no need to add more than about 60 kg of fertiliser per hectare. Explain how the results of the experiment support her decision. (Remember that fertiliser is expensive.) [2]

c Explain why the yield of grain increases when nitrate-containing fertiliser is added. [2]

d Suggest why the results of this experiment might be different if it was repeated in a different place. [2]

e Name **one** mineral, other than nitrate, that plants need for healthy growth. Explain why they need this mineral. [2]

1.4 The diagram shows the carbon cycle.

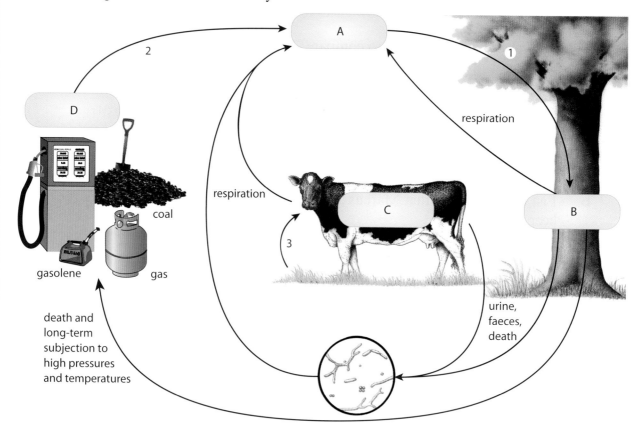

a Match each of these labels to the correct **letter** on the diagram.

i carbon in fossil fuels

ii carbon compounds in plants

iii carbon dioxide in the air

iv carbon compounds in animals [3]

b   Match each of these labels to the correct **number** on the diagram.

   i   feeding

   ii   combustion

   iii photosynthesis   [2]

c   Name **one** compound found in plants that contains carbon.   [1]

1.5 a Carbon dioxide concentration in the atmosphere is increasing.
       This is causing the Earth's climate to change.

       Choose the statements that describe predicted future impacts
       of climate change.

       • The mean temperature at the North and South Poles will decrease.

       • Sea level will rise.

       • There will be more extreme weather events, such as
         typhoons and hurricanes.

       • There will be less sunlight reaching the surface of the Earth.

b   In the past, asteroids have collided with the Earth. Scientists believe
     this has caused mass extinctions.

   i   Explain what is meant by a mass extinction.   [1]

   ii   Explain how an asteroid collision can cause mass extinctions.   [3]

2 Properties of materials

> 2.1 Atomic structure and the Periodic Table

In this topic you will:

- learn more about the structure of the atom
- learn how the structure of the Periodic Table is related to the structure of the elements.

Getting started

1 List the parts of an atom. Give at least one fact about each part.

2 Use the names of the parts and the information about them to write a description of the atom.

Be prepared to share your ideas with the class.

Key words

atomic number

electron shells

electronic structure

electrostatic forces

energy levels

mass number

Periodic Table

The Periodic Table

In Stage 8, you learnt about the first 20 elements and their symbols in the **Periodic Table**. Now you will learn more about the structure of the atoms of these elements.

	metals			1 — atomic number H hydrogen 1 — mass number							2 He helium 4
	non-metals										

3 Li lithium 7	4 Be beryllium 9						5 B boron 11	6 C carbon 12	7 N nitrogen 14	8 O oxygen 16	9 F fluorine 19	10 Ne neon 20
11 Na sodium 23	12 Mg magnesium 24						13 Al aluminium 27	14 Si silicon 28	15 P phosphorus 31	16 S sulfur 32	17 Cl chlorine 35	18 Ar argon 40
19 K potassium 39	20 Ca calcium 40											

- The atoms of the elements increase in mass as you progress from left to right (starting with hydrogen) and downwards in the Periodic Table. For example, an atom of hydrogen has less mass than an atom of sodium.

- Each element has an **atomic number**. This tells you how many protons it contains. The atomic number increases by one with every element.

- Each element has a **mass number**. This tells you how many protons and neutrons each atom in the element has in total.

- Protons have a positive charge. Electrons have a negative charge. Neutrons have no charge.

- An atom has no overall charge, because the number of protons is the same as the number of electrons.

Let's take a look at the metal lithium as an example.

Lithium (metal)

- Atomic number = 3
- Mass number = 7
- Number of protons = 3
- Number of electrons = 3
- Number of neutrons = ?

The atomic number tells you how many protons there are.

3

Li
lithium

7

The mass number tells you how many protons plus neutrons there are.

The mass number tells you that, for lithium, the number of protons and neutrons is seven. We know that there are three protons so we can work out that there are four neutrons (7 − 3 = 4).

The higher the mass number, the more mass the atom has. Hydrogen has an atomic mass of 1. Carbon has an atomic mass of 12. So, one atom of carbon has 12 times more mass than one atom of hydrogen.

Let's compare the mass of a piece of sodium measuring 1 cm³ with the mass of a piece of iron measuring 1 cm³. The mass of the piece of sodium is 0.97 g and the mass of the piece of iron is 7.87 g. The mass of the iron is more than the mass of the sodium.

This measure of the mass for a fixed volume of a substance is called the density. The density is given using the unit g/cm³.

The density of iron is 7.87 g/cm³ and that of sodium 0.97 g/cm³. So, iron is more dense than sodium.

For more information on how to find the densities of solids, liquids and gases and to compare them, see Unit 3, Topic 3.1.

Arranging electrons

In Stage 8, you learnt about the development of a model for the structure of the atom. This used ideas from a number of scientists such as, J. J. Thompson and Ernest Rutherford. They developed the model shown here:

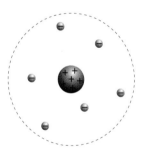

In 1913, the Danish scientist Niels Bohr developed Rutherford's model of the atom further. He had the idea and evidence that the electrons move in different **electron shells** (also called **energy levels**) around the nucleus. He was awarded the Nobel Prize for his work. His idea changed the model of the structure of the atom to the one we use today.

The electrons are arranged in electron shells around the nucleus. This is the **electronic structure**. The first electron shell only has room for two electrons. The second and third electron shells have room for up to eight electrons. The crosses represent the electrons. Remember that the electrons are held in place by **electrostatic forces**.

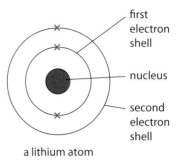

a lithium atom

Look carefully at the diagrams, showing atoms of increasing mass.

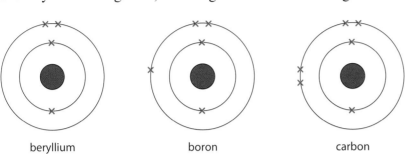

beryllium   boron   carbon

The arrangement of the electrons in an atom is often written as numbers. For example, the electronic arrangement for a boron atom can be written as 2,3. This means that there are two electrons in the first electron shell and three in the next electron shell. The first shell always fills up before electrons go into the second shell.

Questions

1   How many electrons are there in an atom of carbon?

2   How many protons are there in an atom of beryllium?

You will need to look at the Periodic Table to answer the following questions.

3   How many neutrons are there in an atom of boron?

4   Draw a diagram to show the structure of an atom of magnesium.

5   What is the name of the element that has the electronic structure 2,8,3?

6   Draw a labelled atomic diagram of the element fluorine.

7   How is the model of the atom we use today different from the Rutherford model?

Activity 2.1.1

A model of an atom

In this activity, you will build a model of an element.

> **You will need:**
>
> - scissors, hole punch, string, glue, card in different colours (white, red, grey, blue and another colour for the shells).

Method

1 Cut a white circle of card about 6 cm diameter. This will act as the base for the nucleus.

2 Cut out small red circles of about 1.5–2 cm diameter to represent the protons in your chosen element, and grey circles of about 1.5–2 cm diameter to represent the neutrons. Stick these onto one side of the nucleus. Repeat this step, but stick the protons and neutrons onto the other side of the nucleus. Make sure you have the correct number on both sides.

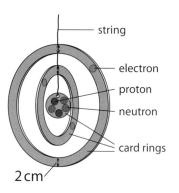

3 Cut out concentric rings of card to represent the electron shells. The rings should be about 2 cm wide. Concentric means circles of different radius sharing the same centre.

4 Cut out small blue circles to represent the electrons in your chosen element. Stick these onto one side of the relevant electron shell. Repeat this step, but stick the electrons onto the other side of each shell. Make sure you have the correct number of electrons on both sides.

5 Assemble the model as shown in the diagram.

6 Make a label for your model that gives the name and symbol for your element, and the number of protons, neutrons and electrons. Hang the label from the bottom of your model.

Look carefully at the model atom you made. How good a model is it? How does it help you to understand the structure of an atom?

Summary checklist

- [ ] I can draw and describe a model of an atom.
- [ ] I can interpret information about the electronic structure of an atom.
- [ ] I can explain how the elements are arranged in the Periodic Table.

> 2.2 Trends in groups within the Periodic Table

In this topic you will:

- learn about the similarities between different elements in the same groups in the Periodic Table
- relate the structure of the Periodic Table to the structure of the elements
- use the Periodic Table to predict the structure and properties of elements
- make careful observations.

Getting started

Use a copy of the Periodic Table to find

- a metal in the same group as magnesium
- a metal in the same period as magnesium
- a non-metallic solid in the same period as magnesium
- a gas in the same period as magnesium.

Compare your answers with a partner and use both of your answers to include all the elements that apply in each answer.

Key words

- alkali metals
- halogens
- noble gases

Group 1: The alkali metals

In Stage 8, you learnt that the columns in the Periodic Table are called groups. The first group, also known as the **alkali metals**, includes the elements lithium, sodium and potassium. The elements have some properties in common. The table below contains data about three of the elements in Group 1.

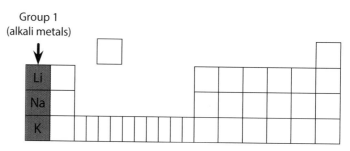

Element	Atomic number	Mass number	Melting point in °C	Boiling point in °C
lithium, Li	3	7	180	1360
sodium, Na	11	23	98	900
potassium, K	19	39	63	777

As you can see, the atomic number increases as you go down the group. The mass number also increases as you go down the group. These increasing numbers tell you that the size of the atom is increasing. When you look at the melting points you can see that they go down as you go down the group. The next element down in the group is the metal rubidium. We can predict it would have a melting point lower than 63 °C.

Questions

1   Where in the Periodic Table do you find the metals?

2   What is the trend in the boiling points of Group 1 elements?

3   What prediction can you make about the boiling point of rubidium?

4   How many more electrons than lithium does sodium have?

Think like a scientist

Observation of the reactions of Group 1 metals with water

You will need:

- safety glasses.

Your teacher needs

- safety glasses, large trough of water, white tile, scalpel or knife, long forceps, samples of the three metals – lithium, sodium and potassium – stored in the normal way, safety screen or screens large enough to protect everyone in the class (including the teacher).

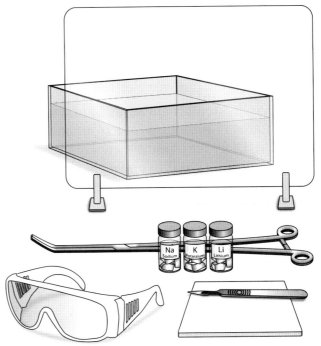

Method

Your teacher will demonstrate the reactions of lithium, sodium and potassium with water. The three elements are stored in a particular way and a small piece of the metal will be cut off and placed one at a time in the trough of water to react.

Watch carefully and record your observations.

Questions

1   Describe the safety precautions your teacher took.

2   Describe what you saw happen when each of the metals reacted with water.

3   Write a word equation for each reaction.

4   What similarities do you notice about the reactions of these metals?

5   What differences do you notice about the reactions of these metals?

6   List the properties that these elements share.

7   Suggest why the next element, rubidium is not used in schools.

8   Why do you think this group is sometimes called the alkali metals?

The structure of the Group 1 metals

The properties of lithium, sodium and potassium are similar and so is their atomic structure.

Lithium has an atomic number of 3 and a mass number of 7. This atom contains 3 protons, 3 electrons and 4 neutrons. The electrons are arranged as 2,1. This means there are two electrons in the lowest electron shell (which is full) and one electron in the second electron shell.

Sodium has an atomic number of 11 and a mass number of 23. This atom contains 11 protons, 11 electrons and 12 neutrons. The electronic structure is 2,8,1. This means there are two electrons in the lowest electron shell (which is full) and eight electrons in the second electron shell (which is full) and one electron in the third electron shell.

Potassium has an atomic number of 19 and a mass number of 39. This atom contains 19 protons, 19 electrons and 20 neutrons. The electronic structure is 2,8,8,1. This means there are two electrons in the lowest electron shell (which is full), eight electrons in the second electron shell (which is full), eight electrons in the third electron shell (which is full) and one electron in the fourth electron shell.

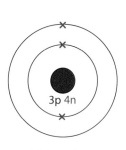

lithium atom

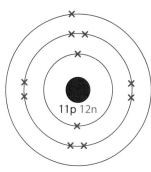

sodium atom

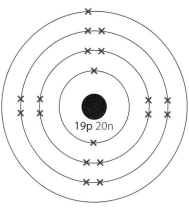

potassium atom

Questions

5   What happens to the size of the atoms as you go down this group?

6   What similarity is there in the structure of these atoms?
(Look at the electron shell arrangements.)

7   Suggest why this group of metals is called Group 1.

8   What are the trends in the structure and behaviour of these elements in Group 1?

Group 7: The halogens (extension material)

Group 7 is another group in the Periodic Table, known as the **halogens**. The group includes fluorine, chlorine and bromine. These elements have a number of properties in common. The first two elements (fluorine and chlorine) are gases at room temperature. Bromine is a liquid. The most reactive is fluorine, then chlorine. Bromine is the least reactive of the three.

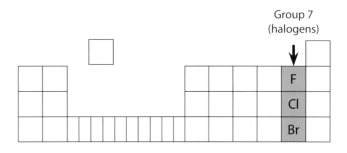

Group 7 (halogens)

Element	Atomic number	Electronic structure	Mass number	Colour	Melting point in °C	Boiling point in °C
fluorine, F	9	2,7	19	pale yellow	−220	−188
chlorine, Cl	17	2,8,7	35	yellowish green	−101	−34
bromine, Br	35		80	brown	−7	59

Questions

9   Are the halogens metals or non-metals?

10   What is the trend in melting points in Group7?

11   What is the trend in colour in Group 7?

12   What is the trend in boiling points in Group 7?

13   What would you predict about the boiling point and melting point of iodine, the next element in Group 7?

14   Would you expect iodine to be more or less reactive than bromine?

15   The electronic structure for bromine is missing from the table. How many electrons do you predict will be in the outer shell?

The structure of fluorine and chlorine

Fluorine has an atomic number of 9 and a mass number of 19. This atom contains 9 protons, 9 electrons and 10 neutrons. The electronic structure is 2,7. This means that the first electron shell has 2 electrons and is full. The second electron shell has seven electrons.

Chlorine has an atomic number of 17 and a mass number of 35. This atom contains 17 protons, 17 electrons and 18 neutrons. The electronic structure is 2,8,7. This means that the first electron shell has two electrons and is full. The second electron shell has eight electrons and is full. The third electron shell has seven electrons.

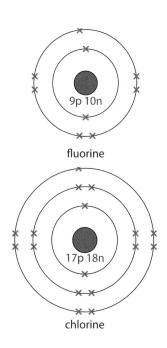

fluorine

chlorine

Questions

16 What happens to the size of the atoms as you go down this group?

17 What similarity is there in the structure of these atoms?

18 Suggest why this group is called Group 7.

Group 8: The noble gases

Group 8 includes the elements helium, neon and argon. They are all gases. They are inert (unreactive) and do not form compounds. They are called the **noble gases**.

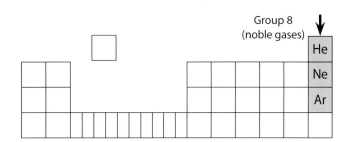

Group 8 (noble gases)

Element	Atomic number	Electronic structure	Mass number	Melting point in °C	Boiling point in °C
helium, He	2	2	4	−270	−269
neon, Ne	10	2,8	20	−249	−246
argon, Ar	18	2,8,8	40	−189	−186

Helium has an atomic number of 2 and a mass number of 4. This atom contains 2 protons, 2 electrons and 2 neutrons. The electrons are arranged with 2 in the first shell. The shell is full.

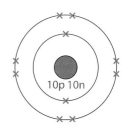

helium

Neon has an atomic number of 10 and a mass number of 20. This atom contains 10 protons, 10 electrons and 10 neutrons. The electrons are arranged with 2 in the first shell and 8 in the second shell. Both shells are full.

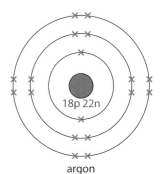

neon

Argon has an atomic number of 18 and a mass number of 40. This atom contains 18 protons, 18 electrons and 22 neutrons. The electrons are arranged with 2 in the first shell, 8 in the second shell and 8 in the third shell. All three shells are full.

argon

Questions

19 What trend in melting points can be seen in Group 8?

20 What happens to the size of the atoms as you go down Group 8?

21 What similarity is there in the structure of these atoms?

22 Suggest why this group is called Group 8.

23 What predictions can you make about the melting point and boiling point of krypton, which is the next gas in this group?

How does the atomic structure of an element relate to its position in the Periodic Table?

Summary checklist

- [ ] I can explain how the structure of the Periodic Table is related to the atomic structure of the elements.
- [ ] I can identify the similarities and differences between the atomic structure of elements in the same group in the Periodic Table.
- [ ] I can use the Periodic Table to predict the structure and properties of elements.
- [ ] I can make accurate observations.

> 2.3 Why elements react to form compounds

In this topic you will:

- describe the structure of an ion and compare it with that of an atom
- explain how ionic and covalent bonds are formed
- explain what a molecule is
- write the formulae of some ionic and covalent compounds.

Getting started

The electronic structure of lithium is 2,1.
Draw the structure of this atom.

The electronic structure of fluorine is 2,7.
Draw the structure of this atom.

When you have drawn them, compare them with a partner's drawings.

Discuss which group in the Periodic Table each of these elements is in.

Be prepared to share your drawings with the class.

Key words

chemical bonds

covalent bond

dot and cross diagram

ion

highest energy level

ionic bond

ionic compounds

molecule

stable

outermost electron shell

Thinking about atomic structure

Atoms have electrons arranged in different electron shells or energy levels around the nucleus. The shell with the **highest energy level** is the one on the outside of the atom. It is called the **outermost electron shell**.

In the different shells, there is room for two electrons in the first electron shell, eight electrons in the second electron shell, and eight electrons in the third electron shell.

The number of electrons in an atom is the same as the number of protons in that atom.

The atomic number tells us how many protons there are in an atom.

The electrons have an electrical charge of -1 and protons a charge of $+1$.

Atoms have no overall charge because there are an equal number of protons and electrons.

Electrons are held in place by electrostatic forces

Why do elements react together?

Atoms are more **stable** when the outermost electron shell (highest energy level) is completely full of electrons.

The elements in Group 8, the noble gases, have their outermost energy level of electrons full, so they do not react to form compounds.

All the other groups do not have full outer shells of electrons so they can react to form compounds. In doing so, they fill the outermost electron shells with electrons. The elements in compounds are held together by **chemical bonds**. These bonds can be formed in two ways:

- the atoms can lose or gain electrons

- atoms can share electrons.

Losing electrons

Sodium reacts with other elements by losing an electron.
When this happens, the sodium atom forms an **ion**.

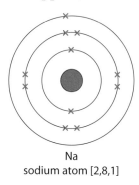

Na
sodium atom [2,8,1]

Na⁺
sodium ion [2,8]⁺

When the sodium atom loses an
electron, it forms a sodium ion.

When a sodium atom loses the electron from the outer shell, which is the outermost electron shell, the next shell becomes the outermost electron shell. This electron shell is full. So, the sodium ion is more stable than the sodium atom. We write the symbol for a sodium atom as Na. When a sodium ion is formed it has one less electron than the atom so there is now one more positively charged proton than negatively charged electrons. So, we write the symbol for a sodium ion as Na^+.

Gaining electrons

An atom can also become an ion by *gaining* electrons.

In some groups in the Periodic Table, the elements have their outermost electron shells almost full. In Group 7, elements such as chlorine have seven electrons in the outermost electron shell. To fill its outermost electron shell, a chlorine atom gains an electron and forms a chlorine ion. The outermost electron shell in the chlorine ion is now full, so the chlorine ion is more stable than the chlorine atom.

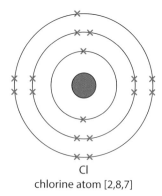

Cl
chlorine atom [2,8,7]

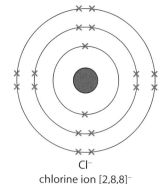

Cl⁻
chlorine ion [2,8,8]⁻

The chlorine atom needs to gain
an electron to make it more stable.

We write the symbol for a chlorine atom as Cl. When a chlorine ion is formed, it has one more negatively charged electron than the atom, so there is now one more electron than the positively charged protons. So, we write the symbol for a chlorine ion as Cl^-.

Ionic bonding

A sodium ion and a chlorine ion can form an ionic chemical bond to form the compound sodium chloride. In an **ionic bond** there is an attraction between the positively charged ion, sodium, and the negatively charged ion, chlorine.

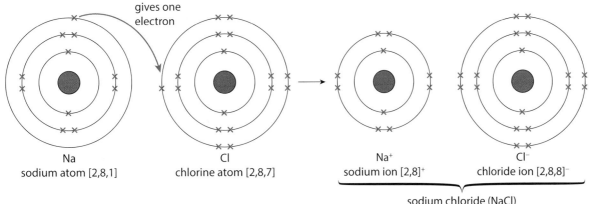

Na	Cl	Na⁺	Cl⁻
sodium atom [2,8,1]	chlorine atom [2,8,7]	sodium ion [2,8]⁺	chloride ion [2,8,8]⁻

sodium chloride (NaCl)

When the sodium atom loses one electron and becomes a sodium ion, it has 10 electrons and 11 protons. This means that there are 11 positive charges from the protons but only 10 negative charges from the electrons in the ion. This means that the sodium ion has a positive electrical charge of +1. The symbol for a sodium ion is written as Na^+. The electronic structure for a sodium ion is written as $[2,8]^+$.

When the chlorine atom gains one electron and becomes a chlorine ion, it has 18 electrons and 17 protons. This means that there are 17 positive charges from the protons but 18 negative charges from the electrons in the ion. This means that the chlorine ion has a negative electrical charge of −1. The chlorine ion is written as Cl^-.

The charges on the ions of sodium and chlorine form a bond and the two elements are held together to form sodium chloride, NaCl.

Other metals in Group 1 react with Group 7 elements in a similar way. For example, lithium and potassium with chlorine and fluorine:

$$\text{lithium} + \text{chlorine} \rightarrow \text{lithium chloride}$$

$$\text{lithium} + \text{fluorine} \rightarrow \text{lithium fluoride}$$

$$\text{potassium} + \text{chlorine} \rightarrow \text{potassium chloride}$$

$$\text{potassium} + \text{fluorine} \rightarrow \text{potassium fluoride}$$

Look at the electronic structures for the elements lithium, sodium and potassium.

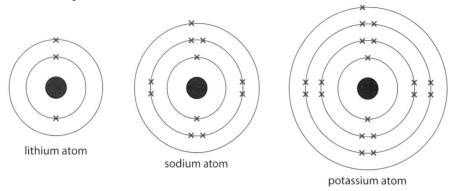

lithium atom

sodium atom

potassium atom

Potassium is the most reactive and lithium the least reactive.

Potassium loses the electron in the outermost electron shell more easily than sodium or lithium can lose theirs. The electrons are held in their electron shells by electrostatic forces between the positive charge on the protons and the negative charge on the electrons. The electron in the outermost electron shell of potassium is furthest away from the protons so it is easier to overcome these forces. It is more difficult for the electron in the outermost electron shell in the lithium atom to escape than in a sodium or potassium atoms as it is more difficult to overcome the electrostatic forces.

Now look at the electronic structures for the elements fluorine and chorine.

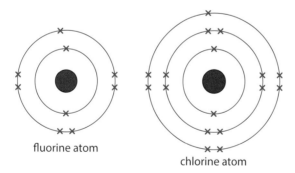

fluorine atom

chlorine atom

Fluorine is more reactive than chlorine.

Fluorine gains an electron in the outermost electron shell more easily than chlorine. The electrons are held in their electron shells by electrostatic forces between the positive charge on the protons and the negative charge on the electrons. The electron in the outermost electron shell of fluorine is closest to the protons so an additional electron is attracted by the electrostatic forces more readily than in chlorine.

Questions

1   What is the electronic structure of a sodium atom?
2   What is the electronic structure of a sodium ion?
3   What is the symbol for a chlorine atom?
4   What is the symbol for a chlorine ion?
5   Draw the electronic structure of a potassium ion.
6   Draw the electronic structure for a fluorine ion.
7   Potassium is more reactive than lithium because it can lose an electron more easily. Why is this?
8   Fluorine is more reactive than chlorine because it can gain an electron more easily. Why is this?

Other ionic compounds

Ionic compounds are those that are made from ions. They form when a metal reacts with a non-metal.

In some elements more than one electron is lost or gained. For example, when magnesium combines with oxygen to form magnesium oxide, MgO.

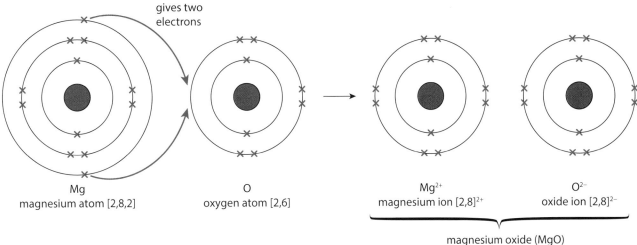

magnesium oxide (MgO)

A magnesium atom has two electrons in the outermost electron shell, its electronic structure is 2,8,2. An oxygen atom has six electrons in its outermost electron shell, 2,6.

The magnesium atom loses the two electrons and forms a magnesium ion, Mg^{2+} The oxygen atom gains two electrons and becomes an oxygen ion O^{2-}. The two ions are attracted to one another and form an ionic bond to form the ionic compound magnesium oxide, MgO.

Magnesium reacts with chlorine to form magnesium chloride (extension material).

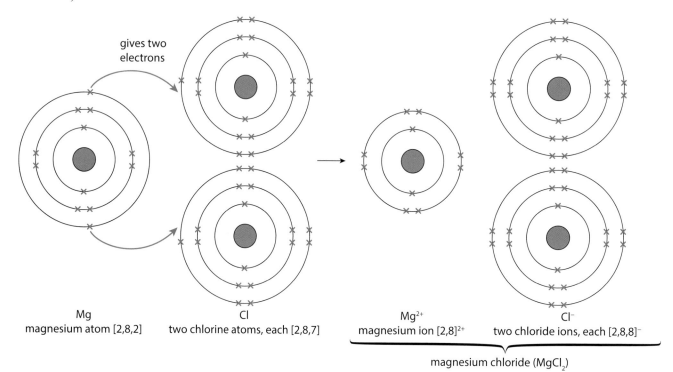

gives two
electrons

| Mg | Cl | Mg²⁺ | Cl⁻ |

Mg
magnesium atom [2,8,2]

Cl
two chlorine atoms, each [2,8,7]

Mg^{2+}
magnesium ion $[2,8]^{2+}$

Cl^-
two chloride ions, each $[2,8,8]^-$

magnesium chloride (MgCl₂)

Extension material: When magnesium forms an ionic compound with chlorine, two ions of chlorine are formed.

The magnesium atom loses the two electrons from its outermost shell and forms a magnesium ion, Mg^{2+}. Two chlorine atoms both gain one electron and become two chloride ions, $2\,Cl^-$. The two chlorine ions are attracted to the magnesium ion and form an ionic bond to form the ionic compound magnesium chloride, $MgCl_2$.

Questions

9   Draw diagrams to explain how the structure of an atom of calcium is different from an ion of calcium.

10 How many ions of chlorine react with one ion of calcium to form calcium chloride?

11 Write the chemical formula for calcium chloride.

12 Write the chemical formula for calcium oxide.

Activity 2.3.1

Forming ionic compounds

You will need:

- coloured paper and/or card, glue, scissors, ruler, large sheet of paper, pair of compasses and/or string and a drawing pin.

Method

1   In pairs, choose one of the following metals: calcium, magnesium, lithium, sodium or potassium.

2   Choose one of the following non-metals: fluorine, chlorine or oxygen.

3   Make a poster to illustrate the structure of the atoms of these elements and show how an ionic bond is formed to make an ionic compound.

4   Make sure you add the name of the elements and their symbols, the name of the compound and its formula.

Peer assessment

When you have completed your poster, swap it with another pair. Suggest two things they have done well and one thing they could do to improve their poster.

Sharing electrons

When non-metals form compounds with other non-metals they do so by sharing electrons to fill their outermost electron shells.

Hydrogen and chlorine

An example of this is when hydrogen and chlorine react to form hydrogen chloride:

- a hydrogen atom has just one electron in its outermost electron shell; in this first shell there is only room for two electrons

- a chlorine atom has seven electrons in its outermost electron shell; in this electron shell there is room for eight electrons

- the atoms share a pair of electrons, so both hydrogen and chlorine have their outermost electron shells full of electrons

- a **molecule** of hydrogen chloride is formed; its formula is HCl.

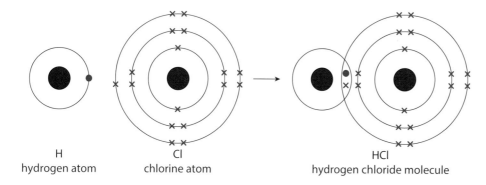

H	Cl	HCl
hydrogen atom	chlorine atom	hydrogen chloride molecule

The electron in the hydrogen atom is shown as a dot and the electrons in the chlorine atom are shown as crosses. This type of diagram is known as a **dot and cross diagram**.

This type of chemical bond where electrons are shared is called a **covalent bond**.

Hydrogen and hydrogen

Covalent molecules are formed when atoms of different non-metals join together to form compounds and when atoms of the same non-metal join together.

For example, two atoms of hydrogen join together to form a molecule of hydrogen:

- an atom of hydrogen has one electron in its outermost electron shell; this electron shell has room for only two electrons

- the hydrogen atoms share a pair of electrons, so both atoms have two electrons in the outermost electron shell so the shell is full and more stable

- a molecule of hydrogen is formed; the formula is written as H_2.

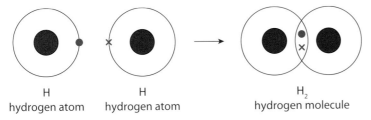

H
hydrogen atom

H
hydrogen atom

H_2
hydrogen molecule

Hydrogen and nitrogen

Another example of a covalent compound is ammonia. This compound is formed when hydrogen and nitrogen share three pairs of electrons:

- an atom of hydrogen has only one electron in the outermost electron shell, but there is room for two electrons in this shell

- an atom of nitrogen has an atomic number of 7, so it has two electrons in the first electron shell and has five electrons in its outermost electron shell, but there is room for eight electrons in this shell

- three atoms of hydrogen combine with one atom of nitrogen and share three pairs of electrons, so all the atoms have their outermost electron shells full of electrons

- a stable molecule of ammonia is formed; its formula is NH_3.

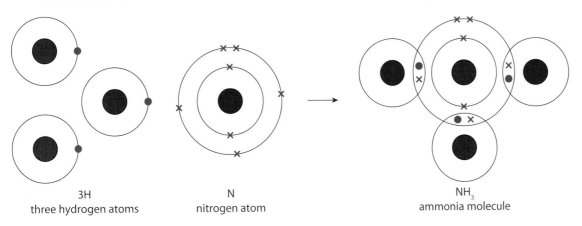

3H
three hydrogen atoms

N
nitrogen atom

NH_3
ammonia molecule

The hydrogen chloride, hydrogen and ammonia molecules can also be represented using diagrams like the ones shown below. There are some more examples of covalent compounds, too.

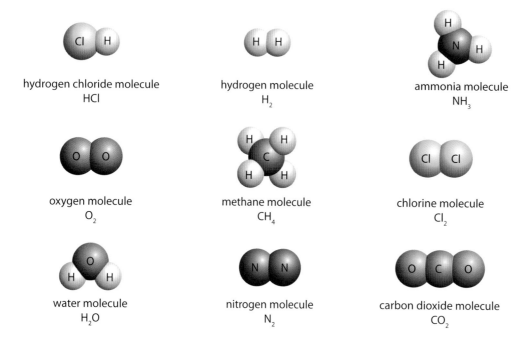

hydrogen chloride molecule
HCl

hydrogen molecule
H_2

ammonia molecule
NH_3

oxygen molecule
O_2

methane molecule
CH_4

chlorine molecule
Cl_2

water molecule
H_2O

nitrogen molecule
N_2

carbon dioxide molecule
CO_2

Questions

13 Which of the nine molecules shown in the diagram above are compounds?

14 Draw a dot and cross diagram to show how a molecule of chlorine is formed.

15 Is the compound calcium chloride an ionic or a covalent compound? Give a reason for your answer.

16 Write the formula for a molecule of methane, a molecule of carbon dioxide and a molecule of nitrogen.

How can I be sure if the bond is ionic or covalent?

Summary checklist

☐ I can show the differences between the structure of an ion and an atom.

☐ I can explain how ionic and covalent bonds are formed.

☐ I can explain what a molecule is.

☐ I can write the formulae of some ionic and covalent compounds.

> 2.4 Simple and giant structures

In this topic you will:

- learn how giant structures are formed
- compare the properties of ionic and covalent substances
- explain how the structures of these substances relate to their properties.

Getting started

- Explain how atoms of sodium and chlorine join together to make the compound sodium chloride.
- Draw diagrams if it helps you to explain.
- Share your ideas with a partner.
- Then work together to explain how this is different from the way that two oxygen atoms join together to form an oxygen molecule.
- Be prepared to share your answers with the class.

Key words

graphite

intermolecular forces

lattice

layers

macromolecule

Giant structures in ionic compounds

Sodium chloride is an ionic compound. The ions of sodium, Na^+, and chlorine, Cl^-, have equal and opposite electrical charges so they are strongly attracted to one another. These forces, called electrostatic forces, act in all directions and form ionic bonds.

The ions in sodium chloride make a giant structure known as a **lattice**.

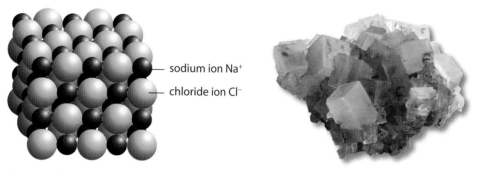

sodium ion Na^+

chloride ion Cl^-

The giant lattice structure of sodium chloride

Sodium chloride crystals

In the lattice structure, a sodium ion, Na^+, is surrounded by six Cl^- ions. Sodium chloride forms crystals with a regular shape because the ions are arranged in a regular pattern.

Giant covalent structures

Many substances that have covalent bonds are formed of simple molecules: oxygen, carbon dioxide and methane, for example. This is because the forces holding the molecules together are very strong but the forces between the molecules are weak. The forces between the molecules are called **intermolecular forces**.

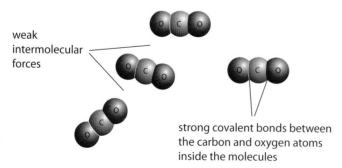

weak intermolecular forces

strong covalent bonds between the carbon and oxygen atoms inside the molecules

Carbon dioxide molecules

However, some covalent substances such as silicon dioxide have giant covalent structures.

Giant structures of carbon

The carbon atoms in diamond form a giant structure. Each carbon atom forms four strong covalent bonds.

Diamond is the hardest material on Earth. It is not just used for jewellery but it is used for cutting and drilling tools. It is so hard because of the strong, rigid, three-dimensional structure of the lattice.

A diamond

Diamond drill bits have small pieces of diamond powder embedded in them

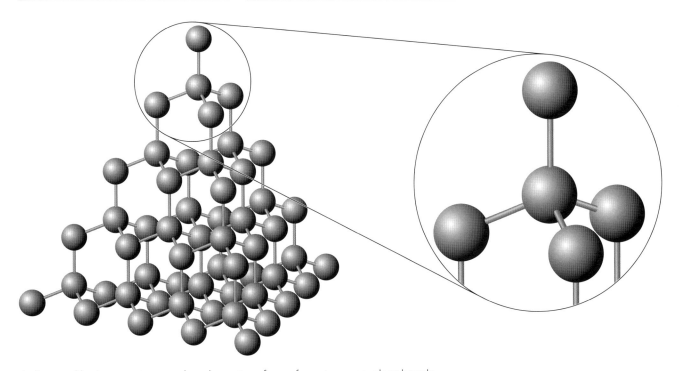

A diamond lattice structure; each carbon atom forms four strong covalent bonds

These large structures are called **macromolecules**.

Carbon also forms a giant structure for a very soft material, **graphite**.

Graphite is used for the 'lead' in pencils, and for lubricating moving parts in machines.

In graphite, the carbon atoms each make bonds with three other atoms. This forms **layers**, which can easily slide over one another. The covalent bonds between the carbon atoms in the layers are strong. The bonds between the layers are weak so the layers slide over each other very easily. This makes the surface very soft and it easily comes away. This is what happens when you make a pencil mark on paper.

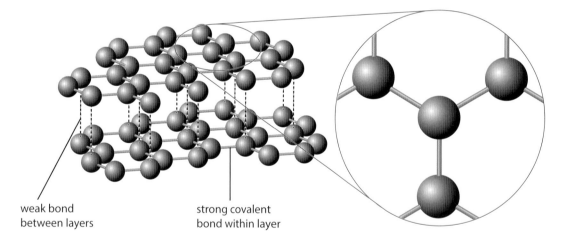

weak bond
between layers

strong covalent
bond within layer

Graphite giant structure; in graphite layers, each carbon atom forms three covalent bonds

Why are the properties of diamond and graphite so different when they are both made up of carbon atoms?

Activity 2.4.1

Building giant structures

You will need:

- poster-making equipment, such as coloured paper and/or card, glue, sticky tape, scissors, paper straws or wires to make covalent bonds, small polystyrene or foam balls or modelling materials to make particles such as atoms or ions.

Method

1   In a group of three, make models of the giant structures of sodium chloride, diamond and graphite. Each model should be labelled and have a list of its properties. Write an explanation of how the structure is linked to the properties of each of your giant structures.

2   Before you begin, discuss how you will construct your models. When you have completed the task, pass your work to another group to assess it.

How did making the models help me to understand the giant structures of sodium chloride, diamond and graphite?

Questions

1   How is an ionic bond different from a covalent bond?

2   When a metal joins with a non-metal, is a covalent or an ionic compound made?

3   Oxygen atoms join together to form an oxygen molecule. Explain what the word molecule means.

4   What is a macromolecule? Give an example.

Covalent and ionic substances have different properties

Melting and boiling points

Ionic substances have very high melting points and boiling points. This is because there are very strong electrostatic forces holding the ions together.

Covalent substances made from simple molecules have low melting points and boiling points because, although the forces holding the molecules together are strong, the forces between the molecules – intermolecular forces – are weak. This means that only a small amount of energy is needed to overcome these forces in order to melt or boil them.

Questions

Use this table to help answer questions 5–9 .

Substance	Melting point in °C	Boiling point in °C
sodium chloride	801	1413
methane	−182	−161
magnesium chloride	714	1412
ammonia	−77	−34
calcium oxide	2613	2850
chlorine	−101	−34.6
water	0	100

5   Is magnesium chloride an ionic compound or a simple molecule with covalent bonds? Give reasons for your answer.

6   Is ammonia an ionic compound or a simple molecule with covalent bonds? Give reasons for your answer.

7   Is ammonia a solid, liquid or gas at room temperature?

8   Why do magnesium chloride and calcium oxide have high melting points?

9   Why do methane and chlorine have low melting points?

10   Look at this photograph of copper sulfate crystals.

What sort of chemical bonds does this substance have?
Give a reason for your answer.

11   A substance has a melting point of 3078 °C and a boiling point of
4300 °C. What sort of chemical bonds does it have? Give a reason
for your answer.

12   Silicon dioxide is a compound formed from two non-metals, silicon
and oxygen. It is the chemical name for sand. It is a hard substance
with a melting point of 1610 °C. Which properties of silicon
dioxide suggest that it has a giant covalent structure?

Conducting electricity

Ionic compounds will conduct electricity if they are dissolved in water
or if they are melted to form a liquid.

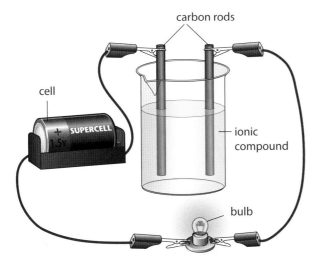

Ionic compounds can conduct electricity because the ions have an electrical
charge. The ions must be free to move about and carry the electrical charge.

Covalent substances made from simple molecules do not conduct electricity.

Think like a scientist

Ionic compounds conducting electricity

You will need:

- safety glasses, surgical gloves, electrical wires, lamp, cell, carbon electrodes, beaker, scalpel or knife, selection of crystals of ionic compounds such as copper sulfate and sodium chloride, selection of crystals of ionic compounds, such as copper sulfate and sodium chloride.

Safety

Some crystals and solutions such as copper sulfate are irritants. Take care when using these and avoid touching them. Wear surgical gloves and safety glasses.

Method

1   Set up your apparatus as shown in the diagram on the previous page, but without the solution. Test to check that the bulb is working before you start.
2   Place a solution of one of your ionic compounds in a beaker.
3   Add your beaker containing the ionic compound to your circuit, but do not connect the final link until you have checked your circuit carefully.
4   Complete the circuit.
5   Repeat this for all the solutions you are using.
6   Record your results.

7   Place one of the crystals in position in the circuit and then complete the circuit. Take care that the connections on the crystal are not touching.

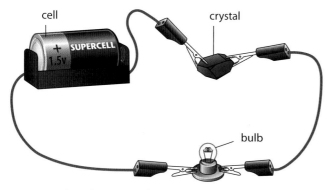

8   Repeat this for all the crystals you are using.
9   Record your results.

Questions

1   Did all your ionic solutions conduct electricity?
2   Explain your answer.

Continued

Questions

3   Did all the ionic crystals conduct electricity?

4   Explain your answer.

5   Predict, with reasons, what would happen if you used a covalent substance in place of an ionic crystal or solution.

Summary of the properties of ionic and covalent substances

Ionic substances	Covalent substances
Compounds made from ions form giant lattices. These ionic compounds have very high melting points and boiling points because the forces between the ions are so strong.	Substances made from simple molecules have low melting points and boiling points because there are only weak forces between the molecules. Atoms that share electrons can form giant structures called macromolecules. These have very high melting points because the atoms are joined by strong covalent bonds.
When ionic compounds are dissolved in water or melted, they can conduct electricity because the ions are free to move about and carry the electrical charge.	Simple covalent molecules do not conduct electricity.

Summary checklist

- [ ] I can explain how giant structures are formed.
- [ ] I can compare the properties of ionic and covalent substances.
- [ ] I can relate the structures of these substances to their properties.

Project: Building the Periodic Table

Scientists often try to make sense of large amounts of information by grouping similar things together. For example, they group similar types of animals together such as mammals, fish, insects and so on.

The same happened with the elements as more and more were discovered. Three important scientists contributed to the Periodic Table that we use today.

The timeline and information below explain a little about their ideas and work.

Your task is to make a report, a presentation using slides or a presentation in any other way to explain and describe the development of the Periodic Table. You should stress the way that scientists collaborate, building on the work of others and changing their ideas once they have more information. You can do this in groups of two or three.

-------- 1817 --------	-------- 1864 --------	-------- 1869 --------
Johann Dobereiner	John Newlands	Dmitri Mendeleev
'law of triads'	every eighth elements had similar properties	modified and extended John Newlands's work

Johann Dobereiner grouped elements in threes based on their properties and their appearance: this is his 'law of triads'.

At about the same time, other scientists began to find out the mass of the atoms of the elements.

This is one of Johann Dobereiner's triads. The numbers are the atomic numbers of the elements.

salt forming elements	
lithium	3
sodium	23
potassium	39

In 1864, there were 63 known elements. John Newlands arranged them in order of the mass of their atoms, starting with the lightest. He noticed that every eighth element in this arrangement had similar properties, a similar element appeared periodically. This pattern did not continue through all the elements.

Continued

In 1869, Dmitri Mendeleev used John Newlands's ideas. He left gaps in the arrangement of elements, so that the pattern of eights continued and the elements with similar properties were grouped together.

Mendeleev predicted the properties of some undiscovered elements that would fill the gaps in his 'periodic table'. These predictions turned out to be correct. His table forms the basis of the Periodic Table we use today.

Here is a list of questions that you may find helpful when preparing your report or presentation.

1   Find out a little background information about Johann Dobereiner.
    Such as: Where and when was he born? Where did he work? When did he die?

2   Explain how Johann Dobereiner arranged the elements.

3   Suggest how John Newlands was influenced by Johann Dobereiner's ideas.

4   Find out a little background information about John Newlands.
    Such as: Where and when was he born? Where did he work? When did he die?

5   Why did the pattern of elements in Newlands's table not continue?

6   Find out a little background information about Dmitri Mendeleev.
    Such as: Where and when was he born? Where did he work? When did he die?

7   Describe how Dmitri Mendeleev modified Newland's table.

8   Suggest why Mendeleev's table did not contain helium, argon or neon.

9   How many elements are known today?

10 Some elements today are made by scientists and are known as synthetic elements. Name some of these. Try to find the names of some of the newest elements.

Make your presentation to the class.

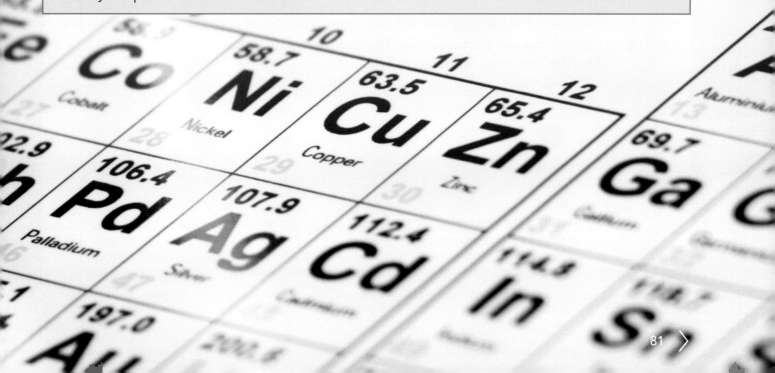

Check your progress

2.1 The table shows some information about four elements. These elements are from the same group in the Periodic Table. They are given in the same order as in the Periodic Table.

Element	Melting point in °C	Boiling point in °C	Reaction with water
lithium	180	1342	Gives off bubbles of gas and gives off heat
sodium		883	
potassium	63		Gives off gas and gives off so much heat that it catches fire
rubidium	39	688	Explodes with such force that the container cracks.

There is a trend in the melting points and boiling points of these elements.
Use the trend to predict the following:

a   the melting point of sodium [1]

b   the boiling point of potassium [1]

c   The elements all react with water to produce a gas. Name the gas. [1]

d   Use the information about the reaction with water to predict the reaction between sodium and water. [1]

e   The following are the mass numbers of the four elements in the table above.

| 23 | 7 | 39 | 85 |

   Match the numbers with the elements. [1]

f   What does the mass number tell you about the atom of each element? [1]

g   Lithium has two electron shells. The electronic structure is 2,1.
   This can be seen in the diagram below.

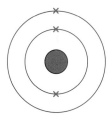

lithium

   Sodium has the electronic structure 2,8,1. Draw a similar diagram to show the electronic structure of sodium. [3]

2.2 The fluorine atom has the electronic structure 2,7. This is shown in the diagram below.

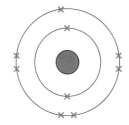

fluorine

    a   Draw a similar diagram to show the electronic structure of a fluorine ion.   **[1]**

    b   Why is a fluorine ion more stable than a fluorine atom?   **[1]**

    c   The symbol for a fluorine atom is F. Write the symbol for a fluorine ion.   **[1]**

2.3 For each of the following, state whether this applies to a substance with covalent or ionic bonds.

    a   When a metal joins with a non-metal to form a compound.   **[1]**

    b   When two atoms share electrons.   **[1]**

    c   When two non-metals join together.   **[1]**

    d   When a compound that is dissolved in water conducts electricity.   **[1]**

    e   When atoms gain or lose electrons.   **[1]**

2.4 The diagram shows a molecule of methane.

    Write the formula for a molecule of methane.   **[1]**

2.5 The diagram shows the lattice structure of sodium chloride.

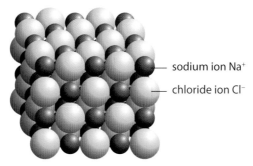

— sodium ion Na⁺

— chloride ion Cl⁻

    a   What holds the lattice together?   **[1]**

    b   What does this lattice structure tell you about the melting point and boiling point of sodium chloride?   **[1]**

3 ▶ Forces and energy

⟩ 3.1 Density

In this topic you will:

- discover what is meant by density
- find out how to calculate density
- compare the densities of solids, liquids and gases
- understand and predict whether objects will float or sink in water.

Getting started

Work in groups to discuss answers to these questions.

1. What is the scientific meaning of the word volume?

2. Which of these has a larger volume?
   - 1 kg of rock
   - 1 kg of feathers

3. Which of these has a larger mass?
   - 1 cm³ of polystyrene
   - 1 cm³ of iron

Key words

density
hollow
irregular
regular
solid

Mass and volume

People often think that materials such as rocks or metals are heavier than objects such as feathers or polystyrene. This is not always true. A very large block of polystyrene may have a larger mass than a small piece of metal.

Think about the food containers and the nails in the pictures.

The food containers are made from polystyrene. They feel very light, because they have a large volume and a small mass. The containers are also hollow, which means they have a space filled with air inside them.

The nails are made from iron. The nails feel heavy because they have a high mass and a small volume. The nails are also solid. The word solid in this case means that each nail has no space with air inside. The word solid can be used as the opposite of hollow.

One of the polystyrene food containers has a larger mass than one of the nails. However, the same volume of iron has a larger mass than the same volume of polystyrene.

We use the word density to describe this difference.

Calculating volume

When calculating the volume of a **regular** block of material, we measure the lengths of the sides. When talking about a block of material, regular means that we can use an equation to calculate its volume.

This block of wood has a regular shape. The lengths of its sides have been measured.

You can work out the volume of the block by multiplying the lengths of the sides:

$10 \times 6 \times 4 = 240 \text{ mm}^3$

4 mm
6 mm
10 mm

The unit is mm³ because the lengths of the sides are in millimetres.

It does not matter in what order you multiply the sides.

Try multiplying the numbers in a different order. You will get the same answer.

If the shape of the material is **irregular**, then we work out the volume using the displacement method. Irregular means the sides or angles of the shape are not equal. The object is placed into a measuring cylinder of water. The increase in volume of the water is the volume of the object.

This piece of rock has an irregular shape.

It is placed into a measuring cylinder containing 40 cm³ water:

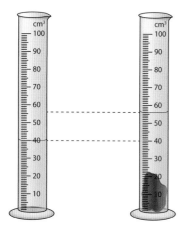

The water rises to the 56 cm³ mark. So, the volume of the rock is:

$56 - 40 = 16 \text{ cm}^3$.

The unit is cm³ because the measuring cylinder measures in cm³.

Calculating density

We say that iron has a higher density than polystyrene. Density means mass per unit volume.

A solid block of iron measuring 1 cm × 1 cm × 1 cm has a mass of 7.9 g.

A solid block of polystyrene measuring 1 cm × 1 cm × 1 cm has a mass of 0.05 g.

We can calculate density using the equation:

$$\text{density} = \frac{\text{mass}}{\text{volume}}$$

or using the formula triangle shown here.

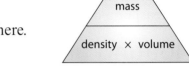

Because density is mass divided by volume, the unit of density is the unit of mass divided by the unit of volume. For example:

- if mass is in g and volume is in cm^3 then density will be in g/cm^3
- if mass is in kg and volume is in m^3 then density will be in kg/m^3.

This leads to the definition of density: density is mass per unit volume of a substance.

Using the example of the block of iron	Using the example of the polystyrene
volume = 1 cm × 1 cm × 1 cm = 1 cm^3 mass = 7.9 g density $= \dfrac{7.9}{1}$ $= 7.9\ g/cm^3$ We say that iron has a density of 7.9 g/cm^3.	volume = 1 cm × 1 cm × 1 cm = 1 cm^3 mass = 0.05 g density $= \dfrac{0.05}{1}$ $= 0.05\ g/cm^3$ We say that polystyrene has a density of 0.05 g/cm^3.

Comparing densities

This table shows the densities of some materials:

material	helium	air	wood	water	concrete	aluminium	osmium
density in g/cm^3	0.00018	0.0012	0.35 – 0.95	1.0	2.4	2.7	22

Look at the densities of the materials in the table. Helium and air are gases. Gases have lower densities than liquids or solids because the particles in a gas are far apart.

As particles in a material get packed closer together, the density of the material increases. So, the materials with the highest densities are all solids.

For the elements, the density usually increases as the atomic number increases. Osmium has atomic number 76 and is more dense than iron, which has atomic number 26.

Did you know, the substance with the highest density in the universe is found in collapsed stars? The forces in collapsed stars are so large that atoms are compressed into very small spaces. This material is called neutronium and has a density of $100\,000\,000\,000\,000\ \text{g/cm}^3$. One teaspoon of neutronium would have a mass of 500 million tonnes.

Floating and sinking

Look at the densities of some of the materials in the table. Compare their densities with the density of water. What do you notice about the densities of materials, such as wood, that float on water?

You can tell whether something will float or sink in water by comparing its density with that of water.

- If something is more dense than water, it will sink in water.

- If something is less dense than water, it will float in water.

Some objects, such as floats that are used in swimming pools, are designed to have a very low density. These objects are made from materials such as polystyrene, or they are hollow with only air inside.

Modern ships are built from steel that has a density of $8–9\ \text{g/cm}^3$. That is much more than the density of water, which is $1.0\ \text{g/cm}^3$. Some of the largest ships have a mass of over $500\,000\,000\ \text{kg}$. So, how do they float in water?

Ships are not solid blocks of steel. There are large spaces inside ships that contain only air. That means the ship has a very large volume, so the average density of the *whole* ship is less than the density of water. The average density is the mass of all the materials in the ship, including the air, divided by the total volume of the ship.

The density of a ship changes when its mass changes. Cargo, passengers and fuel all add mass to a ship, which increases its density. The density of the ship in the picture is too high, because of the mass of the cargo.

Liquids of different density

When liquids are added together carefully, the less dense liquids will float on the more dense liquids. The liquids that do not mix will form separate layers.

The picture shows what happens when some different liquids are added together.

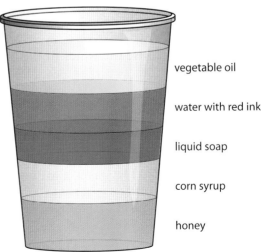

vegetable oil

water with red ink

liquid soap

corn syrup

honey

Crude oil is less dense than water. So, when crude oil spills out of ships or out from oil wells, the oil floats on the water. The photograph shows black oil being washed up on a beach. Oil spilling from ships is a major source of water pollution.

Gases and liquids

Gases are less dense than liquids because the particles in a gas are much further apart than in a liquid.

Drops of rain fall down because the water in the drops is more dense than air.

The gas in fizzy drinks is carbon dioxide. Carbon dioxide has a density of $0.002 \, \text{g/cm}^3$. The liquid in most drinks has a density close to $1.0 \, \text{g/cm}^3$, as the drinks are mostly water. This difference in density explains why the bubbles of gas in a fizzy drink rise to the top. The gas is a lot less dense than the liquid.

Gases of different density

Gases have lower densities than solids or liquids, but not all gases have the same density. Helium is one of the least dense gases. Helium is sometimes used to fill balloons. A balloon filled with helium will float in air because the balloon and gas is less dense than the air. The balloons in the picture have floated up through the air.

Hydrogen gas is even less dense than helium, but is not used to fill balloons because hydrogen forms an explosive mixture with air.

Solids and liquids are very difficult to compress because their particles are already in contact. Gases are easy to compress because their particles are far apart. When a gas is compressed, the same number of particles is in a smaller volume, so the density of the gas increases. Also, if a gas expands, the same number of particles is in a larger volume, so the density of the gas decreases. Heat causes a gas to expand. That explains why a hot air balloon can float because the hot air inside the balloon is less dense than the colder air outside.

Questions

1 Look at the densities of these materials:

- pine wood 0.41 g/cm^3
- polycarbonate 1.2 g/cm^3
- polyethene 0.95 g/cm^3
- water 1.0 g/cm^3

a Which of these materials has the lowest density?

b i Which of these materials will sink in water?

ii Explain why the material will sink in water.

2 a Copy and complete the equation for density.

density =

b A block of aluminium has a volume of 5.0 cm^3 and a mass of 13.5 g. Calculate the density of the aluminium. Give your answer in g/cm^3.

c Explain whether the block of aluminium will float or sink in water.

3 The diagram shows a block of wood.

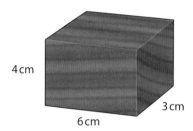

4 cm
3 cm
6 cm

a Calculate the volume of the block of wood. Give your answer in cm^3.

b The block of wood in the diagram has a mass of 54 g. Calculate the density of the wood. Give your answer in g/cm^3.

c Explain whether the block of wood will float or sink in water.

4 Sea water is placed in a tank. The volume of the sea water is $10\,m^3$.
The mass of the sea water is $10\,300\,kg$.

    a Calculate the density of the sea water.
Give your answer in kg/m^3.

    b Pure water has a density of $1000\,kg/m^3$. Explain what will
happen to a block of material with a density of $1020\,kg/m^3$
when placed into:

        i sea water

        ii pure water.

5 Copper has a density of $8.96\,g/cm^3$.

    a Calculate the mass of copper that has a volume of $20\,cm^3$.

    b Calculate the volume of copper that has a mass of $4.5\,g$.

6 A toy car is placed into a measuring cylinder of water as shown
in the diagram.

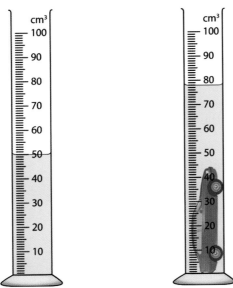

    a Use the diagram to calculate the volume of the toy car.

    b The toy car in the diagram has a mass of $84\,g$. Calculate
the density of the toy car. Give your answer in g/cm^3.

    c The toy car in the diagram is made from steel and plastic.
Steel has a density of $7.8\,g/cm^3$. Suggest **two** reasons for the
difference between this value and the density you calculated
in part **b**.

7 This table shows the densities of three liquids.

liquid	density in g/cm³
kerosene	0.81
mercury	14.00
water	1.00

These three liquids are poured into a measuring cylinder and form three separate layers, as shown in the diagram.

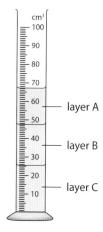

Use information in the diagram and in the table to identify the liquids in the three layers, A, B and C.

8 Zara wants a party balloon that will float in air. She will hold the balloon on a string, as shown in the diagram.

State the property of the gas in the balloon needed to make the balloon float in air.

9 A hot air balloon floats in air because the density of air decreases as its temperature increases. Suggest why hot air balloons usually fly in the early morning and late evening and not in the middle of the day.

Activity 3.1.1

Densities of some regular objects

In this activity, you will calculate the densities of some different materials, using the mass and volume of regular objects.

You will need:

- a balance, a calculator, a ruler that can measure in millimetres, some regular objects made from different materials.

Method

1 Measure the length, width and height of each object. You should measure to the nearest 0.1 cm.

2 Calculate the volume of each object in cm^3.

3 Measure the mass of each object in grams. Remember to check that the balance is reading 0.0 g before you place the material on the balance.

4 Calculate the density of each material using the volumes and masses that you measured.

5 Record your results in a table.

Questions

1 The density of water is 1.0 g/cm^3. Use this value and your calculated densities to predict which materials will float and which will sink in water. If you have time, you could test these predictions.

2 Explain the importance of making sure the balance is reading 0.0 g before you place the material on the balance.

3 Some blocks of material may be old and slightly damaged, such as the one shown in the diagram.

    a Explain why your calculated value for the volume of these damaged objects may not be correct.

    b Explain whether the masses of these damaged objects will be correct.

    c Suggest how any differences in volume and mass would affect the calculated value of density.

Think like a scientist

Densities of irregular objects

In this investigation, you will calculate the densities of irregular objects.

You will need:

- a balance, measuring cylinders of various sizes, water, a calculator, small irregular objects that will sink in water and will fit inside the measuring cylinders.

Safety

Do not drop heavy objects into glass measuring cylinders; either use a plastic measuring cylinder, or hold the glass measuring cylinder at an angle, so that the object slides down slowly.

Method

1   Measure the mass of each object in grams. Remember to check that the balance is reading 0.0 g before you place the object on the balance.
2   Use the displacement method to calculate the volumes of your objects in cm³.
3   Calculate the density of each object using the volumes and masses that you measured.
4   Record your results in a table.

Questions

1   Explain why you should read the volume on a measuring cylinder with your eye at the same level as the surface of the liquid.
2   Explain how you would use the displacement method to calculate the volume of an object that floats in water. Remember that the displacement method only gives the correct volume of an object that is completely under the water.
3   Explain how you would use the displacement method to calculate the volume of an object that sinks in water but is too big to fit in a measuring cylinder.
4   Sofia and Zara are calculating the densities of irregular objects. Zara calculates the density of a small toy made from wood to be 5.27 g/cm³. Sofia says this result is anomalous. Explain whether this result is likely to be correct or anomalous.

Continued

Self-assessment

For each of these statements, decide on how confident you are.
Give yourself 5 if you are very confident and 1 if you are not confident at all.

- I understand how to calculate the volume of a regular object.
- I understand how to calculate the volume of an irregular object.
- I know the equation for density.
- I can use density to predict whether an object will float or sink in water.

Summary checklist

☐ I can recall what is meant by density.
☐ I can recall the equation for density.
☐ I can use the equation for density and can calculate density, mass or volume.
☐ I know how to use density to predict whether an object will float or sink in water.

> 3.2 Heat and temperature

In this topic you will:

- understand the difference between heat and temperature.

Getting started

Work in groups to discuss answers to these questions.

1   Describe how you could increase the temperature of water in a beaker.

2   a   Which of these needs more thermal energy to increase its temperature by 10 °C:

- a glass containing 0.25 kg of water

- 375 000 kg of water in a swimming pool?

   b   Explain your answer.

Heat

You will remember that we described thermal energy in Stage 7. Thermal energy can be transferred between objects. Thermal energy can be stored in an object, but the thermal energy that is stored will eventually dissipate into the surroundings. Thermal energy is measured in joules.

When the thermal energy of an object increases, the particles in the object start to vibrate faster. The energy of the particles increases.

Heat is a measure of the energy in the particles.

Heat is the total thermal energy of the vibrating particles in an object.

Look at the glasses of water in the pictures:

The volume of water is the same in both glasses. One has a higher temperature than the other, meaning that the thermal energy (heat) is greater. The water at the higher temperature contains particles that are moving faster. The number of particles in both glasses of water is the same, but the total thermal energy (heat) of the particles in the water with the higher temperature is higher.

The water in both glasses is at the same temperature. There is a larger volume of water in one glass, so it has more particles. As there are more particles, the total thermal energy (heat) of all these particles is greater than in the water with fewer particles. That means the larger volume of water has greater total thermal energy (heat) than the smaller volume, even when their temperatures are the same.

Temperature

Temperature is **not** the same as heat. Temperature gives us information about two things:

- the direction that thermal energy will be transferred
- the average energy of the particles in an object.

The ice cream in the picture is at a lower temperature than the surroundings.

The ice cream has been taken from a freezer at −20 °C. The air in the room is at 24 °C, which is a temperature difference of 44 °C (from −20 to 24 °C). Thermal energy is transferred from the air to the ice cream because of this temperature difference.

The larger a temperature difference between two objects, the faster the thermal energy transfer.

Temperature also gives us information about the energy of the particles.

Heat tells us about the *total* energy of the particles.

Temperature tells us the *average* energy of the particles.

This means temperature is a good way of comparing the particle energy between objects of different size or made from different materials.

Look at the picture of the hot soup and the cold water.

The soup is at a higher temperature than the water.

The soup and the water in the picture are made from different materials, so the types of particles are different. The mass and volume of the soup and the water are also different, so the numbers of particles are different.

When we say the temperature of the soup is higher than the temperature of the water, we mean the *average* energy of the soup particles is higher than the *average* energy of the water particles.

Another way to think of this is that 100 particles in the soup have more energy than 100 particles in the water.

Heat and temperature in a sparkler

A sparkler is a small hand-held firework.

When you hold a sparkler, some of the sparks may fall on your hand. The sparkler can be at a temperature of about 1000 °C, but one spark does not cause serious burns. Why not?

The reason is the mass of the spark is very small and the temperature difference between the air and the spark is very large.

As there are fewer particles in the spark than in the main part of the sparkler, the total particle energy is much smaller. Therefore, the total thermal energy or heat of the spark is very small.

As the temperature difference between the spark and the air is large, thermal energy will be transferred from the spark to the air quickly. In the short time the spark takes to fall to your skin, its temperature, and heat, have both decreased significantly.

How low can you go?

As the temperature of an object decreases, the particles move more slowly. A scientist called Kelvin in the 1800s predicted that particles would eventually stop moving if the temperature is low enough. Kelvin also predicted that if particles stop moving, this would be the lowest possible temperature.

Kelvin called this temperature absolute cold. We now call this temperature absolute zero. Absolute zero is −273 °C.

It is not actually possible to make particles stop moving completely, but scientists have created temperatures within billionths of a degree of absolute zero in laboratories!

Remember:

*   heat is the *total* thermal energy in an object, which is the total energy of all the particles
*   temperature is the *average* energy of the particles in an object.

Questions

1   **a**   Which of these is the unit of heat?

J   °C   N   m³

    b   Which of these is the unit of temperature?

J   °C   N   m³

2   The diagram shows two blocks of copper, A and B.

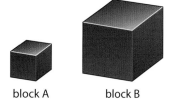

-   block A has a mass of 10 g and a temperature of 25 °C
-   block B has a mass of 80 g and a temperature of 25 °C.

block A   block B

    a   Compare the temperatures of blocks A and B.

    b   Compare the heat of blocks A and B.

3   **a**   Describe what is meant by the heat of an object.

    b   Describe what is meant by the temperature of an object.

4   The diagram shows three objects, A, B and C that are in contact with each other. The three objects are at different temperatures when they are first placed in contact.

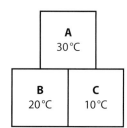

In which direction will thermal energy be transferred?

A → B only

A → C only

A → B and A → C only

A → B and A → C and B → C

5   Zara makes this statement:

> If object X has a higher temperature than object Y, then X must always have more heat than Y.

Is Zara's statement true or false?

Explain your answer.

Activity 3.2.1

The Mpemba effect

In this activity, you will investigate how the temperature of water affects the time taken to freeze the water.

You will need:
- identical containers – such as plastic cups – to hold a small volume of water, access to a freezer, water, measuring cylinder, heat source, thermometer, permanent marker, timer.

Safety

If using plastic cups, do not use water at a temperature higher than 60 °C, so the cups do not melt.

Method

1   Prepare a range of cups by writing your chosen temperature on the side of each cup. For example, one cup each at 10 °C, 20 °C and 30 °C.

2   Add equal volumes of water at the chosen temperature to each cup. A volume of 10–20 cm^3 is enough.

3   Place the cups in the freezer and start the timer.

4   Check the water at equal time intervals for signs of freezing. Record the time taken for each sample to form ice across the surface of the water.

While waiting for the water to freeze, begin to answer the questions.

Questions

1   Draw a table to record your results.

2   Assume the temperature inside the freezer is −18 °C.

    Calculate the temperature difference between −18 °C and the temperature of each sample of water that you used. Remember that you will be subtracting a negative number from a positive number.
    For example, 40 °C − (−18 °C) = 58 °C.

3   What is the link between temperature difference and the speed of thermal energy transfer?

4   Describe any trends in your results.

Think like a scientist

Measuring heat and temperature

In this investigation, you will make measurements of both heat and temperature. Work in groups of three of four.

> You will need:
>
> * the apparatus shown in the diagram.

Safety

Do not touch the immersion heater while it is switched on.

Clamp the immersion heater so that it does not touch the bottom of the cup.

Method

Set up the equipment as shown in the diagram.

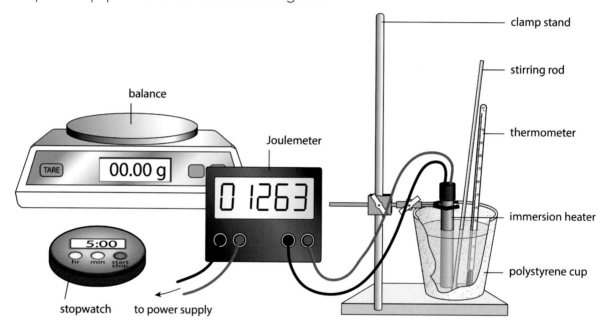

1   Put a known mass of water into the polystyrene cup.
2   Measure and record the temperature of the water at the start of the experiment.
3   Set the joule meter to zero or record the reading at the start.
4   Switch on the immersion heater and start the timer.
5   Use the stirrer to mix the water just before every minute and measure the water temperature every minute.
6   Record the reading on the joule meter every minute.

Continued

7   Continue with the temperature measurements until the temperature of the water has increased by 10 °C.

8   Switch off the immersion heater and allow it to cool.

Questions

1   Record your results in a table.

2   Plot a line graph with temperature on the y-axis and energy on the x-axis.

3   Describe the trend in the results.

4   If you were to repeat this experiment, list three variables that should be kept the same.

5   Most of the thermal energy from the immersion heater is transferred to increase the temperature of the water. List **three** other ways that thermal energy can be transferred in this investigation.

6   Suggest **two** ways to ensure that more thermal energy from the immersion heater is transferred to the water.

Self-assessment

Decide how well you did each of these things:

- making measurements at the correct time
- recording results in a table
- drawing the graph of the results.

Choose one thing that you could do better next time.

How will you do this better next time? What will you change?

Summary checklist

☐   I know what is meant by heat.
☐   I know what is meant by temperature.
☐   I know the difference between heat and temperature.

> 3.3 Conservation of energy

In this topic you will:

- learn that energy cannot be created or destroyed
- understand that because energy is conserved, there is no increase or decrease in energy
- understand that thermal energy is dissipated from hotter places to colder places.

Getting started

1   Thermal is an energy store. List as many other types of energy store as you can remember.

2   Choose two of your energy stores. Describe how the energy can be changed between these energy stores.

3   Describe what is meant by dissipated energy.

Key words

conserved
created
destroyed
system

Energy is conserved

People often talk about conserving energy when they mean using less energy. For example, you switch off a lamp when you leave the room.

In physics, saying that energy is **conserved** means something different from saying less energy is being used.

When we say that energy is conserved, we mean that the total quantity of energy stays the same. This happens when energy is stored, changed, transferred or even dissipated.

Look at the energy diagram for an electric lamp (extension material).

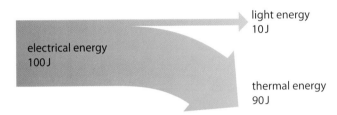

The energy diagram shows that every time 100 J of electrical energy is supplied to the lamp, 10 J of this is changed to light energy and 90 J is changed to thermal energy. The light energy is useful and the thermal energy is wasted.

The electrical energy is called the energy input and the light and thermal energy together are called the energy output.

The total energy input of 100 J is the same as the total energy output of 10 J + 90 J = 100 J.

This shows how energy is conserved in an electric lamp.

The energy diagram for the engine in a car has more energy outputs (extension material).

In the energy diagram for a car engine, the energy input and outputs are shown as percentages. Notice that the energy input is 100% and the total energy output adds up to 100%. Once again, energy is conserved.

In these examples, the electric lamp and the car engine are types of **system**. In physics, a system is something that has been chosen to be studied, especially in terms of energy changes.

The total energy output can never be greater than the total energy input in any type of system. This is because energy cannot be **created**. Created means to make something, or to bring something into existence.

Wasted energy, such as thermal energy, is dissipated. Dissipated means this energy spreads out into the surroundings and becomes less useful. Although this energy is dissipated, it is not **destroyed**. Destroyed is the opposite of created. Destroyed means to damage something or to end its existence.

The law of conservation of energy states that energy cannot be created or destroyed, only changed or transferred.

Questions

1   **a**   Write down the law of conservation of energy.

    b   Decide whether each of these statements is true or false:

       i   The total energy input to a mobile phone is greater than the total energy output.

       ii   The total energy output of a washing machine is greater than the total energy input.

       iii   The total energy input to a wood fire is equal to the total energy output.

2   (Extension question) For each of these energy diagrams, calculate the missing energy value, **X**.

    a   An electric motor

    b   A television

    c   A bus engine

3   a   In a wood fire, 70% of the chemical energy in wood is changed to thermal energy. The remaining energy is changed to light and waste chemicals.

Calculate the percentage of the chemical energy in the wood that is changed to light and waste chemicals.

b   In an oil-burning power station, 55% of the chemical energy in the oil is changed to thermal energy and 10% is used in the power station. The remainder is changed to electrical energy.

Calculate the percentage of the chemical energy in the oil that is changed to electrical energy.

4   Sofia has an LED flashlight that uses 18 J of electrical energy. 7 J of the electrical energy is wasted as thermal energy. Sofia says that 12 J of the electrical energy is changed to light.

Explain whether Sofia is correct.

Activity 3.3.1

Conservation of energy

In this activity, you will observe energy being transferred from one moving object to another.

You will need:

*   two identical plastic water bottles with lids, water, string, scissors, ruler, two strong supports – such as clamp stands – about 70–80 cm apart.

Method

1   Fill the two water bottles completely with water so there is no air inside. This is to make sure both bottles have equal mass.

2   Tie a piece of string about 10 cm long to the neck of each bottle.

3   Stretch a piece of string between the two supports and tie securely at each end. The string must be high enough for the water bottles to hang down without touching the surface below. This is the supporting string.

4   Tie the two bottles to the supporting string so they hang about 40–50 cm apart and hang down at equal heights, as shown in the diagram.

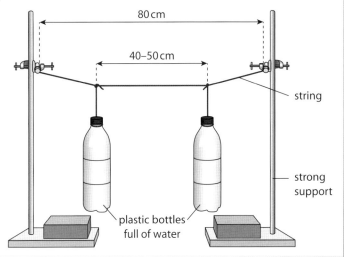

Continued

5 Looking at the equipment as shown in the diagram, pull the bottom of one bottle towards you so that it will swing at 90° to the supporting string.

6 Observe what happens to the two bottles.

Questions

1 Describe what you observe in the movement of the two bottles.

2 Explain this observation using the law of conservation of energy.

3 Explain why the bottles will eventually stop moving.

Activity 3.3.2

Bottle racers

In this activity, you will make household objects move using conservation of energy.
Work in pairs.

> You will need:
> * empty plastic bottle with a small hole in the lid and another small hole in the base of the bottle, paperclip, elastic band, pencil or stick.

Method

1 Attach a paperclip to the elastic band and pass the other end of the elastic band into the bottle through the hole in the base.

2 Pull the elastic band out through the open top of the bottle and pass this end through the hole in the lid. Pass the pencil though this end of the elastic band.

3 Put the lid back onto the bottle.

4 The picture shows a completed bottle racer.

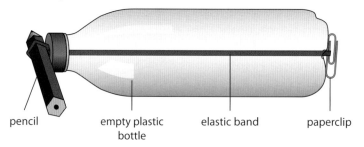

pencil   empty plastic bottle   elastic band   paperclip

5 Rotate the pencil **once** so that the elastic band twists inside the bottle.

6 Place the bottle on its side on the floor.

7 Release the bottle. It should not move.

8 Find the number of times you need to rotate the pencil to make the bottle move.

Continued

Questions

1   State the part of the bottle racer that stores the energy.

2   Name the energy store in the bottle racer before it starts to move.

3   Name the energy that is transferred to the bottle to make it move.

4   If you rotate the pencil more times, what happens to the movement of the bottle racer?

    Explain these observations.

    You could extend this activity by finding the number of times the pencil must be rotated to make the bottle move up a slope.

Summary checklist

☐   I can recall the law of conservation of energy.

☐   I know that the total energy input to a system is equal to the total energy output.

☐   I can use the law of conservation of energy to calculate missing energy values.

> 3.4 Moving from hot to cold

In this topic you will:

- discover that thermal energy always transfers from hotter places to colder places
- understand what is meant by heat dissipation.

Getting started

Work in groups.

Imagine you are in a hot room. It is colder outside than inside. When someone opens a window, the room feels colder.

Discuss what happens in terms of thermal energy to make the room colder.

Key words

colder
hotter

Feeling heat

When you put your hands around a hot drink, you can feel heat in your hands. This will only happen if the drink is **hotter** than your hands. Hotter means at a higher temperature.

Thermal energy moves from the drink, through the container and into your hands.

colder
(lower temperature)

hotter
(higher temperature)

colder
(lower temperature)

Thermal energy moves from the hotter drink to your colder hands.

Thermal energy always moves from hotter places to **colder** places. Colder means at a lower temperature.

We make use of this in many ways:

When you put food into a refrigerator, thermal energy transfers *out* of the food, and the food becomes colder.

There is water inside a car engine to remove thermal energy from the metal engine parts. This stops the engine overheating.

Animals sometimes go in water to cool down. Thermal energy moves from the animal's body into the colder water.

When thermal energy is removed from a hot object, we say that the thermal energy has dissipated.

Feeling cold

Imagine you are holding ice. The ice feels cold.

It is easy to think that the cold from the ice moves into your hand, but that does **not** happen. Cold is **not** an energy store and cold **cannot** move. Cold means there is less thermal energy.

When you hold the ice, thermal energy transfers away from your hand and into the ice. You feel cold because thermal energy has been transferred away from your hands. You can damage your skin by holding ice for too long, as your skin needs the correct quantity of thermal energy to function.

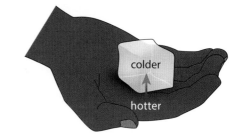

When it is colder outside and you open a window, the inside cools down. This is because thermal energy from the hotter inside moves to the colder outside. Cold *air* may enter the room, but thermal energy from the warmer air is still transferred to the colder air.

Dissipation

You met the word dissipation in Stage 7. Dissipation is used to describe energy that spreads out and becomes less useful.

When thermal energy moves from a hotter place to a colder place, we say that thermal energy has dissipated from the hotter place.

The rate, or speed, of thermal energy transfer increases when the temperature difference between the hot place and the cold place increases.

Remember that energy is always conserved, so the thermal energy has not disappeared or been destroyed, it has just spread out and moved to a colder place.

Some scientists think that, billions of years in the future, all the thermal energy in the universe will have dissipated. At that time, everything in the universe will be at the same low temperature and no more energy changes or transfers will be possible.

Questions

1 Copy and complete the sentence using the best words.

Thermal energy moves from ………….. places to …………... places.

2 Marcus buys hot food and takes the food home.

    a What will happen to the temperature of the hot food on the way home?

    b Explain your answer using the words thermal energy.

3 Arun takes ice cream out of the freezer. The temperature of the ice cream is $-18\,°C$ when he first takes it from the freezer. The temperature of the air in the room is $22\,°C$.

Explain what will happen to the temperature of the ice cream.

4 Sofia and Zara visit an indoor ski slope. The temperature of the air at the indoor ski slope is $-2\,°C$. Both girls wear gloves.

The gloves keep the cold away from my hands.

Sofia

The gloves keep the heat in my hands.

Zara

Explain whether Sofia or Zara is correct.

5 This diagram shows a car engine.

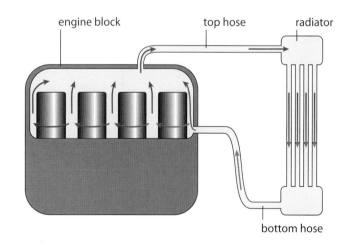

engine block   top hose   radiator

bottom hose

The engine block gets hot. Water flows through the engine in the direction shown by the arrows. Cold water enters the engine block through the bottom hose.

    a Explain how the water keeps the engine from getting too hot.

    b Hot water comes out of the engine through the top hose. The water is cooled as it passes through the radiator. The radiator is exposed to air at the front of the engine.

    Explain what happens to the thermal energy in the water as it passes through the radiator.

Activity 3.4.1

Hot coffee

In this activity, you will do a thought experiment.

Imagine you are making hot coffee for a friend. Your friend drinks hot coffee with a small volume of cold milk added. Your friend will arrive in five minutes. Your friend does not like cold coffee!

There are two methods, A and B, for preparing the coffee.

Method A: Pour the hot coffee into a cup. Leave the coffee for five minutes, and then add the cold milk.

Method B: Pour the hot coffee into a cup and add the cold milk. Then leave this mixture for five minutes.

In each case, think about what should happen. This is called a thought experiment.

Questions

1   Which method, A or B, will result in the coffee being hottest after 5 minutes, or will there be no difference?

2   Explain your choice.

3   Imagine you will do an experiment to compare methods A and B. Make a list of the variables you would need to keep constant to make the comparison fair.

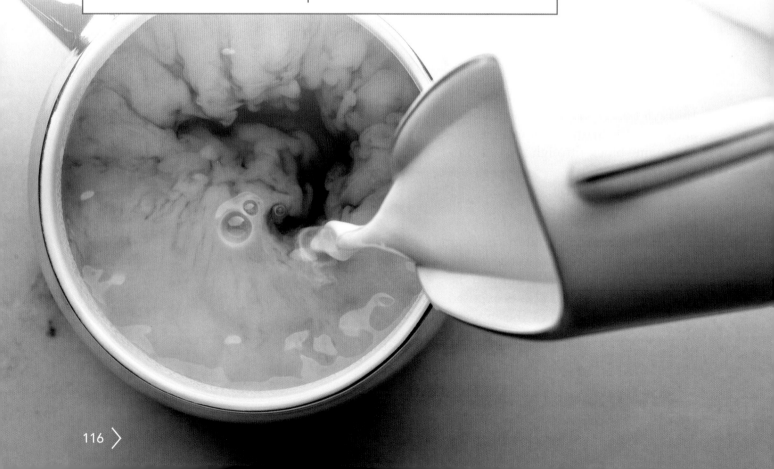

Think like a scientist

Temperature change from heat dissipation

In this investigation, you will measure the temperature change in water caused by heat dissipation.

Work in groups of two or three.

You will need:

- 2 V or 6 V lamp, lamp holder, cells, wires and connectors, 50 cm³ (or smaller) beaker, water, thermometer, timer.

Safety

This experiment must be carried out in the school laboratory. Make sure that **only** the glass part of the lamp is in the water. **Never** put a lamp in water at home!

Method

1   Set up the apparatus as shown in the diagram.

2   Use as small a volume of water as possible.

3   Make sure that **only the glass part** of the lamp is in the water.

4   Record the temperature of the water.

5   Switch on the lamp.

6   Record the temperature of the water every minute.

7   Continue to record the temperature of the water until the temperature stops changing.

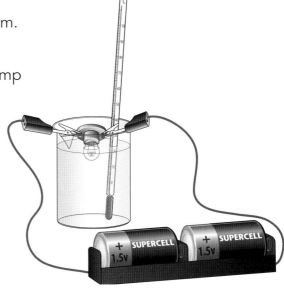

Questions

1   Record your results in a table.

2   Plot a line graph of your results.

3   Explain the change in temperature of the water in the first few minutes after switching on the lamp.

4   Explain why the temperature of the water eventually stops increasing.

5   An LED is a device that changes electrical energy to light energy. LEDs change a bigger percentage of electrical energy to light energy than a lamp. Use this information to predict any differences in results if the experiment were repeated with an LED. Assume everything else in the experiment stays the same.

Summary checklist

☐ I know that thermal energy moves from hotter places to colder places

☐ I know that the spreading out of thermal energy is called dissipation.

> 3.5 Ways of transferring thermal energy

In this topic you will:

- describe how thermal energy can be transferred by conduction
- describe how thermal energy can be transferred by convection
- describe how thermal energy can be transferred by radiation.

Getting started

Work in groups to discuss the answers to these questions.

1 Describe how particles are arranged in:

   a   a solid   **b**   a liquid   **c**   a gas

2 Describe what happens to the particles when each of these substances is heated:

   a   a solid   **b**   a liquid   **c**   a gas

Key words

- conduction
- convection
- convection current
- emit
- expand
- radiation
- vigorously

Heat and particle movement

When any substance is heated, the particles in that substance start to move faster.

In solids, the particles move by vibrating around fixed positions. This vibration gets faster when the solid is heated. As the particles vibrate more **vigorously**, they take up more space. Vigorously means with more energy, more speed and more force. That means solids **expand** when heated. Expand means to increase in size.

In liquids, the particles also vibrate, but the particles are not in fixed positions. When the liquid is heated, the particles vibrate faster and move around faster. Again, as the thermal energy increases, the particles take up more space. That means the liquid expands when heated.

In gases, the particles are far apart and move in straight lines until they collide with another particle or the walls of the container. When the gas is heated, the particles move faster and collide with more force and more frequently. The particles will take up more space in a heated gas, so gases also expand when heated.

Conduction

When particles are vibrating, they will push against the particles beside them. The faster and more vigorous the vibration of the particles, the greater the push. This will cause the particles beside to vibrate more vigorously as well.

This is how thermal energy is transferred by **conduction**. Conduction of thermal energy works best in solids where the particles are close together and can only move by vibrating. The diagram shows how thermal energy is transferred by conduction through a solid.

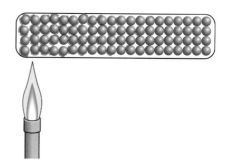

Metals are the best conductors of heat because of the way the particles are arranged. The electrons that are free to move in a metal help to pass along the vibrations.

Wood, plastics and fabrics, such as wool and cotton are poor conductors.

Just as with electricity, the opposite of a conductor is an insulator. We say that poor conductors of thermal energy are good thermal insulators.

Some objects are made from materials that are chosen because of their ability to conduct thermal energy.

Look at the pan in the picture. The pan is made from metal because metal is a good conductor of thermal energy. That helps the food to heat faster. The handle is made from plastic because plastic is a good thermal insulator. That makes the handle comfortable to touch. The spoon is made from wood, which is also a good insulator.

Clothes for cold weather are made from materials that are good insulators. That slows the conduction of thermal energy away from the body.

Conduction does not work well in liquids because the particles move around more when heated, rather than just vibrating.

Conduction also does not work well in gases because the particles are far apart and the collisions are not very frequent.

Conduction cannot happen in a vacuum as there are no particles to vibrate in a vacuum.

Convection

When liquids and gases are heated, the particles move faster and take up more space.

Taking up more space means the volume increases. The number of particles does not change, so the mass of the liquid or gas does not change.

You will remember from Topic 3.1 that density $= \dfrac{\text{mass}}{\text{volume}}$

From this equation, you can see that when volume increases and mass stays the same, then density will decrease.

You will also remember from Topic 3.1 that less dense substances float in more dense substances.

Imagine a gas or liquid that is heated at the bottom. The particles at the bottom will start to move faster and take up more space. This part of the liquid or gas will become less dense and start to float up through the colder, more dense parts. This upward movement of warmer liquid or gas is called **convection**.

Colder, more dense parts of the liquid or gas then sink down to occupy the space. These colder parts are then closer to the source of heat and they get heated. The particles in these parts then occupy more space and start to float.

This movement around the heated liquid or gas is called a **convection current**. The convection current causes all of the liquid or gas to eventually become heated.

The diagram shows how a convection current heats all the air in a room.

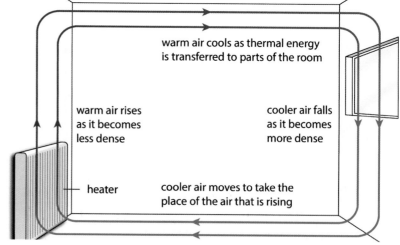

warm air cools as thermal energy is transferred to parts of the room

warm air rises as it becomes less dense

cooler air falls as it becomes more dense

heater

cooler air moves to take the place of the air that is rising

The next diagram shows how a convection current heats all the water in a cooking pan.

Convection can happen in liquids and gases because the particles are free to move.

Convection cannot happen in a solid because the particles are not free to move. The particles in a solid can only vibrate about fixed positions.

Convection cannot happen in a vacuum as there are no particles to move.

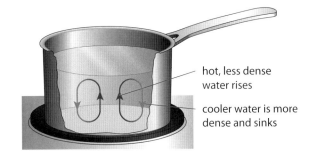

hot, less dense water rises

cooler water is more dense and sinks

The cooking pan is heated only at the bottom, but convection currents in the water heat all of the water.

Radiation

There is a vacuum in the space between the Sun and the Earth, so conduction or convection would not transfer thermal energy from the Sun to Earth. That means thermal energy must be transferred in a different way.

This different way is called **radiation**. Radiation is a type of wave that we cannot see. Thermal energy can be transferred by radiation very quickly. The thermal energy from the Sun only takes aboutnine minutes to reach Earth!

All objects give out thermal energy through radiation. The hotter the object, the more radiation it will **emit**. Emit means to give out.

The Sun and other hot objects emit thermal energy by radiation. Cooler objects absorb thermal energy by radiation from hotter ones.

Radiation can pass through a vacuum because radiation does not need particles.

Radiation can also pass through transparent solids, liquids and gases.

The colour and texture of an object affects its ability to emit or absorb thermal energy by radiation.

The best emitters and absorbers of radiation:

* are dull
* are black
* have a large surface area.

The worst emitters and absorbers of radiation:

* are shiny
* are white or silver
* have a small surface area.

Shiny, white or silver surfaces reflect radiation away.

Penguins have black feathers on their backs to absorb as much thermal energy from radiation as possible.

Buildings in many hot countries are painted white so they absorb less thermal energy from radiation.

Conduction, convection and radiation

Most objects gain or lose thermal energy by a combination of conduction, convection and radiation.

Look at the picture of the room heater.

The room heater in the picture has hot water flowing through the inside. Thermal energy from the hot water is transferred to the metal of the heater by conduction. Thermal energy from the metal is transferred to the air, also by conduction. When the warm air expands, this warm air rises, which heats the air above by convection. The metal surface of the heater also emits thermal energy by radiation.

The room heater uses conduction, convection and radiation to heat the room.

Some objects are designed to reduce the effects of conduction, convection or radiation.

Vacuum flasks are containers used to store hot liquids such as tea, coffee or soup. The flask is designed to slow the transfer of thermal energy by reducing conduction and radiation.

Inside a vacuum flask there is a glass bottle with a silver surface. The glass bottle is surrounded by a vacuum, and the bottle only makes contact with the outside of the flask at the top, as shown in the diagram.

The silver surface of the bottle reflects thermal energy in the form of radiation back into the hot drink. The vacuum surrounding the bottle prevents conduction of thermal energy from the drink to the outside.

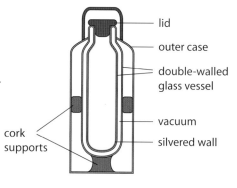

lid
outer case
double-walled glass vessel
vacuum
silvered wall
cork supports

Inside a vacuum flask

Double-glazed windows reduce thermal energy transfer into or out of buildings. The picture shows double-glazed windows. There are two layers of glass separated by a thin layer of argon gas. Argon is a poor conductor of heat. In the picture, you can also see insulation inside the wall of the house. There is a space between the two layers of the brick wall that is filled with foam. The foam is a poor conductor and also fills the space to prevent convection currents from forming inside the wall.

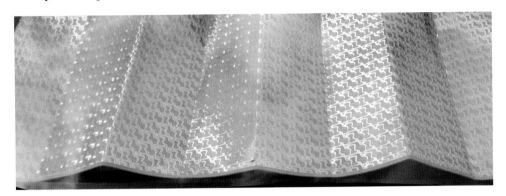

Car windows can be covered with silver material to reflect radiation from the Sun away from the inside of the car. This helps to stop the car becoming too hot inside when parked on a sunny day.

Questions

1   a   List the three ways that thermal energy can be transferred from one place to another.

    b   Explain which two of these ways cannot occur in a vacuum.

    c   Explain which one of these ways occurs best in solids.

2   Marcus and Arun go out on a sunny day. Marcus wears a white T-shirt and Arun wears a black T-shirt. Their T-shirts are the same apart from the colours.

    Explain any difference in the heat that the two boys will feel when they spend the same time in the Sun.

3   Which method transfers thermal energy:

    a   through a metal cooking pan

    b   from the Sun to Earth.

4   The diagram shows a water tank with an electric heater to heat the water.

    a   Explain how the electric heater heats all of the water in the tank.

    b   Explain why hot water is removed from the top of the tank and not from the bottom.

    c   The total volume of water in the tank does not change. Some tanks have a second electric heater that can be used when not all of the water in the tank needs to be heated. Suggest where the second electric heater would be positioned in the tank.

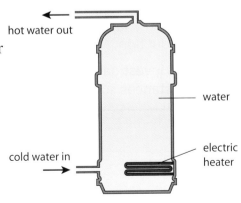

Think like a scientist

Conduction of thermal energy in different materials

In this investigation, you will compare how different materials conduct thermal energy.

Work in groups of two or three.

You will need:
- rods about 30 cm long made from different metals, candle wax, paperclips, a heat source – such as a candle – that can be used to heat one end of the rod, clamp stands.

Safety

Write a risk assessment for this investigation. Check it with your teacher before carrying out the investigation.

Method

1   Melt the candle wax and use the soft wax to attach paperclips to each rod at intervals of about 5 cm.

2   Clamp one rod so that one end of the rod can be heated, as shown in the diagram.

3   Heat one end of each rod and observe what happens to the wax and the paperclips.

Questions

1   To make the comparison a fair test, list the variables that must be kept constant for each rod.

2   List any of these variables that you could not control in your experiment.

3   Describe your observations.

4   Explain your observations using ideas about thermal energy, particles and conduction.

5   This investigation cannot be used to test conduction of thermal energy in substances such as wood or plastic. Explain why.

Activity 3.5.1

Observing convection

In this activity, you will observe a convection current in water.

Work in groups of two or three.

You will need:

- large glass beaker, tripod without gauze, cold water, heat source – such as a candle – coloured ink or water-based paint, pipette.

Method

1   Fill the beaker with cold water to about three-quarters full.

2   Use the pipette to place a small volume of coloured ink at one side of the bottom of the beaker. Take care not to mix the coloured ink with the water.

3   Place the heat source under the beaker below the position of the coloured ink as shown in the diagram.

4   Do not stir the water while heating.

5   Observe what happens to the coloured ink.

Questions

1   Record your observations in a series of labelled drawings.

2   Add a written explanation of what is happening in your drawings. Use ideas about particles and density.

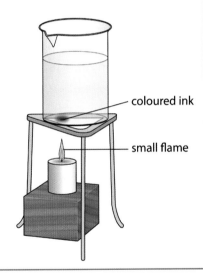

coloured ink

small flame

Think like a scientist

Emitting thermal energy by radiation

In this investigation, you will compare how different colours emit radiation.

Work in groups of two or three.

You will need:

- three or more identical empty food or drink cans, paint (matt/dull black, white and silver – other colours optional), three or more thermometers, hot water, measuring cylinder, funnel, timer, graph paper.

Method

1 Paint three identical cans dull black, white and silver. Allow the paint to dry until the next lesson.

Question

1 You will be placing hot water in each can and investigating how long the water takes to cool in each can. Write a prediction for this investigation, explaining any differences between the three cans.

black   white   silver

Method (continued)

2 Measure the volume of water that will be needed to fill one of your containers to within about 1 cm from the top.

3 Heat enough water to fill four cans (or one more than the number of cans you will use).

4 Stop heating the water when the temperature is about 60 °C.

5 Measure an equal volume of water into each can. Use the funnel to help get all of the water into the cans.

6 Place a thermometer in each can and record the temperature of the water every two minutes.

Questions

2 Record your results in a single table with separate columns for each colour of can.

3 Plot a line graph of your results. Draw the lines for each colour of can on the same graph. Use a key to identify each line.

4 Describe the trends in your results.

5 Explain whether your results matched your prediction.

6 Explain how you could recognise any anomalous results in this investigation.

Continued

7   Make a list of the variables that must be kept the same in this investigation.

8   This investigation was to compare how the colours emitted thermal energy by radiation. Describe an investigation to compare how these coloured cans would absorb thermal energy by radiation.

Summary checklist

☐ I know that thermal energy can be transferred by conduction, convection or radiation.

☐ I know how conduction and convection happen using a particle model.

☐ I know that radiation does not require particles.

☐ I know why conduction works best in solids and cannot happen in a vacuum.

☐ I know why convection happens best in liquids and gases and cannot happen in solids or a vacuum.

☐ I know which colours and textures are the best emitters and reflectors of radiation.

> 3.6 Cooling by evaporation

In this topic you will:

- understand how evaporation causes cooling.

Getting started

Work in groups to discuss the answers to these questions.

The boiling point of water is 100 °C. Water can evaporate at much lower temperatures, such as 15 °C.

1   Explain the difference between boiling and evaporation.

2   Explain how evaporation at temperatures lower than boiling point occurs. Use ideas about particles and energy in your answer.

Key words

porous
random

Evaporation

Evaporation is the change of state from liquid to gas.

Think of a liquid such as water at room temperature. The particles in the water are moving around in **random** directions. Some of these particles move faster than others, and the speed of the particles is also random. The word random means unpredictable.

The particles in the water that are moving faster have more energy. Some of these particles have enough energy to escape from the surface of the liquid and become particles of a gas. Some of these are pulled back into the liquid, but others have sufficient energy to leave and not get pulled back. This is summarised in the diagram.

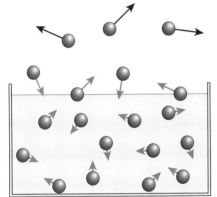

highest energy particles can escape from the liquid

medium energy particles can escape from the liquid but get pulled back into the liquid

lowest energy particles remain in the liquid

Not all of the particles in the liquid are shown. Remember, particles in a liquid are in contact with each other.

Evaporation and cooling

You will recall from Topic 3.2 that temperature is a measure of the average energy of particles.

Think about the water again. Remember that the particles in the water have different energies.

When the particles with the highest energy escape from the water, this will lower the average energy of the particles that remain. Therefore, the temperature of the water will decrease, so evaporation causes cooling.

You can feel the effect of this when you get out of a swimming pool.

When the water on your skin evaporates, the particles with the highest energy escape causing the water to cool. The thermal energy in the water droplets on your skin comes from your skin. Therefore, the energy provided to change the state of the water from liquid to gas comes from your skin. As your skin loses thermal energy, this causes cooling.

When we are too hot, our skin produces sweat. Many people think that the liquid on the skin alone causes cooling, but since the sweat was produced in the skin, it is at the same temperature as the skin.

When the sweat evaporates, its temperature drops. Thermal energy from the skin is then transferred to the cooler sweat and the process continues to lower the skin temperature.

Some animals that do not sweat very much cover themselves in water to cool down. The evaporation of the water gives the cooling effect.

In very humid conditions, sweat may not be able to evaporate. This can be dangerous, as body temperature can increase without this cooling effect.

The picture shows a type of water cooler.

The water cooler is made from **porous** clay. The word porous means that water can slowly soak through the clay. When filled with water, some water soaks through the clay to the outside. This water evaporates into surrounding air, cooling the water inside the water cooler.

Some air coolers use evaporation of water to cool air. The picture shows one of these coolers.

The air cooler contains a sponge that is soaked in water. A fan blows warm air from the room through the sponge. The warm air provides the thermal energy to evaporate the water, and so the thermal energy of the air decreases, cooling the air.

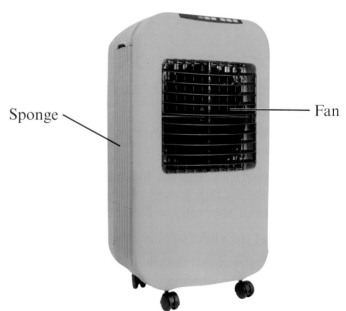

Sponge

Fan

Evaporation and cooling of other liquids

Different liquids have different forces holding the particles together. Some liquids have forces between particles that are weaker than those in water and some are stronger.

Some liquids, such as perfumes, have weaker forces between the particles. Perfumes are designed to evaporate quickly and easily so you can smell them.

If you put equal volumes of perfume and water at the same temperature on your skin, the perfume will feel colder. Perfume evaporates faster than water, so removes thermal energy faster.

Other liquids, such as liquid soap, have stronger forces between the particles. Liquid soap evaporates much more slowly than water. If you put equal volumes of liquid soap and water at the same temperature on your skin, the water will feel colder. Water evaporates faster than liquid soap, so removes thermal energy faster.

Safety note: Do not put any liquid on your skin apart from water, soap or perfume. Soap should be washed off skin using plenty of water.

Questions

1 The boiling point of water is 100 °C.

Copy and complete these sentences about water using words from the list. Each word can be used once, more than once or not at all.

least	most	different	the same
	evaporate	condense	freeze

The energies of the particles in water at 25 °C are ....

Particles with the .... energy stay in the liquid.

Particles with the .... energy can leave the liquid.

When liquid water turns to gas, the water is said to ....

2 Hot water at 80 °C is placed in a beaker and left in a room temperature of 20 °C. Most of the cooling of the water is caused by radiation and conduction. Which of these also causes the temperature of the water to decrease? Write **one** letter.

A freezing B condensation C evaporation D boiling

3 a Explain what happens to the average energy of particles in a liquid during evaporation.

b What happens to the temperature of a liquid during evaporation?

Explain your answer.

4 a Explain how sweat can cool the skin.

b Explain why skin can become too warm when sweat cannot evaporate.

5 Isopropanol is a liquid that can be applied to the skin to reduce the chance of cuts becoming infected. Isopropanol evaporates quickly. Isopropanol at room temperature feels cold when applied to the skin. Explain why.

Think like a scientist

Making an air cooler

In this activity, you will make an air cooler that works by evaporation.

> **You will need:**
> - an old towel, frame to hang towel, tray that can hold water and is long enough to contain one edge of the towel, water, desktop fan, thermometer, stand for thermometer.

Safety

You will be using an electric fan and water in this activity. Keep the water away from electric cables, wall sockets and the fan itself. Keep the fan as far from the wall socket as possible. Make sure the fan can be switched off at the socket immediately if water spills. Only operate switches with dry hands.

Method

1   Make sure the thermometer is dry. Place the thermometer in the stand or clamp the thermometer for all air temperature measurements.

Question

1   Explain why you should **not** hold the thermometer in your hand when measuring the temperature of the air.

Method (continued)

2   Measure the temperature of the air in the room.

3   Switch the fan on and measure the temperature of air coming from the fan.

4   Soak the towel in water and hang the wet towel on the frame.

5   Fill the tray with water and position the wet towel so the bottom edge is in the water.

6   Move the fan to about 10 cm from the wet towel and switch it on, so air is blowing at the wet towel.

7   Measure the temperature of the air between the fan and the wet towel.

Questions

2   Explain any differences in temperature that you measured in steps 2, 3 and 7.

3   Explain any other differences that you would predict if a dry towel were used in place of the wet towel.

Activity 3.6.1

Feeling the effects of evaporation

In this activity, you will feel the effects of cooling by evaporation.

> **You will need:**
> - water, liquid soap, ethanol or isopropanol (also known as isopropyl alcohol or rubbing alcohol), dropper pipette, paper towels, access to hand-washing facilities or running water.

Safety

No other liquids should be used in this activity except ones that are intended for use directly on the skin.

Method

1   Use the dropper pipette to put one drop of water on the back of your hand, as shown in the diagram.

2   Use a finger from your other hand to spread the drop of water thinly on your skin.

3   Gently blow on the wet skin.

4   Remember how this feels.

5   Dry your hand using a paper towel.

6   Repeat steps 1–4 with the liquid soap. This time wash your hand with plenty of water to remove the soap before drying.

7   Repeat steps 1–4 with the ethanol or isopropanol. Wash your hand to remove any ethanol or isopropanol before drying.

Questions

1   Explain why you spread each liquid thinly in step 2.

2   Write a description of what you feel on your skin with each liquid.

3   Use your answer to question 2 to suggest

    a   which of the liquids evaporates fastest

    b   which of the liquids evaporates slowest.

4   Explain why it would be difficult to present the results of this activity in a bar chart.

5   Suggest how you could change this activity to get results that could be presented in a bar chart.

Summary checklist

☐ I know how evaporation can lower the average energy of particles in a liquid.

☐ I know how evaporation can cause cooling effects.

Project: Load lines

Background

Load lines, sometimes called Plimsoll lines, are painted on the sides of many ships. The picture shows an example of load lines.

The load lines are on the side of a ship, half way between the front and the back.

When cargo or passengers go onto a ship, the ship goes further down into the water. The load lines show how far down a ship can be in water and still be safe. The letters stand for different types of water and different conditions.

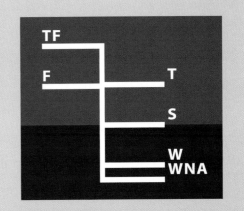

Your task

Find out what the letters on the load lines stand for.

Use a block of wood to model a ship. You will prepare different water conditions and test how your model floats in each. Your water conditions will model those shown on the load lines on a ship.

You can then mark load lines on your model.

You will also explain how the different water conditions affect how the ship floats.

Work in groups.

You can use equipment such as:

* a large bucket or deep sink to hold water
* a large block of wood to model your ship
* salt to add to the water
* a balance to weigh the salt
* a thermometer to measure the temperature of the water
* a method of heating water.

Continued

To give the best results, a block of wood that floats with a minimum of 10 cm of wood below the water surface is suggested.

Fresh water is water such as in rivers and lakes. You can model fresh water by using pure water with no added salt.

Sea water contains salt. Find out how much salt (sodium chloride) you will need to add to water to make your own sea water.

Winter sea water has a minimum temperature of −2 °C.

Summer sea water has a maximum temperature of 27 °C.

Make a presentation of your results.

Remember to:

- include what the letters on the load lines stand for
- explain the different water conditions and how you modelled them
- explain how the model ship floated in each, using ideas about density
- explain why load lines are important in real ships.

Check your progress

3.1 Which of these is the correct equation to calculate density?

Give **one** letter. [1]

A density = weight × volume

B density = $\dfrac{\text{mass}}{\text{volume}}$

C density = $\dfrac{\text{volume}}{\text{mass}}$

D density = $\dfrac{\text{weight}}{\text{volume}}$

3.2 Which statements are true about the density of air?

Give **two** letters. [2]

A The density of air is 0 g/cm³ because air has no mass.

B The density of air is less than that of solids because the particles in air are further apart.

C The density of air is more than that of liquids because the particles in air are closer together.

D The density of air is more than that of a vacuum because a vacuum has no particles.

3.3 An object has a mass of 60 g and a volume of 50 cm³.

a Calculate the density of this object. Show your working and give the unit with your answer. [3]

b The density of water is 1.0 g/cm³. Explain whether this object will float or sink in water. [1]

3.4 Two beakers, X and Y, contain water at the same temperature.

Beaker X contains 50 cm³ water.

Beaker Y contains 100 cm³ water.

a Explain how the average energy of the particles in beakers X and Y compare. [2]

b Explain how the heat of the water in beakers X and Y compare. [2]

3.5 a State the unit of temperature. [1]

b State the unit of heat. [1]

3.6 Copy and complete the law of conservation of energy.

Energy is always ...., meaning that energy cannot
be .... or .... **[2]**

3.7 An electric lamp uses 50 J of electrical energy.

5 J of energy is changed to light energy. The remainder is wasted as thermal energy.

Calculate the quantity of wasted energy. Give the unit. **[2]**

3.8 A small metal ball is heated to a temperature of 200 °C. The heated ball is dropped into water, which is at 4 °C.

   a Explain what happens to the temperature of the ball **and** the temperature of the water just after the ball enters the water. **[2]**

   b After a few minutes, the temperature of the ball and the temperature of the water stop changing. Which statement is true when these temperatures have stopped changing?

     Give **one** letter. **[1]**

   A The temperature of the water will be higher than the temperature of the ball.

   B The temperature of the ball will be higher than the temperature of the water.

   C The temperatures of the water and the ball will be the same.

   D The temperatures of the water and the ball will be lower than 4 °C.

3.9 A metal spoon is initially at room temperature. The metal spoon is placed in a cup of hot tea.

Explain why the handle of the metal spoon increases in temperature. **[3]**

3.10 The diagram shows the convection currents in the air around a heater.

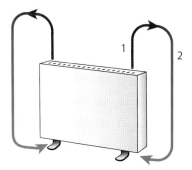

    a   Explain what is happening to the air at position 1 in the diagram.   **[3]**

    b   Explain what is happening to the air at position 2 in the diagram.   **[3]**

3.11 Two cars are parked in the sun on a warm day. They are identical except that one is black and the other is white.

    Both cars are parked for three hours.

    Explain whether there is any temperature difference inside the black car and the white car after three hours.   **[3]**

3.12 Explain how sweat can cool the skin, even when the sweat is at the same temperature as the skin.   **[3]**

4 ▷ Maintaining life

＞ 4.1 Plants and water

In this topic you will:

- find out how plants absorb water
- discover how water moves from a plant's roots to its leaves.

Getting started

All living things need water to stay alive.

For example, living things need water to dissolve chemicals inside their cells, so that chemical reactions (such as respiration) can happen.

With a partner, think of as many sentences as you can that start with:

Living things need water …….

Try to include some good scientific information in each of your sentences. When everyone is ready, take turns with other pairs to share one of your sentences with the rest of the class. Build up a collection of all the different ideas on the board.

Key words

root hairs
xylem vessels

How root hairs absorb water

Plants, like all living things, are made mostly of water. Plants need to absorb water almost all of the time. They do this through their roots. The roots absorb water from the soil.

Soil is made up of tiny particles of rock. The particles are usually irregularly shaped, and all sorts of different sizes. They do not pack together tightly. There are spaces between them, which are filled with air and water.

You may remember that special cells called **root hairs** grow out of the surface of roots. Root hair cells provide a really big surface through which water and mineral ions can be absorbed into the plant.

This photograph of root hairs was taken with a microscope. Root hairs are very tiny, but you can just see them without using a lens.

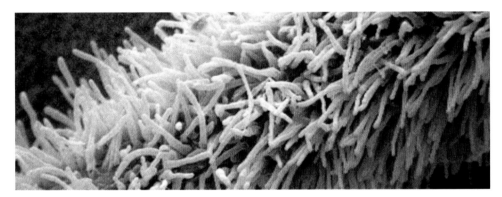

This diagram shows a root hair growing in between soil particles. Each root hair is part of a single cell.

Water moves into the root hair cell from the soil. It passes through the cell wall and the cell membrane of the cell, and into the cytoplasm.

Minerals, including magnesium and nitrate, also move into the root hair cell, along with the water. Magnesium and nitrate are in the form of ions (see Topic 2.4), dissolved in the water between the soil particles.

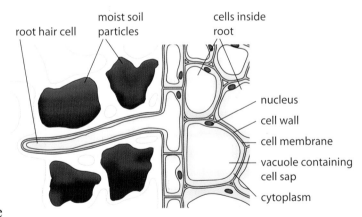

Questions

1   Root hair cells are different from other plant cells. Describe how the structure of a root hair cell helps it to carry out its function.

2   Why do plants need nitrate ions and magnesium ions?

How water moves up the plant

This diagram shows what a root looks like if you cut it across. You can see the root hairs on the outside of the root. In the centre, there are some very special cells called **xylem vessels**. These are the water transport system of the plant.

After water has been absorbed into a root hair cell, it moves from the outside of the root towards the inside. It goes into the xylem vessels in the centre of the root.

Xylem vessels are long, tube-like cells. They are dead cells – all of their contents, such as cytoplasm and a nucleus, have disappeared. All that is left is their cell walls, with an empty space inside. Their end walls have completely disappeared too. Many xylem vessels stack on top of one another, making long, empty tubes that reach all the way from the roots, up to the highest parts of the plant.

The wood in a tree trunk is made up of xylem vessels. They carry water from the roots all the way to the top of the tree.

This photograph shows some xylem vessels. It has been taken with a microscope. The actual diameter of a xylem vessel is only about 0.05 mm – although, as you can see in the photograph, they come in a range of different sizes.

a xylem vessel, which transports water and mineral ions up the plant

cross-shaped area where xylem tissue is found

root hair, for absorbing water and mineral ions

root cap that protects the tip of the root as it grows through the soil

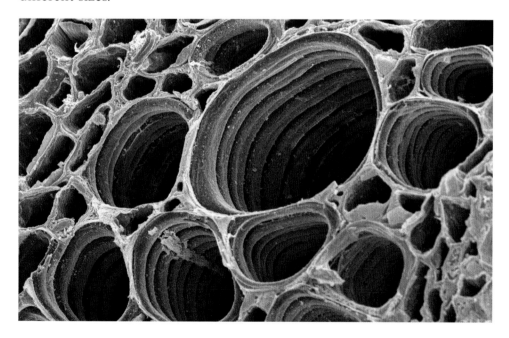

Xylem in roots and stems

These two diagrams show the position of xylem in the roots (left) and stems (right) of a plant. They are cross-sections – you are looking down on a cut surface across a root and across a stem. The xylem vessels are shown in red.

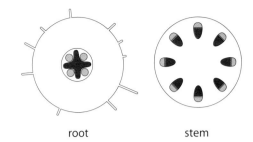

root   stem

Activity 4.1.1

Annotating a diagram

Work with a partner, or in a group of three, for this activity.

On a large sheet of paper, make a big copy of the unlabelled, circular diagram showing the position of xylem vessels in a root. Make sure that you leave enough space around your drawing to add some writing.

Use the information on the three-dimensional diagram on the previous page, and in the text on this page, to add annotations to your diagram.

The annotations should describe what each part does, so that someone looking at your diagram can understand how water is absorbed by the root, and how it is transported upwards from the root.

Self-assessment

Put your completed diagram onto the wall, alongside other learners' diagrams.

How do you think that your diagram and annotations compare with theirs?

What features make one diagram better than another?

Think like a scientist

Investigating transport in a celery stalk

In this experiment, you will try to follow the path of water as it moves up through a stalk.

You will need:

- a stalk of celery, pak choi or another plant that has a thick stalk – it works best if there are leaves at the top of the stalk, a small container, such as beaker or Petri dish, some water mixed with a coloured dye (e.g. blue ink, or methylene blue stain).

Safety

Be sure to put the stalk onto a non-slip surface before you try to cut it.
Cut away from you, so that if the blade slips, it does not hit your hand.

Continued

Method

1 Put some of the coloured water into your small container. You need no more than 1 to 2 cm depth.

2 Cut across the lower end of the stalk (not the leaf end), making sure that the cut end is clean and is not blocked or damaged.

3 Stand the stalk in the coloured water. Make sure you stand the cut end in the water.

4 Every five minutes or so, look at the stalk. You may be able to see the blue dye moving up through it. This can sometimes happen very quickly, or sometimes very slowly – so be prepared!

5 When the dye has reached the top of the stalk, take the stalk out of the container. Rinse the blue dye off the end of the stalk, using tap water.

6 Put the stalk down onto a cork board or other non-slip surface. Use a knife to cut across the end of the stalk, about half way up. You should see something like this:

Questions

1 Make a drawing of the cut end of the stalk after it has been in the blue dye.

2 Which kind of cells do you think are found in the places where you can see blue spots? Choose from:

   palisade cells   root hair cells   xylem cells

   Label your drawing with the name of these cells.

3 Suggest why it was important to do each of these things, as you carried out your experiment.

   a putting no more than 2 cm of water in the container at the start of your experiment

   b washing the stalk before cutting across it, at the end of your experiment

4 In your experiment, there were no roots on the plant. Try to imagine how the stalk that you used would connect with the roots on a complete plant. Then write a sentence or two to explain how – in a complete plant – water would get to the stalk.

Think like a scientist

Planning an experiment

Method

Now that you have done the experiment to see how coloured water moves up a stalk, you are going to think about how you could modify this method to test a hypothesis. After you have had your plan checked, you may be able to do your planned experiment.

Questions

1   Think about what effect temperature might have on the speed at which the water moves up a stalk. If the temperature increases, do you think the water would move upwards faster, or more slowly? Why do you think that?

2   Write down your idea as a hypothesis.

3   Now think about how you could modify the experiment that you did with the stalk, to test your hypothesis. Discuss your ideas with a partner.

4   Write a description of your planned experiment. Make sure that you include:
    - a list, or drawings, of the apparatus that you will need
    - which variable you will change (your independent variable)
    - what you will measure (your dependent variable), how you will measure it and when you will measure it
    - which variables you will keep the same
    - a risk assessment for your planned investigation – what risks are there, and how will you control them?

In this topic, you have used photographs, a three-dimensional diagram, two-dimensional diagrams (the circular ones showing the xylem in stems and roots) and part of a real plant, to help you to understand how water moves into and up a plant.

How easy do you find it to link these different ways of thinking about a topic together? If you do have any difficulties, what might you be able to do to get better at it?

Summary checklist

☐ I can describe how water and mineral salts are absorbed from the soil into root hair cells.

☐ I can describe how water and mineral salts cross the root to reach the xylem vessels.

☐ I can suggest a hypothesis about the rate of movement of water in a stalk.

☐ I can plan an experiment to test my hypothesis.

☐ I can carry out a risk assessment for my experiment.

> 4.2 Transpiration

In this topic you will:

- find out how water vapour is lost from plant leaves
- summarise why plants need water.

Getting started

When we think of water, we usually think of a liquid. But water can also be a solid and a gas.

With a partner, make a drawing to show the arrangement of the particles in liquid water. Then make another drawing to show the arrangement of the particles in water when it is a gas.

Write a brief description next to each drawing, to explain what the particles are doing.

Now write a sentence to explain what happens when liquid water changes to a gas.

Key words

transpiration
wilted

How water moves through leaves

In the last topic, we saw how water goes into a root, across the root to its centre, and then up through the root and stem towards the leaves. Now we will think about what happens to the water when it reaches the leaves.

This diagram shows a section through part of a leaf. The arrows show how water moves out of the xylem vessels, and into the leaf.

When water arrives at a leaf, it moves out of the xylem vessels and into the leaf cells. The cells that have chloroplasts use some of the water for photosynthesis. But they do not need very much water for that, and most of the water does not stay in the cell. The liquid water in the cell soaks into the cellulose cell wall, and then changes to water vapour – it evaporates. The water vapour diffuses into the air spaces between the cells.

These air spaces connect with the air outside the leaf through tiny holes in the underside of the leaf – the stomata. The water vapour can diffuse through these holes and into the air.

The loss of water vapour from leaves is called **transpiration**.

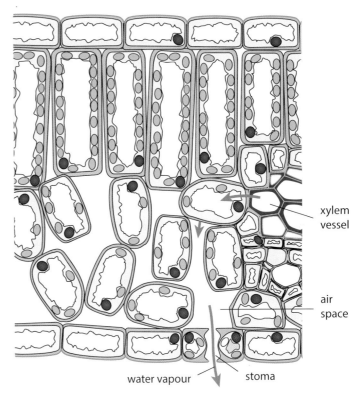

xylem vessel

air space

water vapour stoma

Questions

1   Look at the diagram of the inside of a leaf in Topic 1.2.
    Use the information on that diagram to identify these parts on the diagram on this page

    •   the upper epidermis

    •   the palisade layer

    •   the spongy layer.

2   Most transpiration happens from the underside of a leaf, not the top. Why is this?

Think like a scientist

Investigating transpiration

In this experiment, you will investigate water loss from a plant growing in a pot.

You will need:

- two very similar plants, both growing in the same size pots
- two big, transparent polythene bags
- a balance for measuring the mass of the plants in their pots.

Method

1   Check that the soil in both plant pots is moist. If not, give both of them the same volume of water. Leave the pots for about five minutes, so that any excess water can drain away.

2   Take the first plant, and completely cover the plant and the pot with a plastic bag. Tie the bag very firmly at the top.

3   Take the second plant, and cover the pot and soil, but not the leaves of the plant, with a plastic bag. Tie the bag tightly around the plant stem – but take care not to damage the stem.

4   Measure the mass of both plants in their pots. Record the masses.

5   Each day for at least a week, measure the masses of both plants. Record all of your readings in a results table. (You could put the date in the first column, and the masses of the two plants in the next two columns. Remember to include the units in the column headings.)

Continued

6 Use your results to draw a line graph. You can draw two lines on the same graph – one line for each plant.

Questions

1 What was the variable that you changed (your independent variable) in this experiment?

2 What variables did you keep the same?

3 Compare the changes in mass for the two plants. Use comparative words in your answer, such as 'more' and 'faster'.

4 Explain why one plant lost mass faster than the other. Use the word 'transpiration' in your answer.

Think like a scientist

Which side of a leaf loses most water?

In this experiment, you will hang a number of leaves up to dry. The leaves will be treated differently, so that the surfaces that can lose water vapour are not all the same.

When the leaves lose water, they lose mass. You can compare the mass lost from each leaf to find out which treatment is best at helping the leaf to conserve (keep) its water.

You will need:

- eight leaves, all from the same kind of plant, and all roughly the same size

- some petroleum jelly

- at least eight paperclips, or another way of fixing the leaves to your 'washing line'

- a 'washing line' that you can hang your leaves from; you may be able to hang some string across the whole room for the whole class to share, or you can set up your own personal washing line with some string held between two retort stands

- a balance to measure the mass of the leaves (it needs to be quite sensitive, because leaves have only a small mass)

- some filter paper or other paper to put on the balance when you measure the mass of the leaves, so that you do not get petroleum jelly on the balance.

Method

1 Choose eight leaves that are as similar to each other as possible.

2 Line the leaves up on a piece of paper. Write a letter next to each leaf, in order: A, B, C, D, E, F, G and H. Make sure each leaf stays next to its letter.

Continued

3   Collect some petroleum jelly. Apply it to some of the leaves like this:
Leaves A and B : no petroleum jelly
Leaves C and D: a thin layer of jelly smeared on the upper surface only
Leaves E and F: a thin layer of jelly smeared on the lower surface only
Leaves G and H: a thin layer of jelly smeared on both surfaces.

4   Measure the mass of each leaf, and record it. Take care not to get petroleum jelly on the balance!

5   Now hang all eight leaves on your washing line. You cannot actually label the leaves, so make sure that you keep them in exactly the same order as on the paper (see the diagram below).

6   While the leaves are hanging up, make a prediction about which ones you think will lose mass most quickly. Write it down and explain your prediction.

7   Allow the leaves to dry for at least one day. Then take them off the washing line and measure their masses again.

8   Record all of your results in a results table.

9   Identify any anomalous results. If you have any, decide what you will do about them.

10   Calculate the change in mass for each leaf and add this to your table.

11   Where two leaves had the same treatment, calculate the mean change in mass for those two leaves, and add this to your table.

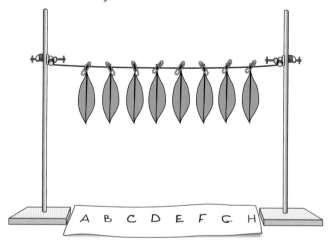

Questions

1   List, in rank order, the treatments that best helped the leaves to conserve (keep) their water.

2   Use your knowledge of leaf structure and transpiration to explain the reasons for the order that you have described in your answer to question **1**.

Continued

3 Did the two leaves that had the same treatment both lose exactly the same mass? If not, suggest why.

4 Suggest why you used two leaves for each treatment. Would it have been better to use more leaves for each treatment? Explain your answer.

5 Imagine that you are asked to do this experiment again. Suggest two improvements you would make (other than using more leaves for each treatment). For each of your suggestions, explain why this would improve the strength of the evidence you collect.

Self-assessment

How well did your results chart work? Do you think you designed it well?
Was it easy to write your results into it?

Activity 4.2.1

Conserving water in the desert

Work with a partner for this activity.

In Stage 8, you studied the different habitats in a desert ecosystem.

Think about the kind of plants that live in a desert, where it is very hot and dry.

How are these plants adapted to:

- get as much water as possible from the soil

- reduce the amount of water that they lose through transpiration?

Be ready to share your ideas with the rest of the class.

Why plants need water

In this topic and the previous one, you have learnt how plants absorb water and transport it to their leaves. But why do plants actually need all this water?

Water for support

The photograph shows one reason why plants need water – it helps them to stand upright.

The plant on the left has been given plenty of water. The plant on the right has not been watered for several days.

Plant cells contain a lot of water, especially inside their vacuoles. A plant cell that has plenty of water is strong and firm. When all the cells in a plant are like this, they press on one another and make the whole plant firm and well supported.

When a plant cell doesn't contain enough water, it becomes soft and floppy. When all the cells in a plant are like this, the plant collapses. We say that it has **wilted**.

Water for transport

As water moves through the xylem vessels, it carries dissolved mineral salts. This is how these mineral salts are transported from the roots to all the other parts of the plant.

Water for cooling

When water evaporates, it takes heat away with it. So when water evaporates from the cell wall of a cell in a leaf, it cools the cell. This is important for plants that live in very hot places.

Water for photosynthesis

Water is one of the reactants in photosynthesis. In photosynthesis, plants change water and carbon dioxide to glucose and oxygen.

Summary checklist

☐ I can describe how water moves from xylem vessels to the outside of a leaf.
☐ I can describe where in a leaf water changes from liquid water to water vapour.
☐ I can explain that transpiration is the loss of water vapour from the surface of leaves.
☐ I can explain why plants need water.
☐ I can measure small masses accurately and precisely, and record my measurements in a results chart.
☐ I can evaluate how strong the evidence I collect in my experiment is, and suggest improvements to my experiment.

> 4.3 Excretion in humans

In this topic you will:

- find out what substances humans excrete
- study the structure of the human excretory system
- learn how the kidneys help with excretion.

Getting started

In the previous topic, you looked at why plants need water.

Discuss these questions with a partner.

1   Are any of the reasons why plants need water the same as for humans?

2   Can you think of any reasons why humans need water that are not the same as for plants?

3   Are there any reasons why plants need water that are not the same as for humans?

Key words

bladder
excretion
excretory system
kidneys
renal
urea
ureter
urethra
urine

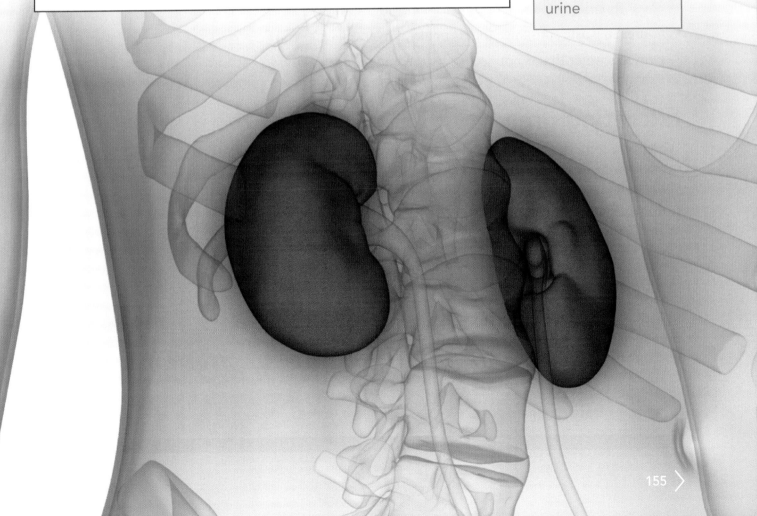

What is excretion?

In Stage 7, you learnt that **excretion** is one of the characteristics of all living things. Excretion means getting rid of waste materials.

In fact, this does not include *all* waste materials. Excretion really only applies to waste materials that have – even for only a short while – been truly inside the body.

Think about what happens when a person eats food. It travels down, along the long tube that takes it from the mouth to the anus. It is a strange idea, but actually the food that travels all the way through this tube has never really been part of their body. Only things that move out of the digestive system, and into the person's blood or their body cells, are really part of their body.

This means that the waste from the digestive system, which animals (including humans) get rid of as faeces, does not count as excretion. It has never been part of the body.

So, if getting rid of faeces is not excretion, what *does* excretion include?

Excretion includes all the waste substances that organisms make in their cells, plus any substances that they have too much of, that have been part of their body. For animals, including humans, these include:

- carbon dioxide, which body cells make in respiration
- **urea**, a waste substance that is made in liver cells
- excess water that is not needed by the body.

Excreting urea

When we eat food, any proteins in the food are broken down to smaller molecules inside the digestive system. These small molecules go into the blood. The blood transports them to the liver.

If we have more protein than we need, the liver changes the smaller molecules into urea. Urea is a poisonous substance. If it builds up in the body, it makes a person ill.

As soon as urea is made in a liver cell, it is taken away from the liver in the blood.

The urea is removed from the blood by the **kidneys** in the **excretory system**. This system is also known as the **renal** system. 'Renal' means 'to do with kidneys'.

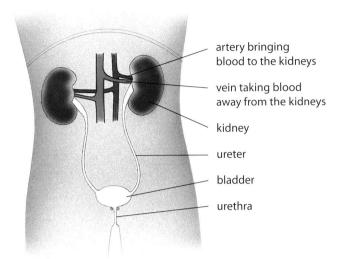

artery bringing
blood to the kidneys

vein taking blood
away from the kidneys

kidney

ureter

bladder

urethra

As the blood flows through the kidneys, the kidneys filter the blood. They remove all of the urea from it. The kidneys also remove excess water from the blood. The urea dissolves in the excess water. The solution made of urea dissolved in water is called **urine**.

The urine made in each kidney flows down a tube called a **ureter**. This carries it to the **bladder**, which can store it for a while. The urine can flow out of the bladder to the outside world through another tube, called the **urethra**.

Activity 4.3.1

Excretory system words and meanings

Work in a group of four or five for this activity.

You need eighteen identical pieces of card.

On nine of the cards, write one of the words in the Key words list at the start of this topic.

On the other nine cards, write the meanings of the Key words. Discuss this in your group first, to make sure that everyone agrees that the meaning is correct.

Shuffle the cards. Place them all face down.

One person picks up two cards. If they are a word and its meaning, they keep the cards and have another turn. If they do not match, they replace them face down and the next person has a turn.

Keep going until all the cards have been claimed. The winner is the person with the most cards.

This topic has a lot of new words beginning with u.

People often get mixed up between urea and urine. They also confuse ureter and urethra.

What have you done to help you to remember how to spell each of these words, and avoid mixing them up?

Questions

1   What is another name for the excretory system?

2   In Stage 8, you learnt about respiration. Carbon dioxide is a waste substance that humans excrete. How is carbon dioxide excreted from the body?

3   Humans excrete urea, which is made from excess proteins in the body. Suggest why plants do not produce urea that they have to excrete. (Think about how plants get their proteins.)

Summary checklist

☐   I can explain what excretion is.

☐   I can describe the structure of the excretory (renal) system.

☐   I can explain that the function of the kidneys is to filter the blood and remove urea.

☐   I can state that urea is excreted in urine.

> 4.4 Keeping a fetus healthy

In this topic you will:

- think about how the development of a fetus is affected by the health of the mother

- find out how diet, smoking and drugs can affect fetal health.

Getting started

In Stage 8, you learnt about the different nutrients that a person needs to stay healthy.

Can you list all of these, and say what each one is needed for?

Do you think a woman is likely to need the same diet when she is pregnant as before she was pregnant?

Key words

fetal

fetus

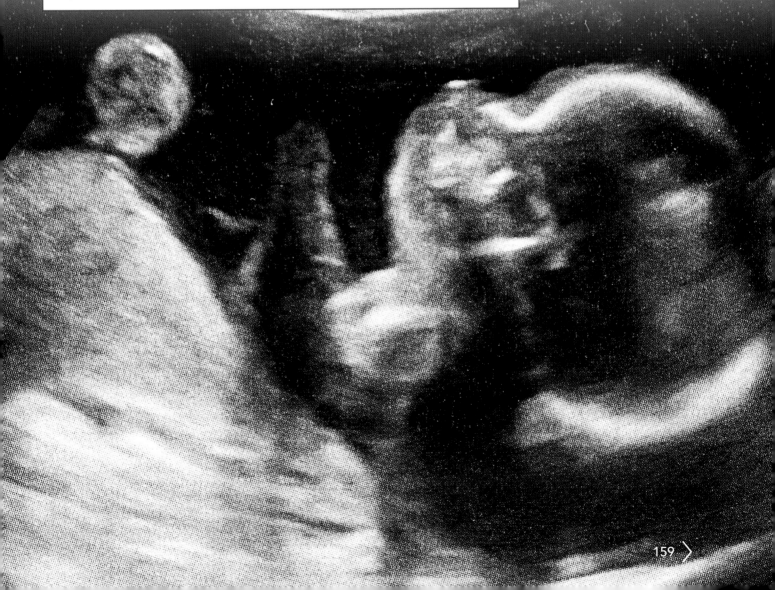

A healthy pregnancy

For the first nine months of its life, a new human being grows inside its mother. During these nine months, it is called a **fetus**. A fetus is a baby before it is born. Every pregnant mother hopes that her baby will be healthy when it is born.

You have learnt a lot about the human body. You know about the nutrients that it needs, how it uses respiration to release useful energy, and how it excretes waste substances. A fetus growing in its mother's body needs to do all of these things.

The fetus relies on its mother to supply it with everything that it needs, and to remove the substances it needs to excrete. If the pregnant mother makes sure that she stays healthy, this helps the fetus to stay healthy too.

The substances that the fetus needs are brought to it in its mother's blood. But the mother's blood does not mix with the blood of the fetus. The two blood systems come very close together, but do not touch. The substances that the fetus needs diffuse from the mother's blood to the fetus's blood. The substances that the fetus needs to excrete diffuse in the opposite direction.

Diet

Eating well is always important, but it is especially important during pregnancy. A good diet during pregnancy has a big effect on **fetal** health.

When she is pregnant, a woman needs to eat a balanced diet. This means that she should eat some of all the different nutrients that are needed to stay healthy. She needs to eat a little bit more than usual because some of the nutrients that she eats are passed to the growing fetus.

Protein is needed to help the fetus to produce new cells and grow, so the mother must make sure she eats plenty of foods containing protein. The mother also needs protein for herself, to keep her muscles strong and working well. She also needs extra protein to make extra haemoglobin – she needs more because her blood has to transport oxygen to give to her fetus, as well as enough for herself. Of course, her fetus also needs to make haemoglobin for itself.

Carbohydrate supplies energy. Glucose is a carbohydrate, and cells get their energy by combining glucose with oxygen in respiration. Both the mother and her fetus need carbohydrate for this, so she needs to eat enough carbohydrate to make sure they both have enough energy. But she should not eat too much, or the extra could be changed to fat and make her put on too much weight, which is not healthy.

Vitamins and minerals are very important. Iron is needed to make haemoglobin, so the mother needs to eat plenty of foods containing iron. Sometimes, it can help if the mother takes iron pills during pregnancy, if she cannot get enough in her diet. Calcium is essential for helping the baby to grow strong bones, and to keep the mother's bones and teeth in good health. The mother also needs to make sure she gets plenty of vitamins in her diet.

Questions

1   List **three** substances that move from the mother's blood into her fetus's blood.

2   List **two** substances that the fetus excretes, which are removed by the mother's blood.

3   You learnt about vitamins A, C and D in Stage 8. Explain why a pregnant mother needs plenty of each of these vitamins in her diet.

4   Suggest some foods that a pregnant woman could eat that would supply her with plenty of protein, carbohydrate, iron, calcium and vitamins A, C and D.

Activity 4.4.1

Display about diet during pregnancy

Work in a group of three or four for this activity.

You are going to make a display about the importance of eating well during pregnancy.

First, you need to collect your information.

Here are some ideas:

* Look on the internet for information about advice for pregnant women and what they should eat.

* Talk to people you know who are mothers. Did they eat differently when they were pregnant? Did they find it easy to eat a healthy diet?

* Find pictures that relate to diet during pregnancy.

* If you visit a doctor's surgery or health centre, ask if they have any leaflets about how to eat well during pregnancy.

Use your information and pictures to produce a bright and interesting display that will catch people's attention and explain why a good diet is important during pregnancy.

Self-assessment

When you have finished your display, look carefully at other people's work.

What have they done really well? What could be better?

Does seeing other people's displays make you want to change your own?

Smoking cigarettes

In Stage 8, you learnt how smoking can harm health. Tobacco smoke contains carbon monoxide, nicotine and tar. When a pregnant woman smokes, carbon monoxide and nicotine diffuse from her blood into the fetus's blood. It is as though the fetus is smoking too.

Carbon monoxide in the blood reduces the amount of oxygen that haemoglobin can transport. This means that the fetus's cells get less oxygen, so they cannot respire as much and they cannot release as much energy as they normally would. This can affect the development of the fetus. Babies born to mothers who smoked during pregnancy tend to be smaller than babies born to non-smoking mothers.

Nicotine is an addictive drug. It can damage blood vessels, so it is not good for a developing fetus to have nicotine in its blood.

In many countries, cigarettes come with warnings about health. This packet has a warning for pregnant mothers.

Drugs

A drug is something that is taken into the body, and that affects the way the body works.

Some drugs are good for health. Antibiotics are drugs that kill bacteria in the body. They are used to cure the infections caused by bacteria. Antibiotics are an example of a medicinal drug. Some painkillers, such as aspirin, are also medicinal drugs. Without medicinal drugs, many more people would die or suffer pain from illnesses that we can now cure.

But other drugs are not so good for us. We have seen how nicotine, the drug in cigarettes, can harm the health of both a pregnant woman and her fetus. Any drug that we do not need can cause harm. These drugs can be even more harmful to a fetus than to an adult person.

Most drugs that a pregnant woman takes will go into her fetus's blood. So the fetus is taking the drug too.

One country has these recommendations for women during pregnancy:

- If she regularly takes a prescribed drug for her own health, she should check with her doctor or a pharmacist to see if it is safe for her to keep on taking it. She should not stop taking it without checking first.

- She should check with her doctor whether it is safe for her to take drugs that do not need a prescription such as aspirin.

- She must stop smoking.

- She should avoid alcohol.
- She should never take illegal drugs at all, but it is especially important to avoid these during pregnancy.
- There is some evidence that caffeine – a drug in coffee and cola drinks – harms a developing fetus. Most doctors recommend that pregnant women should not drink a lot of coffee or cola.

Summary checklist

- ☐ I can explain why a pregnant woman needs to eat a well balanced diet.
- ☐ I can name some nutrients that a woman should eat more of when she is pregnant.
- ☐ I can explain why a pregnant woman should never smoke.
- ☐ I can explain why she should check with a doctor or pharmacist before taking any drugs.

Project: How scientists linked smoking to health

It is not easy to do experiments on human health. For example, if we want to find out how smoking affects fetal health, we cannot ask some women to smoke during pregnancy, and others not to smoke, and then compare the health of their babies.

Instead, scientists try to collect information from as many people as possible. They look for correlations between smoking and fetal health. They publish details about how they did their study, and their results. Other scientists can then look at this information and decide for themselves what they think the results show.

In this project, you will contribute to a class presentation or display, about the work that scientists have done about how smoking affects health.

Here are some questions to research. Choose one of them, or think of another question of your own about how scientists have found out about the effects of smoking on health.

Some of the questions have several parts – do not worry if you do not have time, or cannot find information, about every part.

- When did scientists first begin to think that smoking was bad for health? What made them think this? How did they share their ideas?

- What evidence is there that smoking is bad for health?

- What evidence is there that smoking has a negative effect on the development of a fetus?

- How have people responded to this evidence? Has the number of people smoking decreased in most countries? Has the number of women smoking during pregnancy decreased in most countries?

Check your progress

4.1 Choose the word that matches each description.

bladder   kidney   urea   ureter   urethra   urine

a   This organ filters the blood.   [1]

b   A tube that carries urine from the kidneys to the bladder.   [1]

c   A waste substance made in the liver from excess proteins.   [1]

d   Where urine is stored before leaving the body.   [1]

e   A tube that carries urine to the outside of the body.   [1]

f   A liquid containing urea dissolved in water.   [1]

4.2 Copy and complete these sentences about plants and water.

Choose words from the list.

You can use each word once, more than once or not at all.

air   gas   leaves   liquid

root hairs   soil   stomata   xylem vessels

Plants take up water from the .... into their ....   [2]

The water flows through .... which carry it to the plant's ....   [2]

In the leaves, a lot of the water changes from .... to ....   [2]

It diffuses out of the leaf through the ....   [1]

4.3 Arun did an experiment using two plants in pots.

The diagram shows the two plants that he used.

Arun measured the mass of each plant at the same time every day for seven days. The table shows his results.

Plant **A**   Plant **B**

Day	1	2	3	4	5	6	7
Mass of plant **A** + pot in g	945	925	901	877	855	832	808
Mass of plant **B** + pot in g	960	952	946	940	936	932	929

Arun used his results to calculate how much mass each plant lost each day.

Day	1 to 2	2 to 3	3 to 4	4 to 5	5 to 6	6 to 7
Loss of mass of plant **A** + pot in g	20	24	24	22	23	24
Loss of mass of plant **B** + pot in g	8	6	6	4	4	

a   What apparatus could Arun use to measure the mass of the plants in their pots?   [1]

b   Calculate how much mass plant B lost from day 6 to day 7.   [1]

c   Calculate how much mass plant A lost during the experiment. Choose the fastest way you can use the data to do this, and show your working.   [3]

d   Calculate the mean loss of mass per day for plant A during the experiment.   [1]

e   During the experiment, was more mass lost from the soil, or from the plant? Use the results in the table to explain your answer.   [3]

f   At the end of the experiment, Arun found little drops of water on the inside of the bag that covered plant B. Explain how they got there.   [3]

4.4   The table shows the recommended daily masses of some nutrients that a woman should try to eat when she is not pregnant, and when she is pregnant.

Nutrient	When not pregnant	When pregnant
Protein in g	45.0	60.0
Calcium in g	0.8	1.2
Iron in mg	15.0	30.0

a   Write **one** sentence about each nutrient, to explain why the woman needs to eat more of it when she is pregnant.   [3]

b   For each nutrient, name **one** food that she could eat that contains plenty of that nutrient.   [1]

c   Suggest why it is **not** recommended that she eats more fat when she is pregnant.   [1]

d   Explain why a woman should not smoke cigarettes when she is pregnant.   [2]

5 Reactivity

> 5.1 Reactivity and displacement reactions

In this topic you will:

- use the reactivity series of metals to predict which metals will displace others from a solution of their salts

- carry out some displacement reactions.

Getting started

Discuss with a partner how you can tell if a chemical reaction has taken place. Share your ideas with another pair. Be prepared to share your ideas with the class.

Key words

reactivity
reactivity series
displacement reaction

The reactivity series

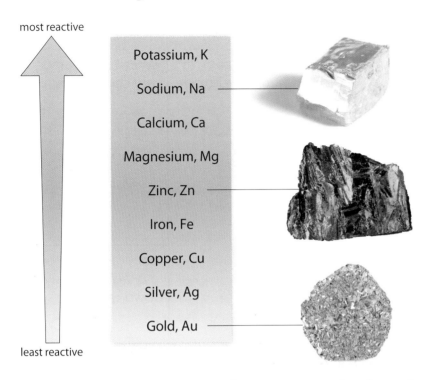

most reactive

Potassium, K

Sodium, Na

Calcium, Ca

Magnesium, Mg

Zinc, Zn

Iron, Fe

Copper, Cu

Silver, Ag

Gold, Au

least reactive

In Stage 8, you learnt that some metals are more reactive than others, by looking at the reaction of the metals with oxygen, water (or steam) and dilute acid. Some metals are much more reactive than others. You can use the results of all the investigations, to place the metals in the order of their **reactivity**.

This list is called the **reactivity series**. It has the most reactive metals at the top and the least reactive at the bottom.

This table shows a summary of the reactions of the metals in the reactivity series.

Metal	Reaction with oxygen	Reaction with water	Reaction with diute acid
potassium (extension material)	burns brightly when heated to form an oxide	very vigorous reaction in cold water, the hydroxide is formed	violent reaction and very dangerous
sodium (extension material)			
calcium	burns brightly in air when heated to form an oxide	slow reaction in cold water to form the hydroxide	reaction, which becomes less vigorous as you go down the list
magnesium			
zinc	slow reaction when heated to form an oxide	reacts with steam but not water to form an oxide	
iron			
copper		no reaction with steam or water	
silver	no reaction		no reaction
gold			

Questions

1   a   The metal lithium is missing from the reactivity list, suggest where it should be placed.

    b   Give your reasons for placing lithium in this position.

2   a   Platinum is a precious metal that is used for jewellery. Platinum stays shiny for a long time. Where in the list would you place the metal platinum?

    b   Give your reasons for placing platinum in this position.

3   Small samples of three metals, A–C, have been added to dilute hydrochloric acid, as shown opposite. Which metal is most reactive? How could you tell?

4   Write a word equation for the reaction between zinc and sulfuric acid.

5   Write the word equation for the reaction between magnesium and oxygen.

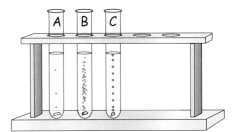

Activity 5.1.1

Learning the order

In this activity, you will try various methods to help you learn the order of the metals in the reactivity series. Work with a partner.

Method 1: Mnemonics

Make up a mnemonic to help you remember the sequence of the metals in the reactivity series. (A mnemonic is a sentence in which the first letter of each word is the same as the first letter of the things you want to remember.) You could use either the first letters of the names of the metals or their symbols. Ask your partner to test you and then you test your partner. Write down your mnemonic for the reactivity series on a poster and share it with the class.

Method 2: Ordering cards

Write the names of the metals on individual pieces of card or paper. Try to arrange the cards in the correct order as fast as possible. Who was the most accurate? Who was the fastest?

Method 3: Pick a card

Use the cards from Method 2. Place them face down on the desk. One of you picks a card and shows it to your partner. The partner must name a metal that is more reactive than the one on the card and a metal that is less reactive than the metal on the card. If there are no metals more or less reactive than the one on the card, the partner must state that fact. Take it in turns to pick a card.

What methods do I find most helpful when I need to learn facts?

Displacement reactions

If you place a clean iron nail in a beaker containing copper sulfate solution, there is an interesting reaction.

The blue copper sulfate solution changes to a slightly paler colour. The most remarkable thing that happens is that the nail looks a different colour. It has become copper coloured. What has happened in this reaction?

The word and symbol equations for this reaction are:

copper sulfate + iron → iron sulfate + copper

$$CuSO_4 + Fe \rightarrow FeSO_4 + Cu$$

The iron nail has become coated with copper. Iron is more reactive than the copper that it has 'pushed out' from the copper sulfate and has reacted to form iron sulfate. This 'pushing out' is called displacement, so this type of reaction is called a **displacement reaction**. A more reactive metal can replace a less reactive one in a salt.

If a copper nail was placed in a solution of iron sulfate there would be no reaction because copper is less reactive than iron. Copper cannot displace the iron in the iron sulfate.

Questions

Use the reactivity series to answer these questions.

6   Which is the more reactive metal: zinc or copper?

7   Can zinc displace the copper in copper sulfate?

8   Which is more reactive – silver or magnesium?

9   Can silver displace the magnesium in magnesium sulfate?

Think like a scientist

Displacing metals

> **You will need:**
>
> - solutions of copper sulfate, magnesium sulfate, iron sulfate and zinc sulfate; small pieces of the metals iron, zinc, copper and magnesium; test tubes, test tube rack, forceps, safety glasses.

Method

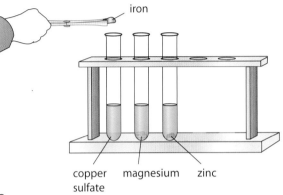

iron

copper sulfate solution   magnesium   zinc

1 Read through all the instructions and prepare a results table. (You will need to think about this carefully – there are lots of different results to record.)

2 Pour copper sulfate solution into three test tubes so that each is about a third full.

3 Add a small piece of iron to one test tube, a small piece of magnesium to the second and a small piece of zinc to the third test tube.

4 Leave the test tubes for a few minutes.

5 Observe carefully and record your observations.

6 Repeat steps 2 to 5 using magnesium sulfate solution and the three metals copper, iron and zinc.

7 Repeat steps 2 to 5 using iron sulfate solution and the three metals copper, magnesium and zinc.

8 Repeat steps 2 to 5 using zinc sulfate solution and the three metals copper, iron and magnesium.

Questions

1 How do you know that one metal has displaced another from its salt?

2 Which of the four metals was the most reactive?

3 Which of the four metals was the least reactive?

Summary checklist

☐ I can use the reactivity series of metals to predict which metals will displace others from a solution of their salts.

☐ I can carry out some displacement reactions safely.

> 5.2 Using the reactivity series and displacement reactions

In this topic you will:

- use displacement reactions to identify an unknown metal
- learn about some useful displacement reactions.

Getting started

Work with a partner. One of you writes down the name of a metal in the reactivity series in the middle of a piece of paper. Pass the paper to your partner and they add the name of the metal that is just above or just below the first metal. Then the first person adds the name of the metal that is just above or below the metals on the paper. Do this until you have completed the reactivity series. Share your list with the class. How well did you do?

Key words

molten

ores

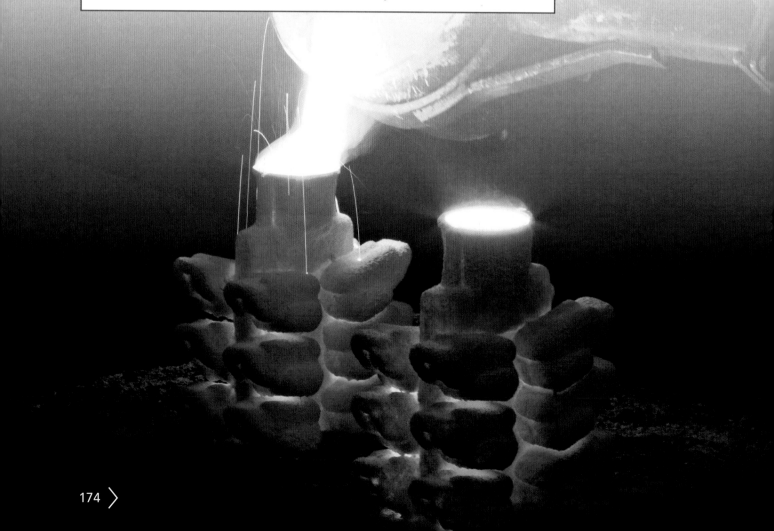

Using displacement reactions

Using the fact that more reactive metals can displace less reactive ones from their salts can be very useful in a number of ways. It is possible to use displacement reactions to help identify an unknown metal.

Think like a scientist

Identifying a mystery metal

Your task is to identify a mystery metal. It is one of the metals listed on the reactivity series. You are going to investigate which metal it could be. You can make observations of the metal; for example, you can investigate its appearance and its reactions with water, oxygen and dilute acid. This will give you some useful information. You could also use displacement reactions.

Part 1: Planning the investigation

Plan an investigation to identify the mystery metal. You must use some displacement reactions.

Safety

You do not know what this metal is, so treat it with care and pick it up using forceps.

Method

1   First, you will need to identify the equipment and chemicals you will use.
2   Write a step-by-step method of what you will do.
3   For each part of the investigation, indicate what information you will get from that part, and how it will help you to identify the mystery metal.

Part 2: Carrying out the investigation

When you have shown your plan to the teacher and had it approved you may carry out the investigation.

Safety

Make sure you have carried out a risk assessment.

Method

1   Record the results of each test you carry out.
2   If you decide to change your plan as you get more information about the mystery metal, ask your teacher first.
3   Keep a record of any changes you decide to make to your plan and the reasons for the change.

Questions

1   What do you think the mystery metal is?
2   Give reasons for your answer. Explain how the results of each test you carried out helped you decide what the mystery metal is.
3   Did you change your plan as you got more information about the metal? Explain how and why you changed your plan.

Using displacement reactions in industry (extension material)

Aluminium is a metal that is above zinc and below magnesium in the reactivity series shown in Topic 5.1. Aluminium will displace iron from solid iron oxide if it is heated.

aluminium + iron oxide → aluminium oxide + iron

This reaction releases a lot of energy. It is an exothermic reaction. The temperature gets so high that the iron that is produced is **molten** (in a liquid state). The melting point of iron is 1535 °C.

In the photograph you can see the reaction being used to weld railway rails together. Often, the rails need to be welded in situ (in other words, on the railway lines and not in a workshop where you have all the welding equipment you will need). The iron oxide and aluminium powder react in a container placed on the rails. The molten iron produced in the reaction is shaped and used to join the rails together. This reaction is called the thermite reaction.

In order for the thermite reaction to take place, the iron oxide and aluminium mixture has to be ignited. This is done using another exothermic reaction – this time between magnesium powder and barium nitrate. This reaction provides the energy to start the displacement reaction between the aluminium and iron oxide.

Displacement using carbon (extension material)

Carbon is not a metal, but it can be used to displace some metals from their compounds. Carbon will displace zinc, iron, tin and lead from their **ores**. An ore is a rock that contains a metal compound.

People discovered that carbon could displace iron around 3500 years ago. They discovered that iron ore heated with charcoal (a form of carbon) at very high temperatures produced molten iron. Today this displacement reaction is still carried out, but on a large scale, in a blast furnace.

The iron ore is mainly iron oxide. This reacts with carbon to form iron and carbon dioxide.

The word equation for this reaction is:

iron oxide + carbon → iron + carbon dioxide

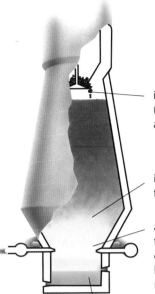

iron ore and coke (a form of carbon) are added

iron being displaced from its ore by carbon

air is blown into the furnace to burn the coke and create the high temperatures needed for the reaction

molten iron collects at the bottom

A modern blast furnace

The controls in a modern blast furnace

Questions

1   Can iron displace aluminium from aluminium oxide? Explain your answer.

2   Why is the thermite reaction useful for welding rails?

3   The early blast furnaces were in areas where there were supplies of iron ore and a lot of coal mining. Why do you think this was?

Think like a scientist

Extracting metals using carbon

In this task you will use carbon to try to displace a metal from its oxide.
Remember that carbon will only displace a metal that is less reactive than itself.

> **You will need:**
>
> - safety glasses, copper oxide powder, charcoal powder, spatula, test tube or boiling tube, heatproof mat, Bunsen burner

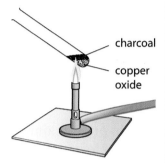

charcoal

copper oxide

Method

Remember your safety! Wear safety glasses.

1   Place a spatula of copper oxide in a test tube or boiling tube.

2   Add a spatula of charcoal powder on top of the copper oxide.
Do **not** mix the powders together.

3   Heat the two layers strongly in a Bunsen flame for five minutes.

4   Allow the tube to cool and then look carefully at where the layers meet.

5   Record your observations.

Questions

1   Has there been a reaction between the copper oxide and the carbon?
Give reasons for your answer.

2   If there has been a reaction, write a word equation for it.

3   What evidence does this experiment give you about the reactivity of carbon?

4   Where would you place carbon in the reactivity series? Give a reason for the position you suggested.

What things do you need to think about when carrying out practical work so that you stay safe?

Summary checklist

☐   I can use displacement reactions to help identify an unknown metal.
☐   I can describe some useful displacement reactions.

> 5.3 Salts

In this topic you will:

- explain what a salt is
- give some examples of salts and their uses
- prepare a salt by reacting a metal with an acid
- prepare a salt by heating a metal oxide with an acid.

Getting started

- With a partner, write word equations for **three** displacement reactions.
- Now write word equations for **two** displacement reactions that cannot happen.
- Write all five equations on a piece of paper and swap them with another pair of learners.
- Can you identify the reactions that would not take place?

Key words

- carbonate
- chloride
- citrates
- crystallisation
- formula (plural: formulae)
- nitrate
- salt
- sulfate

What is a salt?

When you think about **salt**, you probably think of the salt you put in your food as flavouring. This is sodium **chloride**. You have met other salts during your science course: copper **sulfate**, silver **nitrate** and calcium **carbonate**, for example.

Many salts have important uses in everyday life. The photographs show some examples.

Sodium chloride salt is used to preserve food and, as table salt, to flavour food.

Gymnasts use the salt magnesium carbonate to keep their hands dry so that they do not slip on the apparatus.

Calcium sulfate is a salt that is used to make blackboard chalk.

Aluminium sulfate is added to dyes to help them stick to fibres.

These soya seeds are coated with copper sulfate. It stops fungi growing on the seeds when they are planted.

Ammonium nitrate is used as a fertiliser to help crops to grow well.

Acids and salts

Every day, the chemical industry makes hundreds of thousands of tonnes of different salts. Many of the methods for making salts start with acids.

All acids contain hydrogen. The table below gives you the **formulae** of the three common acids you find in the laboratory. The table also shows some examples of the salts that can be formed from these acids.

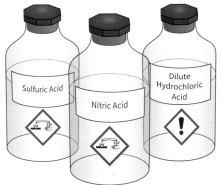

Two other acids you may meet are carbonic acid and citric acid. Carbonic acid is a weak acid that is formed when carbon dioxide reacts with water. Salts made from carbonic acid are called carbonates. Citric acid is found in fruits, such as oranges and lemons. Salts formed using citric acid are called **citrates**.

Name of acid	Formula	Salts formed from the acid	Example of salt	Formula of salt
hydrochloric acid	HCl	chlorides	sodium chloride	NaCl
sulfuric acid	H_2SO_4	sulfates	copper sulfate	$CuSO_4$
nitric acid	HNO_3	nitrates	potassium nitrate	KNO_3

Questions

1   Think about what you have already learnt about acids.

   a   What are the properties of acids?

   b   Name some everyday products that contain acids.

2   Which elements are present in nitric acid?

3   Which elements are present in sulfuric acid? How many atoms of each element make up one particle of sulfuric acid?

4   a   What is similar about the formula for hydrochloric acid and the formula for sodium chloride?

   b   What is different about these two formulae?

5   The illustration below shows a label on a jar of orange jam.

ALLERGY ADVICE: NO NUTS.

SUITABLE FOR VEGETARIANS.

INGREDIENTS: SUGAR, ORANGES, WATER, CONCENTRATED LEMON JUICE, SODIUM CITRATE, CITRIC ACID, BITTER ORANGE OIL.

PREPARED WITH 30 G OF FRUIT PER 100 G.

---

   a   Which ingredient is a salt?

   b   Do some research to find out why this ingredient is added to some kinds of food.

Activity 5.3.1

Researching a salt

Choose a salt to research. You could use one of those mentioned in this topic or choose another. You should use the internet or library to find the answers to these questions:

• How is this salt obtained or made?

• What is the salt used for?

Present what you have found out in an interesting way. You could make a poster, give a short talk or make a slide show.

How can I find out where else salts are used in everyday life?

Making salts using a metal and an acid

You have reacted metals with dilute acids before. It is often a good way to make salts.

The general equation for the reaction of metals with acid is:

$$\text{acid} + \text{metal} \rightarrow \text{salt} + \text{hydrogen}$$

The word and symbol equations for the reaction between zinc and hydrochloric acid are:

zinc + hydrochloric acid $\rightarrow$ zinc chloride + hydrogen

$$Zn + 2HCl \rightarrow ZnCl_2 + H_2$$

Zinc reacting with hydrochloric acid

Questions

6   Which of the compounds in the above equation is a salt?

7   Which acid would you add to the metal magnesium to make the salt magnesium sulfate?

8   Write the word equation for the reaction between iron and hydrochloric acid.

9   Why would it be dangerous to prepare sodium chloride by reacting sodium with hydrochloric acid?

Think like a scientist

Making the salt zinc sulfate

You will need:

- 250 cm^3 beaker, dilute sulfuric acid, measuring cylinder, zinc metal, evaporating basin, pipeclay triangle and tripod, Bunsen burner, tongs, heatproof mat, safety glasses.

Safety

Be careful when heating the evaporating basin as the solution may spit and burn you.

Method

1   Pour about 50 cm^3 of sulfuric acid into a 250 cm^3 beaker.

2   Add 1–5 g zinc metal to the acid in the beaker.

3   Once the mixture stops fizzing pour it into the evaporating dish.

4   Heat the evaporating dish very gently until you see crystals forming at the edge of the solution.

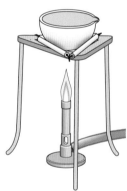

5   Remove from the heat and leave for a few days to form crystals. This is the process of **crystallisation**. If you need to remove the evaporating basin from the tripod, use a pair of tongs and place the evaporating basin on a heatproof mat.

Questions

1   Write the word equation for this reaction.

2   What are the important practical points you will need to consider when you evaporate this solution?

3   Which do you think is the better way to produce large crystals – heating the evaporating dish until there is very little liquid left or leaving it to evaporate slowly?

4   How could you investigate which is the best way to produce large crystals?

Making salts using a metal oxide

Some metals will not react with acids to make salts. For example, silver and copper are too unreactive to displace hydrogen from an acid, so we have to find another way of making salts from unreactive metals. We can do this by starting with a metal oxide.

The general equation for this reaction is:

metal oxide + acid → salt + water

In this example we can make copper sulfate by heating copper oxide with sulfuric acid. The word and symbol equations for this reaction are:

copper oxide + sulfuric acid → copper sulfate + water

$$CuO + H_2SO_4 \rightarrow CuSO_4 + H_2O$$

Think like a scientist

Making the salt copper sulfate

Work out what equipment you will need to make copper sulfate.

Consider the risks you might encounter as you carry out the operation and how you can reduce them.

Safety

Remember not to boil the acid. Use low heat. Be careful when heating the evaporating basin as the solution may spit and burn you.

Method

1 Pour about 100 cm³ of dilute sulfuric acid into a 250 cm³ beaker. Add black copper oxide powder to the acid in the beaker.

2 Heat the mixture very gently, stirring all the time.

dilute sulfuric acid

copper oxide

Continued

3   When the mixture changes colour to blue, turn off the heat. Allow the mixture to cool.

4   Filter the mixture. The filtrate is a solution of copper sulfate. Pour this into an evaporating basin.

filtrate

5   Place the evaporating basin on the pipeclay triangle on the tripod and heat very gently until you see crystals forming at the edge of the solution. Remove from the heat and leave for a few days to crystallise.

Questions

1   Make a list of the equipment you will need.

2   Write a risk assessment for each stage of the process.

3   Suggest why the mixture was filtered.

4   Suggest how you could use a similar method to make copper chloride.

5   Write the word equation for the reaction to make copper chloride from copper oxide.

6   Write the word equation for the reaction between copper oxide and nitric acid.

Summary checklist

- [ ] I can explain what a salt is.
- [ ] I can list some examples of salts and state their uses.
- [ ] I can prepare a salt safely by reacting a metal with an acid.
- [ ] I can prepare a salt safely by heating a metal oxide with an acid.

> 5.4 Other ways of making salts

In this topic you will:

- prepare a salt by using an acid and a carbonate
- prepare a salt using neutralisation
- carry out risk assessments for practical work
- use word and symbol equations.

Getting started

Make a list of the properties of acids and of alkalis (for example: pH of more than 7, all contain hydrogen, turn universal indicator solution blue). Make sure the properties of acids and alkalis are mixed together. Exchange your list with a partner and sort the properties into those of acids and those of alkalis. How well did you do?

Key words

bases
crystallise
erodes
limestone
neutralisation

Metal carbonates and acids

Carbonates – such as calcium carbonate – are salts. Carbonates can be formed by the reaction of a metal with carbonic acid.

We can use carbonates to form other salts by reacting them with an acid.

For example:

sulfuric acid + calcium carbonate → calcium sulfate + water + carbon dioxide

$$H_2SO_4 \quad + \quad CaCO_3 \quad \rightarrow \quad CaSO_4 \quad + H_2O + \quad CO_2$$

hydrochloric acid + calcium carbonate → calcium chloride + water + carbon dioxide

$$2HCl \quad + \quad CaCO_3 \quad \rightarrow \quad CaCl_2 \quad + H_2O + \quad CO_2$$

acid + carbonate → salt + water + carbon dioxide

The line above shows the general equation for these reactions. The rock **limestone** is made of calcium carbonate. It is damaged when it reacts with acid rain and **erodes**.

The skeletons of coral are made from calcium carbonate and react with acids. This happens when the oceans become slightly more acidic as more carbon dioxide dissolves in the water.

This piece of coral is reacting in hydrochloric acid. How can you tell that a reaction is taking place?

Questions

1 Write the word equation for the reaction between magnesium carbonate and nitric acid.

2 Write the symbol equation for the reaction between magnesium carbonate and sulfuric acid.

3 How could you check that the gas given off in these reactions is carbon dioxide?

Think like a scientist

Preparing a salt from acid and a carbonate

You are going to prepare copper chloride, using the reaction between copper carbonate and hydrochloric acid.

Work out what equipment you will need to make copper chloride.

Consider the risks you might encounter as you carry out the operation and how you can reduce them.

Safety

Take care when heating the solution (step 5), as it may spit and burn you.

Method

1 Place 25 cm³ of hydrochloric acid in a small beaker.

2 Add a spatula of copper carbonate.

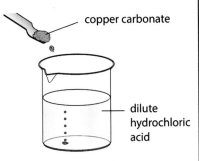

copper carbonate

dilute hydrochloric acid

3 Add more copper carbonate until it stops reacting. You should have a small amount of unreacted copper carbonate left in the beaker. (This is called adding excess copper carbonate. It makes sure that all the acid has reacted.)

4 To purify your copper chloride you will need to remove the excess copper carbonate. Filter the mixture. The unreacted copper carbonate will be trapped in the filter paper.

filtrate

5 Pour the filtrate into an evaporating basin and heat it gently. This will remove the water and leave you with pure copper chloride.

6 Stop heating the evaporating basin when you see some crystals around the edge of the solution.

7 Leave for a few days to cool and evaporate slowly to **crystallise**.

Continued

Questions

1   Read through the method and make a list of all the equipment you will need.

2   Carry out a risk assessment for each step of the method.

3   What did you observe when you added copper carbonate to the hydrochloric acid?

4   Which gas is given off during this reaction?

5   Write the word equation for your reaction.

6   Describe the appearance of the copper chloride you have made.

7   Which substances in your word equation are salts?

8   Using your observations from this experiment, what can you say about the solubility of copper carbonate and copper chloride in hydrochloric acid? (Think about what happened when you filtered the liquid from the beaker.)

9   Suggest how you could use copper carbonate to make copper sulfate.

How did writing a risk assessment help you to think about what you could do to avoid any safety problems?

Salts in rocks

The blue-green colours in these rocks in the Atacama Desert in Chile tell you that they contain copper salts. This bright blue-green mineral in the rock is called malachite. It is made from copper carbonate.

Forming salts by neutralisation

Alkalis react with acids to neutralise them. When an acid is neutralised by an alkali, a salt is produced. For example, when sodium hydroxide reacts with hydrochloric acid, the salt sodium chloride is formed. The other product is water.

sodium hydroxide + hydrochloric acid → sodium chloride + water

$$NaOH \quad + \quad HCl \quad \rightarrow \quad NaCl \quad + \quad H_2O$$

The general equation for **neutralisation** reactions is:

acid   +   alkali   →   salt   +   water

Questions

4   How can you test to see if a liquid is an acid or an alkali?

5   What word is used to describe a solution that is neither acid nor alkali?

6   What are the properties of alkalis?

Think like a scientist

Preparing a salt by neutralisation

Work out what equipment you will need to make a salt by neutralisation.

Consider the risks you might encounter as you carry out the operation and how you can reduce them. Before you begin the practical work, answer questions **1** and **2**.

Safety

Take care when heating the filtrate (step 8), as it may spit and burn you.

Method

1   Place hydrochloric acid in a burette.

2   Measure out $20 \, cm^3$ of the sodium hydroxide into a small flask.

3   Add a few drops of universal indicator solution.

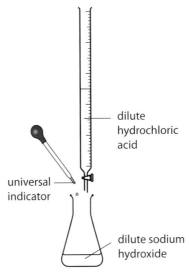

universal indicator

dilute hydrochloric acid

dilute sodium hydroxide

4   Add the acid from the burette slowly, swirling the flask (moving it gently round) as you add the acid.

5   When the universal indicator changes to green you have produced a neutral solution.

Continued

6   Add a spatula of charcoal powder to the green solution. Mix it with a glass rod. The charcoal takes the green colour of the universal indicator out of the solution.

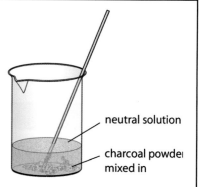

neutral solution

charcoal powder mixed in

7   Filter the mixture.

8   Place the filtrate into an evaporating basin and heat gently.

9   Stop heating when you see some crystals around the edge of the solution.

10   Leave the evaporating basin for a few days. The water will evaporate slowly, leaving crystals of the salt.

Questions

1   Read through the method and make a list of all the equipment you will need.

2   Carry out a risk assessment for each step of the method.

3   What colour is the universal indicator solution in the sodium hydroxide?

4   What colour is universal indicator solution in a neutral solution?

5   Why do you need to swirl the flask as you add the acid?

6   Imagine that you accidently add too much acid from the burette. What could you do to form a neutral solution?

7   What salt is formed in this reaction?

8   Write the word equation for this reaction.

9   Describe the salt crystals you obtained.

Alkalis and bases

When a metal oxide dissolves in water, it forms an alkaline solution.
Metal oxides are called **bases**. Soluble metal bases form alkalis when
they dissolve in water.

For example:

sodium oxide + water → sodium hydroxide

Sodium oxide is a base. The sodium hydroxide is an alkali.

Some metal oxides are not soluble in water, for example iron and copper
oxide. So they do not form alkalis. But they can still react with acids to
form salts.

copper oxide + sulfuric acid → copper sulfate + water

$$CuO \quad + \quad H_2SO_4 \quad \rightarrow \quad CuSO_4 \quad + \quad H_2O$$

Questions

7   What is the difference between a base and an alkali?

8   Write the word equation for the reaction between magnesium
    oxide and sulfuric acid.

9   Write the symbol equation for the reaction between magnesium
    oxide and sulfuric acid.

10 Suggest how you could use iron oxide to make iron chloride.

How does writing an equipment list help me to think about what
I need to do in a practical task?

Summary checklist

☐ I can prepare a salt using neutralisation.
☐ I can write risk assessments for practical tasks.
☐ I can use word and symbol equations.

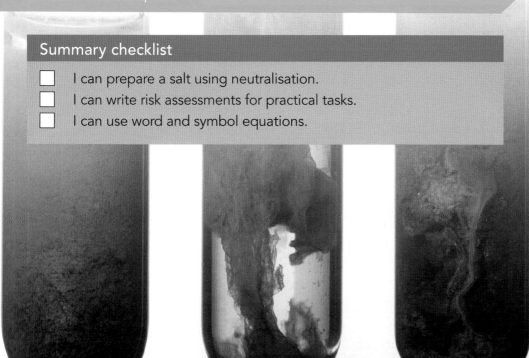

> 5.5 Rearranging atoms

In this topic you will:

- look at the rearrangement of atoms in chemical reactions
- learn what happens to the mass of reactants and products in a reaction
- learn what happens to the energy involved in chemical reactions
- carry out practical work safely.

Getting started

- On a piece of paper write down the formulae for five compounds, write each one on a new line.
- Then write the names of an acid, a salt, an alkali and a metal oxide, write each one on a new line.
- Swap your paper with a partner and try to write the name of the compound against each formula and write the formula against each name.
- How well did you do? Were all the formulae that were written correct?
- Discuss them with your partner.

Key words

crucible

endothermic reactions

exothermic reaction

the law of conservation of energy

the law of conservation of mass

Looking at chemical reactions

In chemical reactions, atoms form new combinations. Atoms that are on their own may join together with other atoms. Atoms that are bonded with other atoms may separate, forming new combinations with other atoms.

In the reaction between iron and sulfur, the iron and the sulfur atoms that were there at the start of the reaction are still there at the end. They have just rearranged themselves. We can represent this reaction by drawing the atoms, writing a word equation or by writing a symbol equation.

Fe	+	S	⟶	FeS
iron	+	sulfur	⟶	iron sulfide

In a chemical reaction, no atoms are lost. No new atoms are produced. The atoms are simply rearranged into new combinations.

When you look at any of the equations for the reactions in this topic you can see that the elements that are present in the reactants are also present in the products.

Here is the equation for the reaction between magnesium and hydrochloric acid.

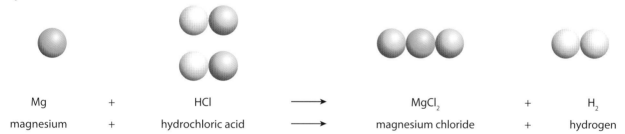

Mg	+	HCl	⟶	$MgCl_2$	+	H_2
magnesium	+	hydrochloric acid	⟶	magnesium chloride	+	hydrogen

The magnesium metal in this reaction is a reactant. The magnesium is still present in the products as part of the salt magnesium chloride. The element hydrogen is present in the reactants as part of the compound hydrochloric acid. In the products it is present as hydrogen gas. The element chlorine is present in the reactants as part of the compound hydrochloric acid and in the products it is part of the salt magnesium chloride.

This is an important idea. No element that is present in the reactants disappears from the products. No new element appears in the products.

Look carefully at the symbol equation. Not only does it tell you which elements are present in the reactants and products but how many of each atom is present. In the reactants there is one atom of magnesium and in the products there is one atom of magnesium. In the reactants there are two atoms of hydrogen and in the products there are two atoms of hydrogen. In the reactants there are two atoms of chorine and in the products there are two atoms of chlorine.

Questions

1 Look back at the reaction between copper carbonate and hydrochloric acid in Topic 5.4.

    a Which product of this reaction contains the element copper?

    b Which reactant contains the element hydrogen?

    c Which product contains the element hydrogen?

    d Which reactant contains the element carbon?

    e Which product contains the element carbon?

2 In the reaction between copper oxide and sulfuric acid in Topic 5.3:

    a Atoms of which elements are present at the start of the reaction?

    b How many of each kind of atom are represented in the reactants shown in the equation?

    c Atoms of which elements are present at the end of the reaction?

    d How many of each kind of atom are represented in the products shown in the equation?

Conservation of mass

Atoms have mass. If no atoms are gained or lost during a chemical reaction, then no mass is gained or lost either.

Zara, Sofia and Arun carry out the reaction between calcium carbonate and hydrochloric acid.

They place some calcium carbonate in a flask, add the hydrochloric acid and place the stopper in the top of the flask. They place the flask on a top pan balance. They each have different ideas about what will happen to the mass in the flask as the reaction takes place.

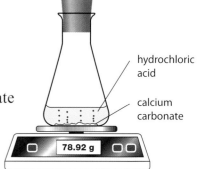

hydrochloric acid

calcium carbonate

I think the mass will decrease because one of the products is a gas and gases are very light.

I think the mass will increase because there are two reactants and three products, so there are more products.

I think the mass will stay the same because there is a stopper in the top and no atoms can enter or leave the flask.

When the three students carry out the reaction they find that the mass has not changed. Arun's idea was correct and so was his reason.

In chemical reactions the elements you begin with are the ones you end the reaction with. Nothing is added or taken away. The mass you begin with is the mass you end with.

This important idea is called **the law of conservation of mass**.

Think like a scientist

The law of conservation of mass

You will need:

- safety glasses, top pan balance, flask with stopper, calcium carbonate, dilute hydrochloric acid

Method

Place some calcium carbonate in a flask, add hydrochloric acid and place the stopper in the top of the flask. Place the flask on a top pan balance. Observe the reading on the top pan balance.

Questions

1   What did you observe happening in the flask?

2   Write a word equation for this reaction.

3   Which salt is made in this reaction?

4   Some students found the mass of each piece of apparatus and each chemical separately before they mixed the chemicals together in the flask, put the stopper in and placed the flask on the top pan balance. Do you think the mass of all the items added together will be the same as the reading on the balance at the end of the reaction? Give a reason for your answer.

Questions

3   A learner reacts 37 g of magnesium with 150 g of sulfuric acid. What will be the total mass of the products of this reaction?

4   If a learner starts with 10 g of magnesium in the reaction above, how much magnesium will be present in the magnesium sulfate that is produced?

Not the results you expect?

When you add calcium carbonate to hydrochloric acid, there is a chemical reaction.

Arun places a flask of hydrochloric acid on a top pan balance and carefully adds calcium carbonate. He measures the mass of the flask and the contents at the beginning of the reaction and after 10 minutes. These are his results:

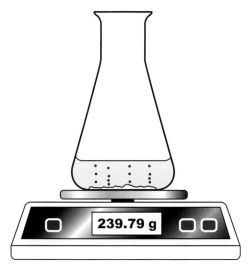

Time in minutes	Mass of flask and contents in g
0	250
10	207

The law of conservation of mass tells you that there must be the same mass at the end of the reaction as at the start. In Arun's experiment the mass appears to decrease. Why is this?

The word equation for this reaction is:

calcium carbonate + hydrochloric acid → calcium chloride + water + carbon dioxide

The carbon dioxide gas escapes into the air because the flask is open. You then cannot measure its mass. So, it appears as if the mass decreases as the reaction continues. The elements present are all present in the products. Remember, water is made from hydrogen and oxygen atoms.

Questions

5   In the reaction between calcium carbonate and hydrochloric acid:

    a   Which **one** of the reactants contains the element oxygen?

    b   Which **two** of the products contain the element oxygen?

    c   Where does the element hydrogen in the water come from in this reaction?

6   Explain what Arun should have done to show that mass is conserved in a chemical reaction.

Another surprising result

Here is another reaction that produces a result that is a surprise to some people.

Some magnesium is placed in a **crucible**, and the mass of the crucible with the magnesium is recorded. The crucible is heated very carefully. The lid of the crucible is lifted from time to time during the heating to allow the air in. After heating, the mass of the crucible with contents is measured again.

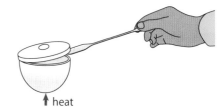

heat

A reaction takes place when the magnesium is heated. After the reaction, the crucible contains white ashes. The mass of the ashes is more than the mass of the magnesium at the start of the reaction.

Some people think that the ashes will be lighter because the ashes look smaller than the magnesium. They see the flames escaping from the crucible, so they think something has been lost.

However, the word equation explains what happens.

$$\text{magnesium} + \text{oxygen} \rightarrow \text{magnesium oxide}$$

There is an increase in mass because oxygen from the air has combined with the magnesium.

A French scientist called Antoine Lavoisier carried out this experiment in 1772. He repeated it many times and found he had an increase in mass every time. He could not explain why this happened. Finally he came up with the idea that when something burns it combines with a gas from the air. He also found that the gas from the air that is involved in burning is involved in respiration as well. He named the gas oxygen.

These early scientists managed to get accurate results with very simple equipment. How can I ensure my results are always as accurate as possible?

Think like a scientist

Burning magnesium in air

You will need:

- the apparatus shown in the diagram.

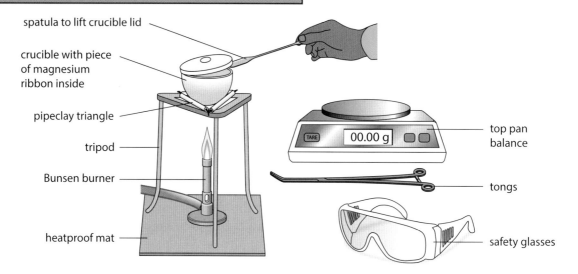

spatula to lift crucible lid

crucible with piece of magnesium ribbon inside

pipeclay triangle

tripod

Bunsen burner

heatproof mat

TARE 00.00 g

top pan balance

tongs

safety glasses

Method

1. Find and record the mass of the crucible and lid.

2. Place a piece of magnesium ribbon in the crucible and find and record the mass of the crucible, lid and magnesium.

3. Calculate the mass of the magnesium.

4. Assemble the apparatus as shown in the diagram. During the heating process you will need to lift the lid from time to time to allow the air to enter. Use a spatula or the tongs and be careful so that none of the ash inside is lost. The contents of the crucible will glow and change. The crucible will remain hot for a long time – do not touch it. Once there is no more reaction, allow the crucible to cool.

5. Find and record the mass of the cool crucible, lid and contents.

6. Calculate and record the mass of the contents.

7. Calculate the difference between the mass of the magnesium and the mass of the product after heating.

Continued

Questions

1   What has happened to the mass after heating?

2   Explain why this has happened.

3   What is the name of the product of this reaction?

4   What safety risks are there in this experiment?

5   Why did you need to lift the lid of the crucible from time to time?

6   What do you need to be careful about to make sure none of the product is lost before you find its mass?

Energy and chemical reactions

All chemical reactions involve energy.

Energy is used to break bonds in the reactants and energy is released when new bonds are formed in the products. When metals react with water or acids, energy is released, as thermal energy or sometimes as light or sound or kinetic energy. For example, in the reaction between potassium and water the potassium catches fire, gets so hot that it melts, burns with a pinkish purple flame and hisses or explodes. It also moves across the surface of the water.

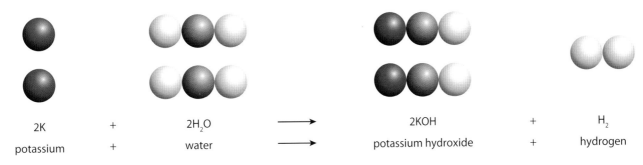

| 2K | + | 2H$_2$O | $\longrightarrow$ | 2KOH | + | H$_2$ |
| potassium | + | water | $\longrightarrow$ | potassium hydroxide | + | hydrogen |

In this reaction, less energy is needed to break bonds in the reactants than is released when bonds form in the products. This is an **exothermic reaction**.

In other chemical reactions it takes more energy to break bonds in the reactants than is released when the bonds form in the products. These reactions are called **endothermic reactions** and they take in energy. For example:

sodium hydrogencarbonate + citric acid → sodium citrate + water + carbon dioxide

This reaction happens when we eat sherbet sweets. They give us a cool refreshing feeling in our mouth when we eat them.

When this reaction takes place, energy is transferred from the environment (your mouth). The energy is transferred to chemical energy stored in the bonds of the products.

Whether a chemical reaction takes in energy or releases energy there is no overall change in the amount of energy during the reaction. This is because energy cannot be created or destroy. This is **the law of conservation of energy**.

Energy may be transferred from one form to another but the same amount of energy remains after the reaction as before. This is true of every chemical reaction.

Summary checklist

- [ ] I can use word and symbol equations to describe chemical reactions.
- [ ] I can explain what is meant by the law of conservation of mass.
- [ ] I can explain what is meant by the law of conservation of energy.
- [ ] I can carry out practical work safely.

Project: Where is the evidence?

When manufacturers want to sell you their products, they make claims about them, or offer you deals to make you think this is the best brand to buy. Sometimes a deal seems very good, such as "50% extra for free" or "buy one get one free". To know if it is a good deal there are some questions you need to ask, such as:

- 50% more than what?

- Is it cheaper than buying the regular size?

- Have they increased the price?

- Does buying two give me a better deal than just buying a larger size?

To find out, you would need to do some research into the sizes and prices of the
packs and work out how much they each cost per 100 g or 100 cm³.

Some manufacturers make claims for their products, such as "80% of women said
that after using this shampoo their hair was stronger". What does this mean?

Continued

Here are some points you will need to consider:

- Stronger than what?
- How do the women know this?
- How could you find out?
- How many women did they ask?

Which type of hair: long, short, curly or straight?

Another claim might be that this painkiller medicine gets to work on your body twice as fast.

Some points you will need to think about here are:

- Twice as fast as what?
- How do you know?
- How can you prove it?
- Would it work the same on everyone?

These advertisements are often worded very carefully because some countries have rules about what advertisements are allowed to say.

Some claims can be investigated, but others are much more difficult because they are subject to opinion.

Work in groups of two or three.

Your tasks:

1   Find out about the advertising rules in your country. Make a poster or other presentation to give a quick overview.

2   Choose one deal or advertisement based on the size of the item purchased, for example "50% extra free" or "buy one get one free". Work out if this is really a good deal or if buying the normal item is better value. Show how you worked this out and present your findings.

3   Choose one advertisement based on claims such as "kills 99% of germs" or "92% of women say this face cream reduced their wrinkles after two weeks". Make a list of the questions you will need to ask. What investigations could you carry out to test these claims? Can you prove if these claims are true?

Make a presentation of your findings.

Check your progress

5.1 Arun places a piece of aluminium metal in a test tube of copper sulfate.

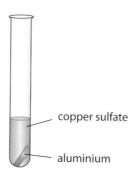

copper sulfate

aluminium

A reaction takes place.

The word equation for this reaction is:

aluminium + copper sulfate → aluminium sulfate + copper

a How can Arun tell that a reaction has taken place? [1]

b Why is this reaction called a displacement reaction? [1]

c Arun then places some zinc in a solution of lead nitrate. A displacement reaction takes place. Write a word equation for this reaction. [2]

d He then places some copper into a solution of sodium chloride. No reaction takes place. Give a reason for this. [1]

5.2 (Extension question) The word equations below represent some displacement reactions.

aluminium + copper sulfate → aluminium sulfate + copper

aluminium + lead nitrate → aluminium nitrate + lead

lead + copper sulfate → lead sulfate + copper

lead + silver nitrate → lead nitrate + silver

a Use the word equations to decide which of the four metals, aluminium, copper, lead or silver, is the most reactive. [1]

b Decide if a reaction will take place when lead is placed in a solution of magnesium sulfate. If you think there will be a reaction, write the word equation. [1]

c Decide if a reaction will take place when iron is placed in a solution of lead nitrate. If you think there will be a reaction, write the word equation. [1]

5.3 The diagram shows an experiment where zinc metal is added to sulfuric acid.

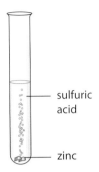

sulfuric acid

zinc

    a   What is the name of the gas given off in this reaction?   **[1]**

    b   How could you test for this gas?   **[2]**

    c   What salt is formed in this reaction?   **[1]**

    d   How do you know when all the acid has reacted?   **[1]**

    e   Write the word equation for this reaction.   **[2]**

5.4 Zara is making crystals of the salt potassium chloride by neutralisation. The diagram shows some of her apparatus set up.

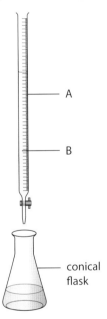

A

B

conical flask

    a   What is the name of the piece of apparatus labelled A?   **[1]**

    b   What is the name of the liquid labelled B?   **[1]**

    c   Describe how she can obtain crystals of the salt.   **[3]**

6 > Sound and space

> 6.1 Loudness and pitch of sound

In this topic you will:

- find out about the amplitude of a sound wave
- find out about the frequency of a sound wave
- learn how amplitude is linked to loudness
- learn how frequency is related to pitch
- learn how to recognise amplitude and frequency from a diagram of a sound wave (waveform).

Getting started

Work in groups to discuss answers to these questions.

1   Describe how a sound wave travels through air. Use ideas about particles in your answer.

2   What is common to all objects that make sound?

Key words

amplitude
frequency
loudness
oscilloscope
peak
pitch
trough
waveform

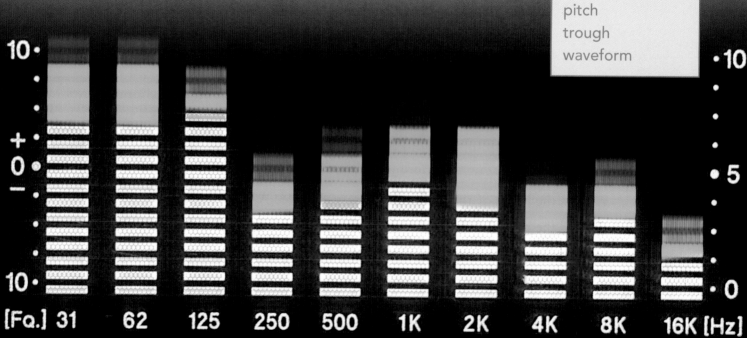

10										·10
+										
0										·5
−										
10										·0
[Fq.] 31	62	125	250	500	1K	2K	4K	8K	16K [Hz]

Loudness and amplitude

In Stage 7 you learnt that sound is made when objects vibrate.

The **loudness** of a sound is a way to describe how quiet or loud a sound appears. Loudness depends on two variables:

- how much the object is vibrating – the greater the distance of each vibration, the louder the sound

- how far away the vibrating object is – the further away the quieter the sound that we hear.

The greater the distance of each vibration in the object, the greater the distance that particles in air will be pushed and pulled.

Sounds get quieter when the distance from the vibrating object increases because of energy dissipation. You learnt about energy dissipation in Stage 7.

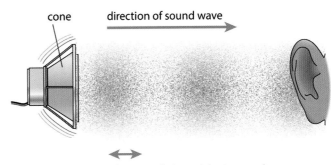

You learnt in Stage 7 that when a sound wave travels forward in air the particles move backwards and forwards, as shown in the diagram.

The movement of particles in air is difficult to draw in a sound wave, but is easier to draw in a graph. The graph shows the distance that the particles move forward and backward with time. The shape of this graph is sometimes called a **waveform**.

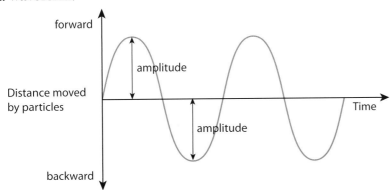

The maximum distance that particles move, either forward or backward in a sound wave, is called the **amplitude**.

You can measure the amplitude in two ways.

The amplitude is the distance from zero to the top, or **peak**, of the graph.

The amplitude is the distance from zero to the bottom, or **trough**, of the graph.

Both these distances are equal in a graph of the same sound wave.

The peak is the highest point of the graph and the trough is the lowest point.

As the distance or range of the vibration increases, the loudness increases. You can also say that as the amplitude of a sound wave increases, the loudness of the sound increases.

A piece of equipment called an **oscilloscope** displays waveforms of sound waves. An oscilloscope uses a microphone to detect the sound and then produces a waveform of the sound on a screen.

In this photo, the microphone is attached to the oscilloscope by the black wire.

The next diagram shows how a quieter sound and a louder sound compare when the waveforms are seen on an oscilloscope.

The louder sound has a larger amplitude than the quieter sound.

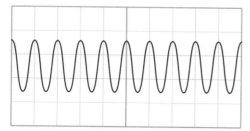

quieter sound has smaller amplitude

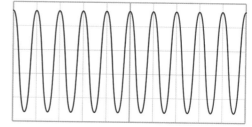

louder sound has larger amplitude

Pitch and frequency

When you vibrate a ruler while holding the ruler at the edge of a desk, the vibrations make sound.

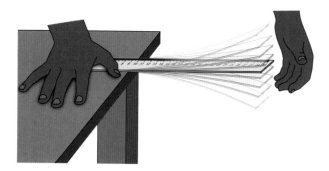

When the vibrating ruler is moved so the length of the vibrating part is shorter, then the **pitch** of the sound changes. The pitch of a sound is how high or low the sound appears on a musical scale.

The reason that the pitch of the sound from the vibrating ruler changes is because the speed of the vibrations change.

The faster the vibrations, the higher the pitch of the sound.

The speed of vibrations is measured by the number of complete vibrations per second. In Stage 8 in the topic on speed, you learnt that per means 'in each'. The number of vibrations in each second is called **frequency**. As the frequency of a sound wave increases, the pitch of the sound also increases.

Frequency is measured in a unit called hertz or Hz.

A frequency of 500 Hz means that 500 complete vibrations happen every second.

Look back at the graph that shows amplitude. The horizontal axis of this graph is time, so a wave with a higher frequency will have more waves in the same time.

As with amplitude, we can use an oscilloscope to compare the frequencies of sound waves of different pitches.

The next diagrams show how a higher pitch sound and a lower pitch sound compare when the waveforms are seen on an oscilloscope.

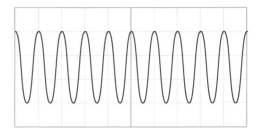

higher frequency has higher pitch

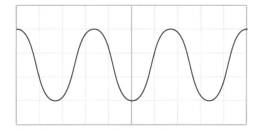

lower frequency has lower pitch

You will also notice from the waves of higher and lower pitch, that their amplitudes are the same. That means the loudness of both these sounds are the same.

Usually, vibrating objects that are shorter make higher pitch sounds than those that are longer.

This picture shows a musical instrument called a gayageum. The strings are plucked to make them vibrate. The pegs, called bridges, can be moved to change the length of each string that vibrates. The shorter the string, the higher the pitch.

Questions

1 **a** Describe the link between amplitude and the loudness of a wave.

   b Describe the the link between frequency and the pitch of a wave.

2 **a** Which of these describes the amplitude of a sound wave?
Write **one** letter.

   A The maximum distance that particles move from their position when there is no wave.

   B The total distance that particles move forward and move backward in the wave.

   C The number of times that particles vibrate backwards and forwards every second.

   D The direction that particles move in the wave compared to when there is no wave.

   b Which of these describes the frequency of a sound wave?
Write **one** letter.

   A The maximum distance that particles move from their position when there is no wave.

   B The total distance that particles move forward and move backward in the wave.

   C The number of times that particles vibrate backwards and forwards every second.

   D The direction that particles move in the wave compared to when there is no wave.

3 This is the waveform of a sound displayed on an oscilloscope screen.

Write down:

   a the letter that represents the amplitude of the wave

   b one letter that shows a measurement that depends on the frequency of the wave.

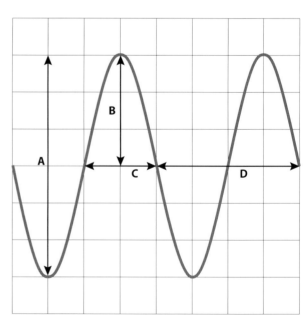

4   Look at the four sound waveforms, A, B, C and D.

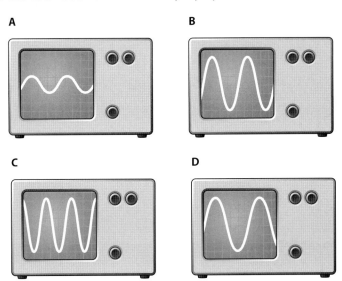

Copy and complete these sentences. Choose your answers from the list below.

increases   decreases   stays the same

a   When the sound changes from A to B, the amplitude of the wave ....

b   When the sound changes from A to B, the loudness of the sound ....

c   When the sound changes from C to D, the pitch of the sound ....

d   When the sound changes from C to D, the loudness of the sound ....

e   When the sound changes from C to D, the frequency of the wave ....

Activity 6.1.1

Pitch and frequency in music

In this activity, you will look at the trends in frequencies of musical notes.

A piano is a musical instrument that makes sound when strings inside the piano vibrate.

The strings are made to vibrate by pressing keys. The piano player presses the keys with their fingers.

The key at the left of the piano makes a string produce a note called A_0

After an interval of notes called an octave, there is another note called A_1

After the next octave, the next note is A_2

These are shown on the diagram.

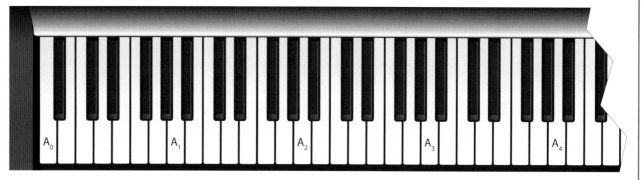

The frequencies of the A notes are shown in the table.

name of note	frequency in Hz
A_0	27.5
A_1	55.0
A_2	110
A_3	220
A_4	440

Questions

1   Describe the trend in the frequencies of the notes shown in the table.

2   Use the information in the table and in the diagram to predict how the pitch of the notes changes from left to right on the piano keys.

3   The piano can also produce the notes A_5 A_6 and A_7

   Use the trend in the table to predict the frequencies of these three notes.

Continued

4 Many pianos have pedals that can be pressed using the player's feet.
One of the pedals decreases the loudness of the note without changing the pitch.
Suggest what this pedal does, if anything, to:

a the amplitude of the string vibration

b the frequency of the string vibration.

Think like a scientist

Vibrations in a ruler

In this investigation, you will investigate the variables affecting the vibration of a ruler.

When you make a ruler vibrate at the end of a desk, the vibrations are too fast to measure. In this activity, you will make a ruler vibrate more slowly so that measurements can be made.

You will need:

- metre rule or half-metre rule made from wood, metal screw clamp (G-clamp), selection of masses, adhesive tape, stopwatch.

Safety

Do not stand with your feet under the ruler. Use masses that will not cause the ruler to break. Make sure the clamp is strong enough to hold the ruler when it is vibrating.

Set up the equipment as shown in the diagram.

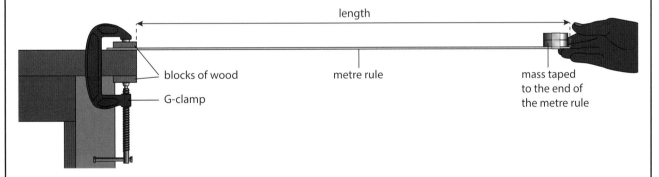

In this investigation, you will keep the length the same and change the mass.

Method

1 Decide on what preliminary measurements are needed to determine the range of masses that will be used. Try to use a minimum of five different masses.

Continued

2 The frequency of the vibration is the number of times the ruler moves from the lowest position back to the lowest position in 1 second. A good method for finding this is to count the number of complete vibrations in 10 seconds, then divide your result by 10. This gives the frequency in Hz, which is the number of vibrations in 1 second.

3 Carry out the investigation using the range of masses that you selected.

Questions

1 Record your results in a table with these columns:
- mass
- number of vibrations in 10 seconds
- frequency.

Remember to include units, where needed, in the column headers.

Remember to include all your repeat measurements in the table.

2 Calculate the average frequency for each mass.

3 In this investigation, state:
- **a** the independent variable
- **b** the dependent variable
- **c** two control variables.

4 Plot a line graph of your results. Put frequency on the *y*-axis and mass on the *x*-axis.

5 Describe the trend in your results.

6 Read the guitar facts, then use your results and the facts about the guitar to answer these questions.

- **a** Suggest how the frequency of vibration of a guitar string depends on the mass of the string.

- **b** Suggest how the pitch of the musical note from a guitar string depends on the mass of the string.

Guitar facts:
- A guitar is a musical instrument that produces sound from vibrating strings.
- Most guitars have six strings.
- The strings are all of equal length.
- The strings have different masses.
- Each of the six strings produces a different musical note.

Continued

c A guitar player can change the pitch of the note from each string by placing a finger on the string and pushing the string down against the metal cross pieces (frets). This makes the vibrating length of the string shorter. Describe how you could change the metre rule experiment to investigate the effect of length on frequency. Include:

- the independent variable and how you would change it
- the dependent variable and how you would measure it
- any control variables
- a prediction of the results.

Self-assessment

For each of these statements, decide on how confident you are.
Give yourself 5 if you are very confident and 1 if you are not confident at all.

- I understand why it is better to count vibrations in 10 seconds rather than in 1 second
- I understand how the frequency of vibration depends on mass
- I know how to write a plan for an investigation that someone else could follow.

Summary checklist

- ☐ I can describe what is meant by the amplitude of a sound wave.
- ☐ I know how loudness of a sound depends on the amplitude of the sound wave.
- ☐ I can describe what is meant by the frequency of a sound wave.
- ☐ I know how the pitch of a sound depends on the frequency of the sound wave.
- ☐ I can recognise changes in amplitude and frequency from a graph of the wave or an oscilloscope display.

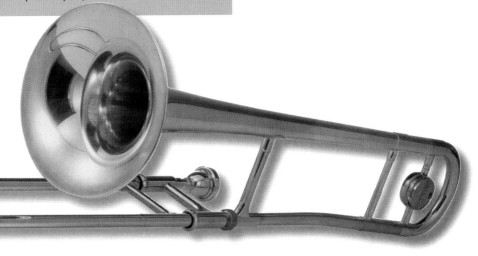

> 6.2 Interference of sound

In this topic you will:

- find out how sound waves can reinforce each other to make louder sounds
- find out how sound waves can cancel each other out to make no sound.

Key words

interference

reinforce

Getting started

Work in groups.

1. Each person in the group should draw a wave on a piece of paper.

2. Compare all the waves that have been drawn in the group.

   a. Sort the waves in order from smallest amplitude to largest amplitude.

   b. Sort the waves again, this time from smallest frequency to largest frequency.

Interference

Water waves are a useful analogy for sound waves. Particles in water waves do not move in the same way as particles in a sound wave, but the analogy helps explain how waves behave.

If you dip your finger in and out of water, you can make waves as shown in the picture.

If you make two sets of water waves, you can watch what happens when the waves meet each other. If you move your fingers at the same frequency and with the same amplitude, you can make a pattern like the one in the next picture.

The effect that is produced when the waves meet each other is called **interference**.

Sound waves also produce interference when they meet each other.

Interference can only happen when the waves are of the same type. Sound waves can interfere with each other. Sound waves cannot interfere with water waves.

Interference is easiest to detect when the waves have the same frequency and the same amplitude.

Interference can produce two effects: the waves can reinforce or the waves can cancel each other.

Waves that reinforce

The word **reinforce** means to make stronger.

If you look carefully at the picture of the water waves interfering, you can see a pattern. Part of the pattern is made by waves reinforcing each other. These parts appear with waves of larger amplitude than either of the individual waves. In this pattern, there are only small areas with waves that have reinforced.

Waves will reinforce when they meet with the peaks together and with the troughs together. This is shown in the diagram.

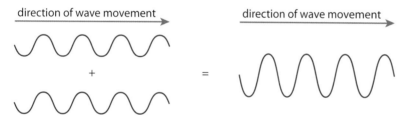

Two waves can interfere to reinforce when the wave peaks arrive together.

If you look carefully at the diagram, you will see that:

- the amplitudes of the two waves that interfere are added together

- the frequency of the two waves that interfere does not change.

When sound waves interfere to reinforce, the amplitude of the sound wave increases.

You will recall from the previous topic that the loudness of a sound wave depends on its amplitude.

That means, that when two sound waves reinforce, the sound becomes louder.

Sound waves can meet and reinforce where there are two sources of the same sound.

The picture shows the stage for a music concert. There are two loudspeakers – one on either side of the stage.

At certain places in the audience, people may hear sounds of a particular pitch louder than usual. This can be caused by the sound waves from the two loudspeakers meeting and reinforcing.

This diagram shows the pattern of sound waves that could be produced from these loudspeakers.

The curved lines in the diagram represent peaks in the sound waves. Where two of these lines cross, the waves will reinforce. A person at that position will hear a louder sound.

Sound waves will also reinforce where two troughs meet, but this is difficult to show in the diagram.

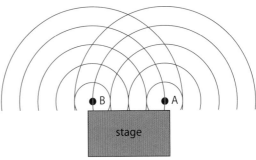

Waves that cancel

Waves will cancel when they meet with the peaks and troughs together. The word cancel in the context of waves means adding together to make zero.

Think of a peak as the wave's maximum *positive* amplitude, and a trough as the wave's maximum *negative* amplitude. When you add a positive number to a negative number of equal size, you get zero; for example, $2 + (-2) = 0$.

This is shown in the diagram.

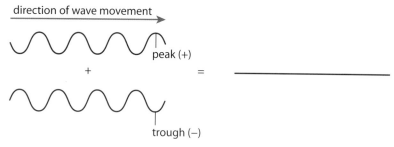

Two waves can interfere to cancel when the wave peaks of one meet troughs of another of equal amplitude.

If you look carefully at the diagram, you will see that the amplitudes of the two waves that interfere are added together to become zero.

When sound waves interfere to cancel, the amplitude of the sound wave becomes zero, the result is no sound. For two sound waves to cancel completely, their frequencies must be the same and their amplitudes must be the same.

Noise-cancelling headphones work by making sound waves cancel. The headphones pick up the sound from the surroundings, then analyse the sound wave and create another sound wave with the same amplitude and frequency, but out of phase with the original wave This new sound wave is used to cancel the sound wave from the surroundings. This is shown in the diagram.

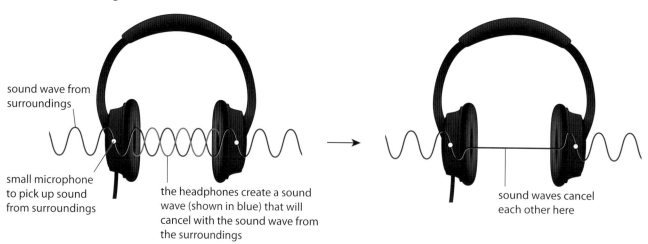

sound wave from surroundings

small microphone to pick up sound from surroundings

the headphones create a sound wave (shown in blue) that will cancel with the sound wave from the surroundings

sound waves cancel each other here

It is not likely that the sound waves from loudspeakers A and B at the concert will ever completely cancel so people hear nothing. This is because the sound waves from loudspeakers A and B at the concert will be reflected off objects, including off people in the audience. These reflected sound waves would add many more waves to the pattern in the diagram, making it very unlikely that only two identical waves will be present to cancel.

Questions

1   a   Which of these will always result in a louder sound being heard?

Write **one** letter.

A	two sound waves cancel	**C**	two sound waves reflect
B	two sound waves reinforce	**D**	two sound waves refract

     b   Which of these will always result in no sound being heard?

Write **one** letter.

A	two sound waves cancel	**C**	two sound waves reflect
B	two sound waves reinforce	**D**	two sound waves refract

2   a   Describe how two sound waves must meet in order to reinforce.

     b   Describe how two sound waves must meet in order to cancel.

3   The table gives information for two waves that will meet to reinforce. Copy the table and complete the missing information about the one wave that is formed.

two waves before reinforcing		one wave after reinforcing	
frequency in Hz	amplitude in mm	frequency in Hz	amplitude in mm
450	0.5		

4   Two sound waves have equal frequencies of 600 Hz. The amplitude of one of the waves is 0.25 mm.

     a   State the amplitude of the other wave required for the two waves to cancel.

     b   State the amplitude after the waves cancel completely.

Activity 6.2.1

Reinforcing and cancelling waves

In this activity, you will use water waves as an analogy for sound waves, to observe reinforcing and cancelling.

> **You will need:**
>
> - shallow tray to hold water, piece of white sheet material to put in the base of the tray, piece of wood with two identical nails that are part-way into the wood as shown in the diagram – the distance between the nails should be less than half the width of the tray.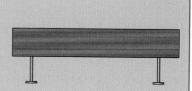

Method

1 Put water in the tray to a depth of about 2–3 cm.

2 Put the white sheet at the bottom of the tray. This is to make the waves easier to see.

3 Hold the piece of wood above the tray so the heads of the nails are just touching the water surface.

4 Move the wood up and down so the heads of the nails make waves in the water.

5 Observe the pattern where the waves meet.

Questions

1 Suggest why both nails are attached to the same piece of wood and not dipped into the water separately. Use the words frequency and amplitude in your answer.

2 Copy and complete the sentences.

    a In the areas where there is larger amplitude, the two waves are said to

       ....

    b In the areas where there is zero amplitude, the two waves are said to

       ....

3 This demonstration can be done with sound, but it is more difficult.

    a Suggest two sources of sound that could be used to produce two sound waves of equal frequency and equal amplitude.

    b Even in a room with no other sounds, it is very difficult to make two sound waves cancel so you do not hear anything. Suggest why.

Think like a scientist

Listening to sound waves reinforcing

In this investigation, you will listen to the effect when sound waves reinforce.

In Stage 7, you learnt that sound waves can reflect. It is possible to make a sound wave reflect so that the reflected wave reinforces the wave from the sound source.

You will need:

- tuning forks or a small sound source with constant frequency, piece of plastic pipe 4 cm or more diameter and about 70 cm long, deep water container such as a large sink or wide measuring cylinder, metre rule.

Method

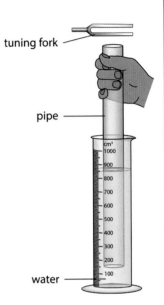

1   Set up the equipment as shown in the diagram.
2   Strike the tuning fork so it makes a sound.
3   Hold the tuning fork over the open end of the pipe.
4   Move the pipe up or down to a new position in the water so the length of pipe above the water changes.
5   Listen for an increase in loudness of the sound from the tuning fork.
6   Strike the tuning fork again, if needed, and adjust the length of the pipe above water so the sound is loudest.
7   Measure the length of the pipe above water.
8   Repeat steps 1–7 with a tuning fork of different pitch.

Questions

1   Find out the frequencies of the tuning forks that you used.
2   Record your results in a table.
3   Describe the trend in the results that links the frequency to the length.
4   Use this trend to explain how the range of notes produced by wind instruments depends on the length of the wind instrument.

Summary checklist

☐   I know how sound waves reinforce.
☐   I know what happens to the loudness of a sound when sound waves reinforce.
☐   I know how sound waves cancel.
☐   I know what happens to the loudness of a sound when sound waves cancel.

> 6.3 Formation of the Moon

In this topic you will:

- describe evidence for the collision theory for the formation of the Moon.

Getting started

Work in groups.

Discuss how the Solar System was formed from a cloud of dust and gas in space.

Key words

collision theory

Where did the Moon come from?

In the early twentieth century, scientists thought that the Moon was formed by splitting away from the Earth, soon after the Earth was formed.

Calculations showed that, if this theory was correct, the Moon would still be slowly moving away from Earth. Accurate measurements made more recently have shown that the Moon *is* still moving away from Earth – at a rate of about 4 cm each year.

These calculations could not completely confirm the theory that the Moon had formed by splitting away from the Earth.

In 1974, it was suggested that the Moon was formed in a different way, called the collision theory.

Collision theory for formation of the Moon

The **collision theory** (also called the giant impact hypothesis) is another theory of how the Moon was formed. There is more evidence that supports the collision theory than any other current theory.

The collision theory refers to a collision that happened relatively soon after the formation of the Solar System.

A newly formed planet, about the same size as Mars, collided with the newly formed Earth.

Scientists have called the colliding planet Theia. The picture – drawn by an artist – shows what the collision between Earth (left) and Theia may have looked like.

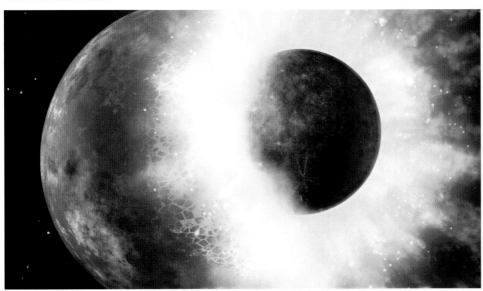

The collision would have caused rocks and dust to break away from both planets. The theory states that Earth was formed from the two planets joined together. The Moon was formed when the rocks and dust was pulled together by gravity. These stages are shown in this diagram:

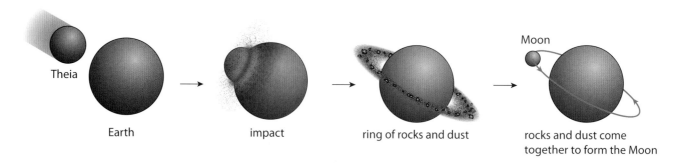

Evidence that supports the collision theory	Evidence that contradicts the collision theory
The Moon is less dense than the Earth. Samples of rock from the Moon show that its surface was once molten. The Moon has a small iron core, similar to the Earth. There is evidence outside the Solar System of similar collisions causing rings of rock and dust. The collision theory fits with the theory of how the Solar System was formed. The composition of rocks on the Earth and the Moon are the same.	The surface of the Earth does not appear to ever have been molten. A collision that formed the Moon would have caused the surface of the Earth to melt. The surface would have later solidified. Venus has no moon. Collisions in the early years of the Solar System would have been common and scientists would have expected Venus to have a moon formed in the same way. The composition of rocks on the Moon would be expected to be more similar to rocks on Theia than rocks on Earth. In fact, the composition of the Moon is more similar to Earth.

Questions

1   The collision theory suggests that an object called Theia collided with Earth.

Which of these planets is closest in size to Theia? Write **one** letter.

A   Mars   B   Earth   C   Neptune   D   Jupiter

2   Which of these statements could explain why the composition of rocks on the Earth and on the Moon is very similar?
Write **one** letter.

A   The Moon is mostly formed from Theia's rocks and the Earth only has a small quantity of Theia's rocks.

B   The Earth is mostly formed from Theia's rocks and the Moon only has a small quantity of Theia's rocks.

C   Rocks from Theia and Earth were completely mixed during the collision.

3   The planet Mars has two moons called Phobos and Deimos. Scientists have evidence that Phobos and Deimos are asteroids that were captured by the gravity of Mars, so they remain in orbit around Mars.

Suggest how the composition of rocks on Phobos and Deimos would compare with the rocks on the planet Mars if Phobos and Deimos were:

a   originally asteroids

b   formed by a collision of another object with Mars.

4   Models of the formation of the Solar System show that collisions between planet-sized objects would have been common soon after the Solar System formed. Suggest why these collisions are no longer common.

Activity 6.3.1

Evidence for the collision theory

In this activity, you will do your own research to find evidence.

Work in groups of three or four.

Use an internet search engine to find out more about the collision theory of the formation of the Moon. Some scientists call it the giant impact hypothesis, so you should also search for that.

Try to find:

- websites other than general encyclopaedia sites
- information that you can understand
- evidence that supports the collision theory
- evidence that contradicts the collision theory
- other theories on how the Moon was formed.

Produce a report on what you find. Write this in your own words as much as possible. Your report can take any form.

Include:

- the websites where each piece of information was obtained
- which websites you thought were most reliable
- whether any of the websites were biased
- why you had to use secondary sources rather than first-hand experience
- which theory you think is correct and why.

Summary checklist

☐ I know the collision theory for the formation of the Moon.
☐ I know the evidence for the collision theory.

> 6.4 Nebulae

In this topic you will:

- discover that nebulae are clouds of dust and gas in space
- learn how stars can form in nebulae.

Getting started

Work in groups to discuss the answers to these questions.

1 Describe how the planets in the Solar System were formed.

2 List ways in which planets and stars are

    a different

    b the same.

Key words

nebulae (singular: nebula)

northern hemisphere

southern hemisphere

stellar nurseries

Nebulae

Nebulae are clouds of dust and gas in space.

The word nebulae is plural. The singular is **nebula**.

The gases found in nebulae are mostly hydrogen and a smaller quantity of helium. The particles of gas and dust are very far apart in nebulae. A nebula the same size as the Earth would have a mass of only a few kilograms!

Most nebulae are very large. Some are more than 10 000 times bigger than the Solar System!

Some nebulae form when giant stars reach the end of their life. These giant stars then explode, sending dust and gas over a wide area of space.

There are many nebulae visible from Earth.

If you live in the **northern hemisphere**, one of the easiest nebulae to see is the Orion nebula, which is visible in winter. The northern hemisphere is the part of the Earth that is north of the equator. You can see the Orion nebula without a telescope. The picture shows what the Orion nebula looks like through a very powerful telescope.

If you live in the **southern hemisphere**, the easiest nebula to see is the Carina nebula. The southern hemisphere is the part of the Earth that is south of the equator. This nebula is also visible without using a telescope. The picture shows what the Carina nebula looks like through a powerful telescope.

Stellar nurseries

A **stellar nursery** is an area in space where stars are formed. The word stellar can be used to describe anything about stars. A nursery is a place to care for young people, animals or plants. In this case, the word nursery applies to young stars.

Some types of nebulae act as stellar nurseries.

In a stellar nursery, the dust and gas can start to collapse together under the force of gravity. When the mass of dust and gas collects together and becomes larger, the force of gravity pulling inward increases. When this force gets very large, the pressure inside the new star also gets very large. The high pressure causes heat. The heat can cause atoms to react with each other, causing the new star to give out heat and light.

The picture shows a stellar nursery photographed from space. You can see the young stars inside the cloud. Some of these stars are only half the mass of the Sun and have not yet reached their full brightness. The light from the stars lights up the dust and gas in the cloud.

Questions

1   a   Describe the features that are common to all nebulae.

   b   Describe the difference between a nebula and a galaxy.

2   Name the two gases most commonly found in nebulae.

3   a   Describe what is meant by the term *stellar nursery*.

   b   Which of these statements is correct?

     A   All nebulae act as stellar nurseries.

     B   Only some nebulae act as stellar nurseries.

     C   No nebulae ever act as stellar nurseries.

4   Outline the process by which a new star forms.

5   The light year, ly, is a unit of distance measurement used in space.

The diameter of the Solar System is 0.001 ly.

The diameter of the Orion nebula is 24 ly.

Calculate how many times bigger the diameter of the Orion nebula is than the diameter of the Solar System.

Activity 6.4.1

Virtual tour of nebulae

In this activity, you will compare nebulae.

Some space agencies maintain websites with up-to-date photographs of nebulae and information about each one.

Many of the photographs are taken with telescopes such as the Hubble Space Telescope.

Questions

1   Find as many different types of nebula as you can. Include at least one that acts as a stellar nursery.

2   Design an information sheet that shows the different types of nebula.

3   Find out about the Hubble Space Telescope. Describe what is different about the Hubble Space Telescope compared to other telescopes used to look into space. Include this information on your sheet.

Summary checklist

☐   I know what nebulae are.
☐   I know that stars can be formed in nebulae.

> 6.5 Tectonics

In this topic you will:

- discover how convection currents cause movement of tectonic plates
- learn about the evidence we have for tectonic plates.

Getting started

Work in groups to discuss the answers to these questions.

1 Describe the structure of the Earth.

2 Link the model of plate tectonics to the structure of the Earth.

3 Describe some of the events that are more likely to occur at the boundaries of tectonic plates.

Key words

jigsaw
continental coasts
fossil record
alignment

Movement of tectonic plates

You may recall from Stage 7 that the outer layers of the Earth are the solid, rocky crust, which rests on the more fluid mantle.

The mantle is heated from the innermost part of the Earth: the inner core. The inner core is estimated to be at a temperature of over 5000 °C! The high temperature of the inner core is due to thermal energy left over from the formation of the Earth, friction inside the Earth and the type of reactions that happen in the rocks.

You may also recall from Unit 3 that thermal energy is transferred through fluids by convection and that convection currents occur in fluids.

The inner part of the mantle gets thermal energy from the core. The fluid in the mantle then expands when heated and becomes less dense that the fluid surrounding it. This hotter, less dense fluid in the mantle rises towards the crust, cools and sinks again, resulting in a convection current.

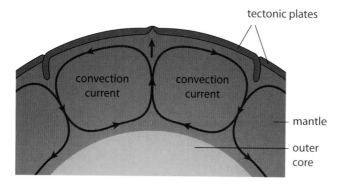

The mantle is a very thick fluid and does not flow easily like water, so the convection currents move very slowly. As the convection currents in the mantle move across underneath the crust, the tectonic plates that make up the crust are pulled along. Just as the convection currents are slow, the movement of the tectonic plates is also slow, varying between 0.6 and 10 cm per year.

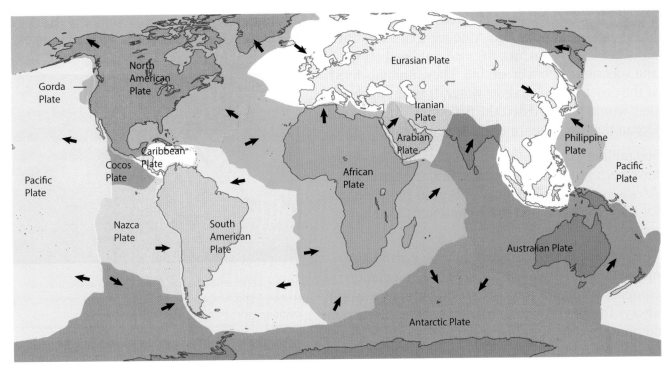

Scientists have mapped the movement of the tectonic plates

Evidence for tectonic plates

When you look at a world map, it looks like the continents could fit together like pieces of a giant jigsaw puzzle. A jigsaw puzzle is a picture that is cut into small interlocking pieces. The object of the puzzle is to put the pieces back together to form the original picture.

Scientists have done this with the continents on Earth. The continental coasts can fit together as shown in the diagram.

Scientists say that this continental jigsaw appearance is evidence for tectonic plates. There is a hypothesis that there was once only one large continent that eventually separated. The separate parts became some of the tectonic plates, and the convection currents from the mantle drove their movement.

The fossil record provides more evidence for tectonic plates and their movement. The fossil record is the name given to the collection of thousands of fossils that provide us with information about the time before humans were on Earth. Fossils are the remains of dead animals and plants that have turned to stone over millions of years.

Fossils of an extinct reptile called *Mesosaurus* have been found in the parts of Africa and South America that would fit together in the jigsaw model of the continents. *Mesosaurus* lived about 275 million years ago and was similar to a crocodile. These animals lived at the coast and in shallow water. It is not likely that they would have crossed the 5000 km-wide Atlantic Ocean that now separates these continents.

300 million-year-old fossils of the plant *Glossopteris* have been found in Antarctica, India, Australia, Africa and South America. This gives more evidence for the hypothesis that these continents were once joined.

Fossils of *Mesosaurus* have been found in both South America and Africa (this one is in Namibia), giving evidence for tectonic plate movements.

You may recall from Stage 8 that the Earth has a magnetic field. Today, the needle of a magnetic compass will point towards north, but that was not always the case. Around 780 000 years ago, the same compass needle would have pointed south! Scientists now know that the Earth's magnetic poles have swapped positions almost 200 times in the last 100 million years.

Magnetic crystals in molten rocks line up to point north in the same way as a compass needle. When the rock solidifies, scientists can use these crystals to tell the direction of the Earth's magnetic field at the time when the rock became solid. The direction that the crystals are pointing is called **alignment**. The word alignment means to line up in a particular way.

The magnetic crystals in rocks found in the middle of the Earth's oceans have been studied. In these locations, called mid-oceanic ridges, magma is coming up from the mantle and solidifying to form new rocks. This action pushes the continents away from each other. The magnetic crystals in the mid-oceanic ridges always have an alignment to north because the Earth's magnetic field is currently in that direction. Rocks further away from these ridges contain magnetic crystals with the opposite alignment. This suggests that these rocks are much older.

Fossils of the plant *Glossopteris* provide more evidence for the movement of tectonic plates.

If the hypothesis of moving tectonic plates was correct, then we would expect there to be more earthquakes and volcanoes at the tectonic plate boundaries. This is indeed the case, as shown on the map.

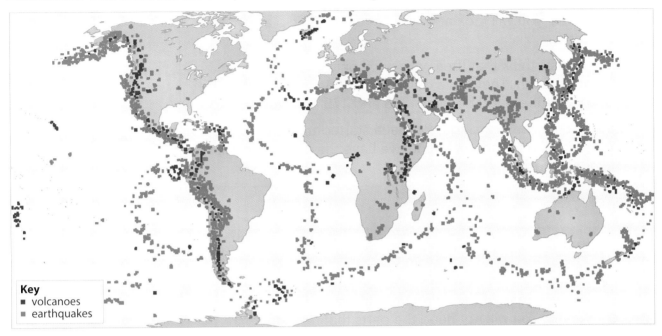

Most of the volcanoes and earthquakes that have been recorded occur close to the tectonic plate boundaries

Questions

1 Describe what makes convection currents in the Earth's mantle.

2 Describe what is meant by the term tectonic plate.

3 The continents of Earth appear to fit together like a jigsaw. Explain how this provides evidence for tectonic plates.

4 Describe how each of these provides evidence for the movement of tectonic plates:

    a   the fossil record

    b   the alignment of magnetic materials in rocks.

5 Scientists think that the Earth's magnetic field has reversed 183 times in 83 million years. Calculate the average time between reversal events.

6 Use the map shown above to discuss the statement 'Earthquakes and volcanoes always occur at tectonic plate boundaries.'

Activity 6.5.1

Pangaea

In this activity, you will look at evidence for tectonic plate movement.

Many scientists think that there was once only one large continent on Earth. They have called this continent Pangaea and they think that it existed between 335 and 175 million years ago.

Around 175 million years ago, Pangaea started to break apart. The parts moved further away until we have the continents that we recognise today.

You will need:

- atlas or printed map of the world that is about A4 size, tracing paper and a pencil, piece of card about A4 size, scissors.

Trace an outline map of the world onto the card. Carefully cut out the continents. You will not need the parts that represent the oceans.

Can you fit your continents together to see what Pangaea might have looked like?

Questions

1 Which continents fit together most easily?

2 Discuss whether Pangaea was made from only one tectonic plate or more than one.

3 Use your continents to predict how a map of the world may look 200 million years in the future.

4 The distance between the coasts of Africa and South America is currently about 5000 km. These continents separated about 140 million years ago. Use this information to calculate the average speed of their separation. Give your answer in centimetres per year.

Summary checklist

☐ I understand what makes tectonic plates move.
☐ I understand what evidence exists for tectonic plates.

Project: Impact craters

Background

Impact craters are formed when a large object from space collides with the rocky surface of a planet or moon.

The word moon can be used with either a capital M or a small m. When used with a capital, as in Moon, the word refers to the large natural object that orbits the Earth. When used with a small letter, as in moon, the word refers to any natural object orbiting another planet.

Impact craters can be found on Earth and you can also see them on the Moon. There are also impact craters on Mercury, Venus, Mars and the moons of Jupiter.

Your task

Find out how impact craters are formed in solid rock.

Next, you will develop an analogy for crater formation.

Work in pairs.

> Your pair will need:
>
> • tray to hold sand, sand, metre rule, 30 cm or 15 cm ruler, balance, various objects such as marbles and small pieces of rock.

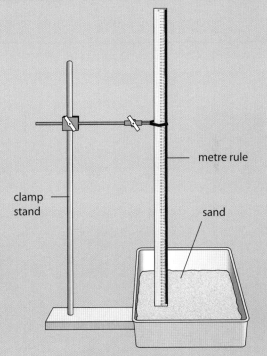

This list includes equipment that you will need to start the investigation. You can develop the investigation to include other equipment.

Set up the equipment as shown in the diagram.

When an object is dropped into the sand, an impact crater will form in the sand.

Safety

• The equipment should be on the floor so that it cannot fall.

• Safety glasses should be worn so that particles ejected from the crater cannot enter eyes.

• Do not stand on tables or chairs to drop objects.

• Make sure objects can only fall into the tray and do not stand with your feet close to the tray.

Continued

- Make a list of variables that you think will affect the diameter and depth of the impact crater.

- Predict how each of these variables will affect the diameter and depth of the crater.

- Investigate each variable in turn, making sure to control each of the other variables.

- Make drawings of the crater to show the shape when seen from the top and also from the side. Add labels to show where you measured the diameter and depth of the crater.

- Record your results in separate tables for each variable.

- Describe any trends in your results for each variable.

- State whether any of your results matched your prediction.

- This investigation is an analogy for impact crater formation on Earth. Describe the strengths and weaknesses of this analogy.

- Suggest any improvements to the method that would make the analogy better.

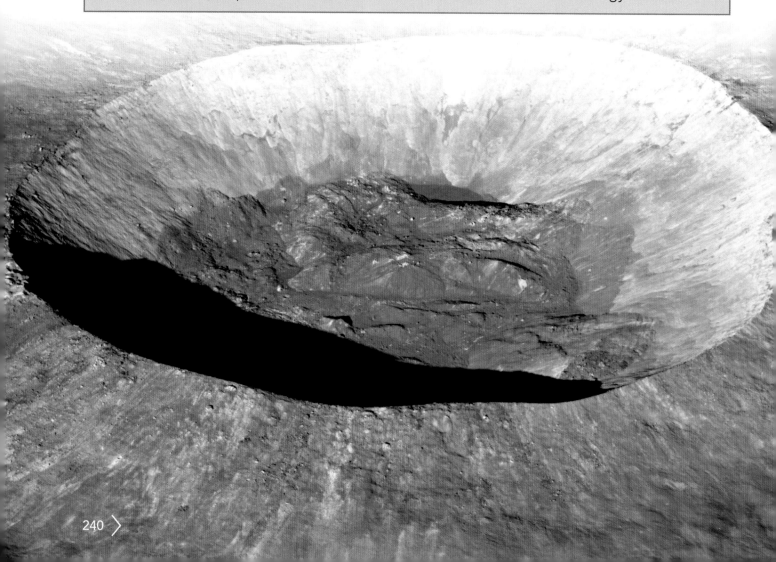

Check your progress

6.1 The graph shows how the particles in a sound wave move with time.

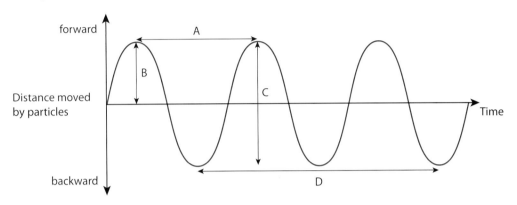

Which measurement shows the amplitude?

Give **one** letter. [1]

6.2 Describe what happens to a sound when these changes are made.
All other variables stay constant.

    a   The amplitude increases. [1]

    b   The frequency increases. [1]

    c   The number of waves per second increases. [1]

6.3 The diagram shows how four different sounds appear as waveforms on an oscilloscope.

A

B
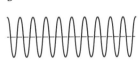

C

D
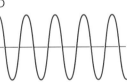

Write the letter of the wave that represents:

    a   the sound with the highest pitch [1]

    b   the quietest sound with the lowest pitch. [1]

6.4 Draw diagrams to show how two sound waves of equal frequency and amplitude can

  a meet each other to reinforce [3]

  b meet each other to cancel. [3]

6.5 Many scientists think that the collision theory explains how the Moon was formed.

  a Describe the events in the collision theory. [4]

  b Describe two pieces of evidence that support the collision theory. [2]

6.6 a Explain what is meant by each of these terms:

  i nebula [2]

  ii stellar nursery. [2]

  b When stars are first formed, they are more difficult to see than older stars that are the same distance from Earth. Suggest two reasons why the young stars are more difficult to see. [2]

6.7 Describe how each of these provides evidence for tectonic plates:

  a the shapes of the present-day continents [1]

  b the fossil record [1]

  c the alignment of magnetic materials in rocks. [1]

7 ▶ Genes and inheritance

> 7.1 Chromosomes, genes and DNA

In this topic you will:

- learn that chromosomes contain genes
- find out what genes and chromosomes are made of.

Getting started

Discuss these questions with a partner. Then share your ideas with the rest of the class.

Atoms and cells both contain a nucleus.

1 Why do you think these very different structures have the same name?

2 Which one is larger?

3 What does the nucleus of a cell do?

Key words

chromosomes
DNA
genes

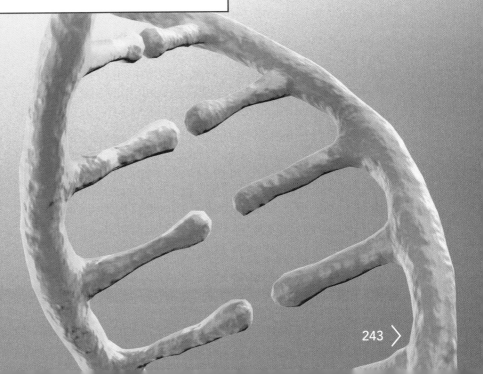

Chromosomes

In Stage 7, you learnt that the nucleus of a cell controls its activities. In this unit, you will learn much more about how it does this.

The nucleus of every cell contains threads called **chromosomes**. Chromosomes were discovered in the nineteenth century. This was when scientists first had sufficiently powerful microscopes, and were first able to see very small things, such as the structure of cells.

When you looked at cells using a microscope, you almost certainly did not see any chromosomes. This is because chromosomes only become visible with a light microscope when a cell is dividing. Chromosomes also need to be coloured using special stains, in order to be able to see them.

This photograph shows a plant cell that is just beginning to divide into two cells. The cells have been stained with a special dye that colours the chromosomes dark red. You cannot really see any of the other structures in the cell.

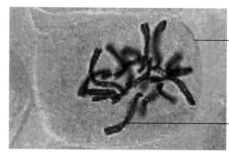

position of cell wall

a chromosome

This photograph shows a chromosome from a fruit fly. Fruit flies have especially thick chromosomes, called giant chromosomes, which are much easier to see than most chromosomes. You can see that this chromosome is a long, striped thread.

Different species of organism have different numbers of chromosomes in the nuclei of their cells. Human cells have 46 chromosomes. Fruit fly cells have eight chromosomes. Mango trees have 40 chromosomes.

Scientists number the chromosomes in a cell according to how long the chromosomes are. In a human cell, the longest chromosome is chromosome 1, the next longest is chromosome 2, and so on.

We have two of each kind of chromosome. This photograph shows all the chromosomes in a human cell. It has been made by cutting and pasting pictures of the individual chromosomes. They have then been lined up in size order. They do not really line themselves up like this!

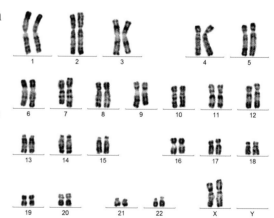

If you look very closely at this photograph, you may be able to see that each chromosome looks like a cross shape. You can see this really clearly in the photograph at the start of the next topic. This is because – just before a cell divides – each chromosome makes a copy of itself. The two copies stay joined together part-way along their length.

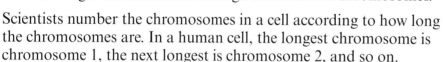

Activity 7.1.1

Making models of chromosomes in a cell

Work in a group of two or three for this activity.

You are going to make a set of chromosomes in a cell of a chosen species of animal.

You can use whatever materials you like to make the models of chromosomes. For example, you could use string or wool. You will also need a large sheet of paper.

First, use the internet to find out how many chromosomes your species has in its cells.

Next, draw an outline of a cell on a large sheet of paper. Do not make it a perfect circle – draw it freehand. Draw a large nucleus inside the cell.

Now make your chromosomes. Remember that there are two chromosomes of each type. So, if your animal has 32 chromosomes, you need to make two sets of 16.

Stick the chromosomes inside the nucleus of the cell.

Write a heading on the sheet of paper to say which species of animal your cell represents.

Self-assessment

How satisfied are you with your model of a cell containing chromosomes?

How does it compare with the models that other groups have made?

What would you do to improve your model, if you had different materials to use, and more time?

Questions

1   Explain why we cannot usually see the chromosomes in a cell, even using a microscope.

2   Red blood cells do not contain a nucleus. Do you think they contain any chromosomes? Explain your answer.

Genes

Each chromosome is made up of hundreds of different **genes**. The genes are arranged in a particular sequence along the chromosome. Each gene helps to control a particular characteristic in the organism. On this diagram of a short chromosome, the stripes represent different genes.

Scientists are still finding out which genes are found on each type of chromosome in humans. On chromosome 1, for example, we know that there are about 2000 different genes. Chromosome 15 is a much shorter chromosome, and it has about 600 different genes.

Discovering exactly what each of these genes do is not easy, but scientists are learning more all the time. For example, we know that two genes on chromosome 15 help to determine eye colour. Everyone has genes for eye colour in the same place on their chromosome 15s. But there are different versions of these genes, so one person could have a chromosome 15 with eye colour genes that give them blue eyes, and another could have a chromosome 15 with eye colour genes that give them brown eyes. That is why the two sisters in this photograph have different eye colours.

DNA

Chromosomes are made of a chemical substance called **DNA**. Each chromosome is one enormously long molecule of DNA.

This means that genes are also made of DNA.

A DNA molecule has a shape like a twisted ladder. This shape is called a double helix. One gene could be a length of DNA with about 2500 of these twists. We cannot see these twists when we use microscopes to look at chromosomes because DNA molecules are much too small to see.

DNA was first discovered in the 1950s. Since then, scientists have found out a great deal about how the DNA in genes helps to determine the characteristics of humans and other organisms. The DNA in a cell determines what the cell does. It contains a complete set of instructions to make a functioning cell, and a whole organism. If you continue to study science to IGCSE or O level, you will find out much more about this.

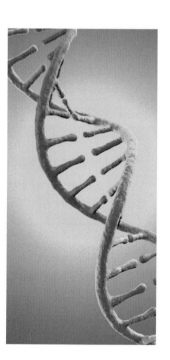

Questions

3 Explain the difference between a chromosome and a gene.

4 All fruit flies have a gene for wing shape, in the same place on their chromosome 2. But some fruit flies have normal wings, and some have very tiny wings – so small that they cannot fly. What can explain this?

Summary checklist
☐ I can explain that chromosomes are made of DNA.
☐ I can explain that each chromosome contains many genes.
☐ I can explain that genes help to determine an organism's characteristics.

> 7.2 Gametes and inheritance

In this topic you will:

- learn what a gamete is
- think about the similarities and differences between male and female gametes
- find out what happens at fertilisation
- explain what determines whether a baby is a boy or a girl.

Getting started

All cells have similar features, but most kinds of cell are specialised to perform a particular function.

1   How many different kinds of animal cells can you think of?

2   What features do they all share?

3   Can you describe how some of them are adapted for their functions?

Key words

egg cell
fertilisation
gametes
inheritance
sex chromosomes
sex inheritance
sperm cell
X chromosomes
Y chromosomes
zygote

Gametes

Most cells in a human body contain 46 chromosomes. Where did these chromosomes come from? To answer that, try to think about how a new human life begins.

Every human being began life as a single cell. This cell was formed when a **sperm cell** joined with an **egg cell**. Sperm cells and egg cells are specialised cells known as **gametes**. A sperm cell is a male gamete, and an egg cell is a female gamete.

This diagram shows a human sperm cell. The photograph shows a group of sperm cells. It was taken with a special kind of powerful microscope called a scanning electron microscope.

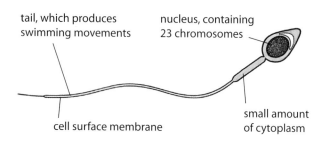
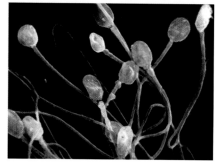

tail, which produces swimming movements

nucleus, containing 23 chromosomes

cell surface membrane

small amount of cytoplasm

Sperm cells are very small cells. They are very active, using their tails to swim vigorously.

This diagram shows a human egg cell. The photograph, like the photograph of the sperm cells, was taken with a scanning electron microscope.

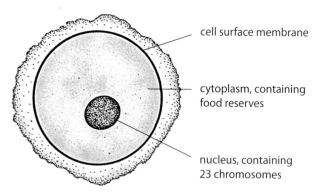
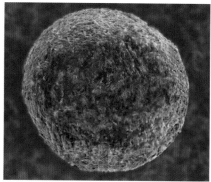

cell surface membrane

cytoplasm, containing food reserves

nucleus, containing 23 chromosomes

Egg cells are much bigger than sperm cells, but they are still very small. A human egg cell is about the same size as a full stop. They need to be larger than sperm cells because they contain food reserves. Another difference from sperm cells is that egg cells cannot move by themselves.

Questions

1   What is a gamete?

2   Draw a table with two columns. Write the headings 'Sperm cell' and 'Egg cell' at the top of the columns. Then make a comparison of these two cells. Try to think of at least three differences between them.

Fertilisation

You may have noticed something odd in the labels on the diagrams of the sperm cell and the egg cell. They each have only 23 chromosomes.

In the previous topic, we saw that human cells each have 46 chromosomes in their nucleus. They have two sets, each set containing 23 chromosomes.

But gametes have only one set of chromosomes. This means that, when a sperm cell joins with an egg cell, the new cell that is produced has two sets. It will have 46 chromosomes.

The joining of a sperm cell with an egg cell is called **fertilisation**.

The diagram and photograph show how fertilisation takes place.

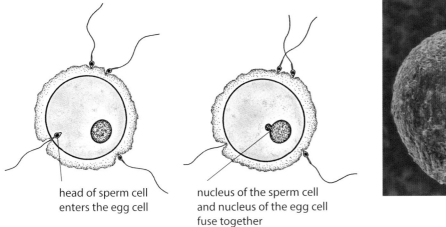

head of sperm cell enters the egg cell

nucleus of the sperm cell and nucleus of the egg cell fuse together

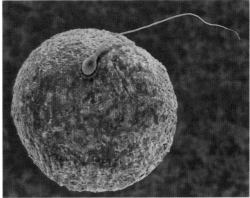

The new cell that is formed when the nucleus of the sperm cell and the egg cell join together is called a **zygote**.

All humans began their life as a single cell like this. Over the next days, weeks and years, this single cell divides over and over again, eventually producing all of the millions of cells in a human body.

Boy or girl?

All of the chromosomes in the cells in a human body came from the person's mother and father. There is one set from the mother, and one set from the father. We can use this information to explain how a baby's sex is determined.

Look at the black and white photograph in the previous topic, where the two sets of chromosomes in a cell from a woman's body have been arranged in order. The last pair, at the bottom right of the photograph, are labelled X.

These two chromosomes are sex chromosomes. They determine whether a person is male or female. In that photograph, there are two X chromosomes. A person with two X chromosomes, XX, is female.

There is another kind of sex chromosome, called a Y chromosome.

Y chromosomes are much smaller than X chromosomes. A person with one X chromosome and one Y chromosome, XY, is male.

This photograph – again taken with a scanning electron microscope – shows a human X chromosome and Y chromosome.

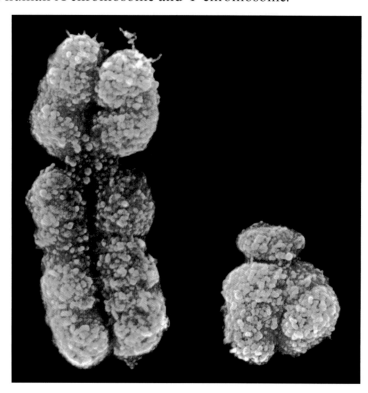

All egg cells contain one X chromosome. Remember that gametes only have one set of chromosomes, so they only have one of each kind. However, sperm cells can have either one X chromosome or one Y chromosome.

So, each time fertilisation happens, either an X-containing sperm cell or a Y-containing sperm cell could join with an egg. If it is an X-containing sperm cell, then the zygote will have two X chromosomes, and will become a baby girl. If it is a Y-containing sperm cell, then the zygote will have one X chromosome and one Y chromosome, and will be a baby boy.

The chance of either of these events happening is about equal. This is why approximately equal numbers of boys and girls are born.

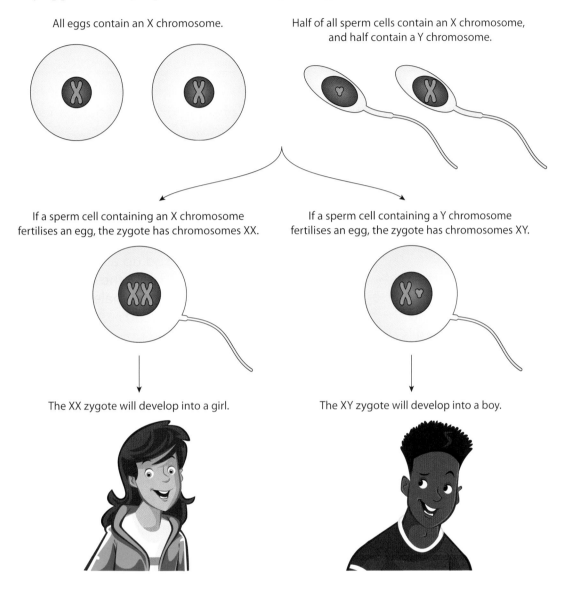

All eggs contain an X chromosome.

Half of all sperm cells contain an X chromosome, and half contain a Y chromosome.

If a sperm cell containing an X chromosome fertilises an egg, the zygote has chromosomes XX.

If a sperm cell containing a Y chromosome fertilises an egg, the zygote has chromosomes XY.

The XX zygote will develop into a girl.

The XY zygote will develop into a boy.

Inheritance

Inheritance means passing on DNA (as chromosomes containing genes) from parents to offspring.

A baby's sex is determined because a baby inherits X or Y chromosomes from its parents. We can use the term **sex inheritance** to describe this.

All organisms also inherit other features from their parents. You will find out more about this in the next topic.

Activity 7.2.1

Modelling sex inheritance

In this activity, you will work in pairs and use coloured pieces of string or wire to represent X chromosomes and Y chromosomes.

You will need:

- two containers – such as plastic pots, 45 short pieces of string or wire all the same size and the same colour – these represent X chromosomes, 15 short pieces of string or wire all the same size as the X chromosome strings but a different colour – these represent Y chromosomes

Method

1   Put 30 X chromosomes into one of the containers. These represent the chromosomes in 30 egg cells.

2   Put 15 X chromosomes and 15 Y chromosomes into the other container. These represent the chromosomes in 30 sperm cells.

3   One person puts their hand into the first pot – without looking – and takes out a piece of string or wire. Then they take out another piece of string or wire from the other pot.

4   Write down the chromosomes in the 'zygote' (fertilised egg) you have produced. Record the result in a table.

5   When you have used up all of the 'chromosomes', add up the total numbers of female and male zygotes that you have produced.

Question

1   From your results, what can you say about the chance of a baby being a boy or a girl?

Peer assessment

Look at how another pair have recorded their results.
Can you easily understand their results table?
Is it as good as yours, or is it better? What makes one table better than another?

Questions

3   Is it correct to say that the sex of a baby is determined by its father, not its mother? Explain your answer.

4   Explain, in your own words, why the numbers of boy and girl babies born each year is approximately equal.

Summary checklist

☐   I can explain what a gamete is, and describe the male and female gametes of humans.

☐   I can explain that fertilisation is the fusion of a male and female gamete.

☐   I can describe how sex is inherited in humans, in terms of X and Y chromosomes.

> 7.3 Variation

In this topic you will:

- learn what is meant by variation
- think about how genes help to produce variation
- investigate and record some examples of variation.

Getting started

In Stage 7, you learnt what a species is.

Think of a way to complete this sentence. Try to include some useful scientific information in your sentence.

A species is ....

Key words

genetic differences

variation

Variation within a species

Organisms that belong to different species usually look very different from one another. Horses look different from donkeys. Lions look different from tigers.

But individual organisms that belong to the same species also have differences between them. You and all of the other people in your class all belong to the same species. But you are all very different from one another.

The differences between individuals belonging to the same species are called **variation**.

Questions

1   These goats all belong to the same species. What similarities are there between them?

2   The goats show variation. What differences can you see between them?

Activity 7.3.1

Measuring variation in humans

Choose four or five features that vary among the members of your class.

Choose at least one feature that you have to measure.

Then complete a results table like this. Change the headings to match the features that you have chosen.

Draw enough rows so that you can complete results for at least eight people.

Person	Hair colour	Eye colour	Shoe size	Height in cm

Collect your results and complete your results table.

Using a bar chart to show variation

A species of plant called kidney vetch has flowers that can have any one of five different colours.

Zara studied the kidney vetch plants growing in a small area of a field. She counted the number of plants with each colour of flower.

She recorded her results like this. Each stroke represents one plant. When she gets to five, she puts the stroke for five across the first four.

red   pink   orange

Colour	Red	Pink	Orange	Yellow	Cream
Tally	⳾⳾⳾⳾	ǀǀ	ǀǀǀ	⳾⳾⳾⳾ ǀǀǀǀ	ǀǀǀ
Number	5	2	3	9	3

yellow   cream

When she had recorded the flower colour of each plant, she added up all the tally strokes and wrote the number in the last row.

Then she used her results to draw a bar chart, like this.

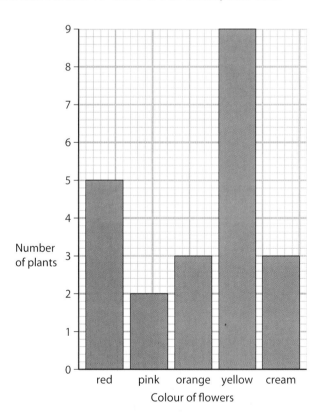

Questions

3   How many plants did Zara find?

4   Which was the most common flower colour?

5   Zara recorded her results in a table and also in a bar chart.
    Which of these do you think shows the results more clearly?
    Explain your answer.

Think like a scientist

Investigating variation in leaves

Some trees have leaves that are divided up into several smaller parts, called leaflets. You are going to investigate the variation in the number of leaflets in a leaf.

You will need:

- one or more trees belonging to the same species, with leaves divided up into leaflets.

Safety

Choose trees where you can collect leaves without having to climb onto anything.

Method

1   Collect at least 20 leaves from the same species of tree.

2   Count the numbers of leaflets on each leaf, and write them down in a list, like this:

    11, 15, 12, 11, 13 .... and so on

3   Draw and complete a tally chart like this. You will need to change the number of columns, depending on your results.

Number of leaflets					
Tally					
Number of leaves					

4   Now you are ready to draw a bar chart. Use the bar chart for the flower colour results to help you.

Questions

1   The median is the middle value for the number of leaflets.
    What is the median value in your results?

Continued

2   The mode is the most common value for the number of leaflets. What is the mode in your results?

3   You can find the mean by adding up all of the numbers of leaflets, and dividing by the number of leaves. What is the mean value in your results?

4   Did you find any differences between the number of leaflets on the leaves of the same individual tree? If you did, do you think that genes could have caused these differences? Explain your answer.

DNA and variation

Look again at the photograph of the goats, near the beginning of this topic. Can we tell what has caused the differences between them?

Each goat in the picture began life when a sperm cell fertilised an egg cell. A sperm cell and an egg cell each contain chromosomes, made of many genes. The genes are made of DNA.

All the sperm cells and all the egg cells of goats contain genes that affect the development of horns. There are several versions of these genes, each made of slightly different DNA. One version of the genes might produce long horns, another short horns and another one perhaps no horns at all. There could also be different genes for making curved horns or straight horns.

Different sperm cells and different egg cells probably contain different versions of these genes. They will also contain different versions of other genes – for example, for height, or coat colour or tail shape. Each gene is different because its DNA is different.

When a sperm cell and egg cell fuse together at fertilisation, the zygote that is produced has a new combination of DNA. The combination is not exactly the same as in its parents, or in its brothers and sisters.

Differences in the DNA of organisms within a species are called **genetic differences**. Genetic means 'to do with genes'.

The people in this photograph belong to three generations of the same family. Some of the DNA from the grandparents has been passed on to their children and grandchildren. You can probably see some similarities between them, because some of their DNA is the same. But everyone in the family has a slightly different combination of DNA from everyone else. There are genetic differences between them.

Environment and variation

DNA is not the only cause of variation between individuals. An organism's environment also affects it.

For example, think again about the variation in the goats. Let us for the moment just think about the two adult goats. They have different coat colours. This is determined by their DNA. Variation in coat colour is caused by genetic differences.

The size of the goat could also be affected by its DNA, but its environment will also affect size. For example, one goat might eat more than another, so it would grow fatter and have a greater body mass. This is not caused by its genes. Not all variation within a species is caused by differences in DNA.

Question

6   Look at your results for the Activity: Measuring variation in humans. For each feature that you investigated, suggest whether the differences are caused by:
   *   genes only
   *   environment only
   *   genes and environment.

Think like a scientist

Measuring variation in humans

You are going to investigate variation in people's wrist circumference. The data you collect are a little bit more difficult to deal with than the leaflet data. This is because they do not fit into definite categories, so you will have to determine the categories yourself.

Method

1   Measure the circumference of the wrist of every person in your class. (If your class has fewer than 20 people, you could measure some other people as well.) Write down your measurements in a list. Remember to include the unit.

2   Think about how you can fit the measurements into different categories. Each category should have the same range of measurements. Look at the table below for an idea. However, you may need to have categories that are not the same as these, depending on the measurements that you made.

Continued

Wrist circumference in cm	Tally	Number of people
8.0 – 8.9		
9.0 – 9.9		
10.0 – 10.9		
11.0 – 11.9		
12.0 – 12.9		
13.0 – 13.9		
14.0 – 14.9		

3 Now put a mark in the Tally column for each measurement that fits into that category.

4 Next, add up all the tally strokes and complete the last column in the table.

5 Now you are ready to draw a frequency diagram to display your results.
Put wrist circumference on the x-axis, and number of people on the y-axis.
The bars in your frequency diagram should touch one another.

Questions

1 What were the smallest and largest wrist circumferences that you measured in your investigation?

2 Which was the most common category of wrist circumference?

Peer assessment

How well do you think you have completed this task?

Did you:
- make sure that you measured the wrist circumference of each person in exactly the same way
- put the measurements into suitable categories
- label the axes of your frequency diagram correctly
- choose good scales for both axes of your graph
- draw the bars carefully and accurately?

Write down one thing that you think you did really well.

Write down one thing that you could do better next time.

Summary checklist

- ☐ I can explain what is meant by variation.
- ☐ I can describe some examples of variation affected by genes.
- ☐ I can explain that when two gametes fuse, they produce a fertilised egg with a new combination of DNA.
- ☐ I can measure and record some examples of variation, and display them in bar charts or frequency diagrams.

› 7.4 Natural selection

In this topic you will:

- learn about the scientific theory of natural selection
- find out about some examples of natural selection in action.

Getting started

The photograph shows a tiny frog, called a waxy monkey leaf frog.

The frogs live in a hot, humid rainforest. They are in danger from many different predators.

Suggest how the frogs are adapted to survive in their environment.

Key words

advantageous
feature
natural selection
resistant

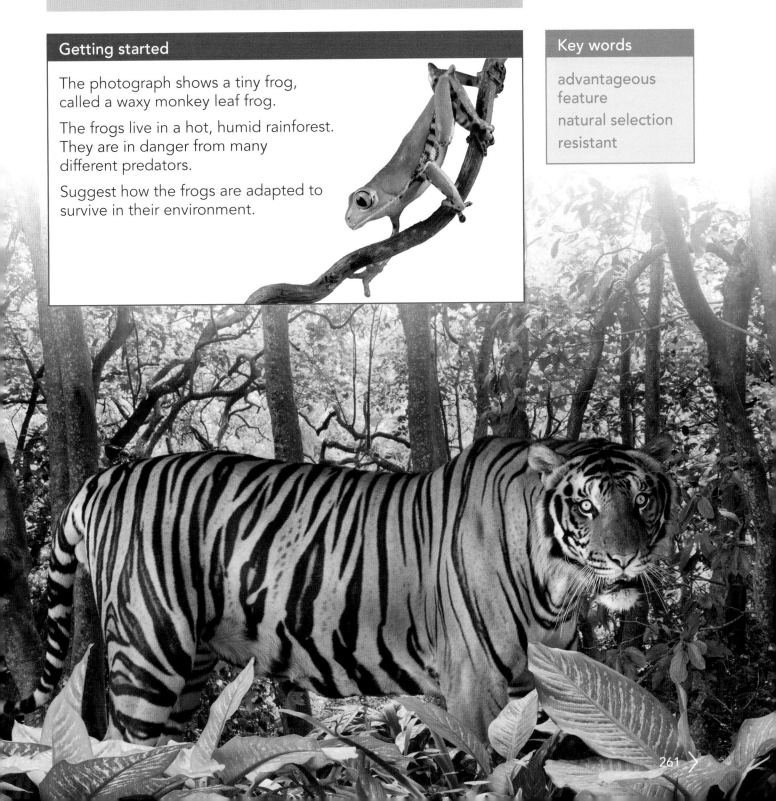

An imaginary story

A long time ago, some animals belonging to a species of herbivore lived on the grassy plains of Africa. They ate leaves from trees. As in all species, there was genetic variation among them. Some individuals had varieties of genes that gave them long necks, and some had varieties of genes that gave them shorter necks.

In some years, the rains did not come. The animals ran short of food. When all the lower leaves had been eaten, only the long-necked animals could get food.

Most of the animals with short necks died of starvation.

When the animals reproduced, they passed on their genes to their offspring. Because only the long-necked animals had survived, it was only their genes that passed to the next generation. Most of their offspring grew up to have long necks.

This imaginary story describes how giraffes might have come to have such long necks. We do not know if this is what happened, and we can never really know. But this theory does help to explain how almost every species is so well adapted to its environment.

You can summarise the theory like this:

1   In every species, there is variation among individual organisms.

2   Some of this variation is caused by differences in their genes.

3   Some individuals have features that make it more likely that they will survive than individuals that do not have these features.

4   The individuals with these **advantageous features** are therefore more likely to reproduce, and pass on the genes that produce the advantageous features to their offspring.

5   Over many generations, the genes that produce these advantageous features get a little bit more common, and the genes that are not so useful get a little bit less common.

This process is called **natural selection**. In the imaginary giraffe example, natural selection has caused genetic changes in the giraffes over time because some varieties of genes have become more common, and some have become less common.

Activity 7.4.1

Does natural selection always produce change?

Think about these questions on your own for a few minutes. Then turn to your partner and discuss your ideas.

1   Imagine a population (group) of organisms that are all really well adapted to their environment. What organisms are you thinking of? Where do they live? How are they adapted to their environment?

2   Now think about what happens over time, if there is no change in their environment. How does natural selection affect this population?

3   Now think about a change in their environment. How does natural selection affect the population now?

Share your ideas with a partner. Do they agree with your ideas? Do you agree with their ideas?

Bacteria and antibiotics

The giraffe story is an imaginary one. We have no evidence that any of this ever happened. But we do have very strong evidence for natural selection in other organisms.

Antibiotics are medicinal drugs that we can take to cure diseases caused by bacteria. There are many different antibiotics. But doctors are finding that some antibiotics do not work anymore. Bacteria have become **resistant** to them.

This is what happened.

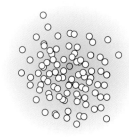

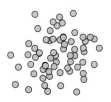

In a population of bacteria, not every one is alike. By chance, one may have a gene that makes it resistant to an antibiotic.

Antibiotic is added, which kills the bacteria that are not resistant.

The resistant one can now multiply and form a population of resistant bacteria just like itself.

Questions

1. Explain what we mean when we say that bacteria have become resistant to an antibiotic.

2. Bacteria have genes. Explain how the development of resistance in bacteria can be explained in terms of genetic changes over time.

3. Doctors advise that we should not use antibiotics unless we really need them. We should save them for when people have serious illnesses. Suggest an explanation for this advice.

Peppered moths

Here is another example of natural selection in action.

Peppered moths live in England. Most peppered moths have pale wings, but some have a gene that gives them dark wings.

Peppered moths fly at night, and spend the daylight hours resting on tree trunks. They are hunted and eaten by birds. The pale colour of peppered moths camouflages them perfectly against lichen-covered tree bark. (Lichen is a plant-like organism that grows on rocks and trees.)

Until the year 1849, almost all peppered moths were pale. Then more and more dark ones started to appear. By 1900, almost all peppered moths near some English cities were dark ones.

What was happening? During this time, the Industrial Revolution was taking place in England. Many factories burnt coal, which polluted the air with smoke. The smoke killed lichens and made the tree trunks dark.

Scientists have done experiments that show that birds can see light moths more easily on dark tree trunks than on lichen-covered ones. And they can see dark moths more easily on lichen-covered tree trunks than on dark ones.

Now we can explain why the dark variety of the moth became more common. When the tree trunks got darker, the pale moths were not camouflaged. They were more likely than the dark ones to be eaten by birds.

The dark moths were more likely to survive and reproduce than the pale moths. They passed on their genes for their dark colour to their offspring. Over several generations of moths, more and more of the offspring inherited these advantageous genes for dark colour. Over time, the dark colour became more and more common. Each generation, more dark moths were born and fewer pale moths.

Today, pollution in England is much less. Lichens grow on tree trunks again. Today, most peppered moths are the pale variety.

Questions

4   Look back at the list of five events that summarise the theory of natural selection.

Use this list to explain how natural selection caused dark peppered moths to become more common than pale peppered moths, during the late nineteenth century in England.

How well do you think you have answered question 4? Did you:

- refer to each of the five points in the list describing how natural selection happens

- pick out events in the peppered moth story that match each of these five points

- give a really clear explanation of how genetic changes over time produced the change in the most common type of peppered moth

- use scientific terms in your explanation (e.g. gene, natural selection, variation)?

Extinction

The proportions of dark and pale peppered moths changed over time, when their environment changed. But imagine what might have happened to the peppered moths if the proportions of pale and dark moths in the population had **not** changed, when the tree trunks became darker. If the moths were still all pale, then most of them could have been eaten by birds. The population of moths might have become so small that the peppered moths all died out. The species might have become extinct.

Changes in the environment can cause a population to become extinct, if the species cannot change over time. Scientists are worried that climate change may cause a very large number of species to become extinct.

Summary checklist

- ☐ I can describe the scientific theory of natural selection.
- ☐ I can explain how natural selection can sometimes produce genetic changes in a population over time.
- ☐ I can describe some examples of natural selection in action.
- ☐ I can explain that environmental change can cause a species to become extinct.

Project: How we learnt about DNA

You are going to work in a group to produce a short report about one of the steps by which scientists discovered what we know about DNA today. Each group's report can then be used to contribute to a display to show a time line of these discoveries.

One of the first people to do scientific experiments about inheritance was Gregor Mendel. He worked in a monastery garden on his own, but today scientists researching DNA work in groups, in well-equipped laboratories. Your time line will help to show how scientific research has progressed from Mendel's time to today.

A portrait of Gregor Mendel   Research into DNA in a modern laboratory

Choose one of these steps to research:

1860s Gregor Mendel does experiments on inheritance of characteristics in pea plants.

1902 Walter Sutton and Theodor Bovari each discover that chromosomes are important in inheritance.

1920 to 1944 Frederick Griffith and Oswald Avery show that DNA is the genetic material.

1953 Rosalind Franklin, Francis Crick and James Watson work out the structure of DNA.

2001 The structure of all the DNA in human cells is worked out, through the international Human Genome Project.

You can use a mix of words, photographs (from the internet) and drawings. It would be good if everyone in the class uses the same size of paper to produce their report, so that they look good when they are all put together to produce the time line. Do not make your report too long – it should fit onto one piece of paper.

Continued

Try to include information about these questions in your report:

- Where did the people who made the discovery work?
- How did they make their discoveries?
- Did the scientists work on their own, or with others?
- How did the discoveries made earlier help your scientists to make their discoveries?
- How did the scientists share their discoveries with other scientists? Did this happen quickly, or did it take a long time?

Check your progress

7.1 Copy and complete the sentences. Choose from the list.
You can use each word once, more than once or not at all.

chromosomes   DNA   four   genes   two

The nucleus of every cell contains several long threads, called ....

In most cells, there are .... copies of each thread.

Each thread contains many ....

The threads are made of a chemical called ....   [4]

7.2 Copy and complete the table. Put a tick in a space if you think the description is
correct. Leave the space empty if you think the description is not correct.   [5]

Description	Egg cells	Sperm cells
contain a nucleus		
are gametes		
can swim		
in humans, contain 23 chromosomes		
contain either an X chromosome or a Y chromosome		

7.3 Arun investigated variation in bean pods. (You can see a picture of a pod on
the previous page.)

He picked 20 bean pods, all from the same species of bean plant. He counted
the number of beans in each pod. These are the results that he wrote down.

7, 3, 8, 6, 3, 4, 7, 5, 5, 8, 6, 4, 6, 7, 5, 5, 6, 5, 4, 8

a   Calculate the mean number of beans in a pod.
Show how you worked out your answer.   [2]

b   Copy this results table. Use Arun's results to complete it.   [2]

Number of beans in a pod						
Tally						
Number of pods						

c   Copy these axes onto a large piece of graph paper.
Then draw a suitable graph to show Arun's results.

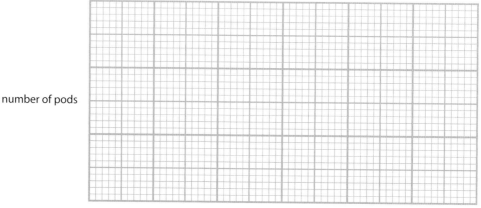

number of pods

number of beans

Add a suitable scale on each axis.

Draw touching bars to show the results.   [4]

7.4 A bacterium called *Staphylococcus pneumoniae* causes a serious infection of the lungs, called pneumonia. The graph shows the percentage of cases of pneumonia in which the bacteria were resistant to penicillin (an antibiotic).

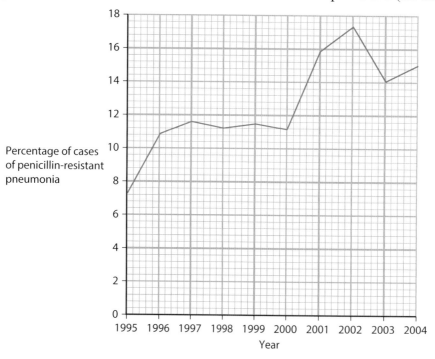

Percentage of cases of penicillin-resistant pneumonia

Year

a   What is an antibiotic?   [1]

b   Describe the trend shown in the graph.   [1]

c   Suggest how natural selection has caused this trend.   [3]

Rates of reaction

> 8.1 Measuring the rate of reaction

In this topic you will:

- learn how the rate of reaction can change
- measure the rate of reaction
- use graphs to discuss and measure the rate of reaction
- explain why the rate of reaction changes.

Getting started

- With a partner, list as many of the ways you can of telling that a reaction has taken place.
- Can you suggest ways in which you could measure how quickly a reaction takes place?
- Share your ideas with the class.

Key words

anomalous result

collecting a gas over water

collisions

gradient

rate of reaction

Rate of reaction

When magnesium ribbon is added to dilute sulfuric acid, you can tell a reaction is taking place because bubbles of hydrogen gas are given off. When you carried out this reaction in the laboratory, you may have noticed that at the start of the reaction a lot of bubbles were given off quickly. As the reaction came to an end, fewer bubbles were produced. Eventually, no more bubbles were produced. This shows that the reaction started quickly, then slowed, and eventually stopped.

How could you measure how quick the reaction was? This is called the **rate of reaction**.

The rate of reaction can be measured by working out how much of one of the products has been made in a given time, or how much of a reactant has been used up in a given time.

In the magnesium ribbon experiment, it is difficult to measure how quickly the reactants are used up or how quickly the magnesium sulfate is formed. The easiest way to measure the rate is to measure how quickly the hydrogen gas is produced. You can do this by measuring the volume of gas produced in a particular period of time.

To collect the gas, you can attach a syringe to the top of a flask so that no hydrogen can escape, as shown in the diagram. You can use the scale on the syringe to measure the volume of gas produced at different times during the reaction.

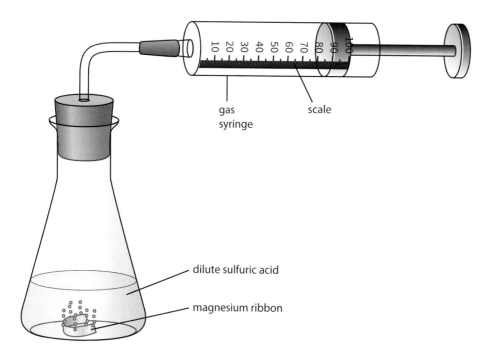

gas syringe

scale

dilute sulfuric acid

magnesium ribbon

Questions

1   Write the word and symbol equations for the reaction of magnesium with sulfuric acid.

2   This three-part table shows the results obtained from an experiment using the apparatus shown above.

Time in s	Total volume of hydrogen gas produced in cm^3	Time in s	Total volume of hydrogen gas produced in cm^3	Time in s	Total volume of hydrogen gas produced in cm^3
0	0	120	40	240	64
30	10	150	48	270	66
60	20	180	54	300	66
90	26	210	60	330	66

How can you tell from the table that the reaction has finished at 270 seconds?

3   Suggest what might happen in the experiment if you used a lot more magnesium and acid, so that more than 100 cm^3 of hydrogen gas was formed. What could be done to reduce the risk of an accident if more than 100 cm^3 of hydrogen as produced?

4   When a graph of the results in the table is plotted, it is easier to see the pattern that they make. The graph shows that one of the results does not fit the pattern. This is called an **anomalous result**.

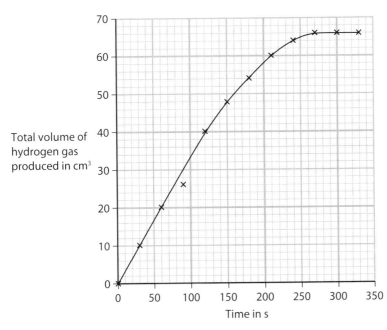

Which of the results is anomalous? Explain how you identified the anomalous result, and say what you would expect the result to be.

When you measure the rate of reaction, you find that the rate of reaction changes as the reaction proceeds. Another reaction you could look at is the one between calcium carbonate and dilute hydrochloric acid.

As carbon dioxide gas is lost from the flask, the mass of the flask decreases. If you measure the mass every 30 seconds, you find that the mass decreases quickly at first but, as the reaction continues, the mass decreases more and more slowly.

Using the graph

A graph of the results from investigations into the rate of reaction can be used to measure the rate of reaction at any given time. The slope or **gradient** of the line tells you how quickly the reaction is taking place.

The steeper the slope, the faster the reaction.

This graph shows the results of an investigation into the rate of reaction between calcium carbonate and hydrochloric acid.

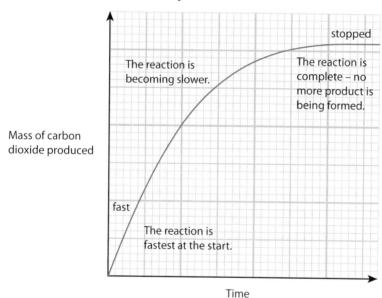

The line is steepest at the start of the reaction. This is when the reaction is fastest. As the slope of the line becomes less steep, the reaction is becoming slower. When the line levels out, it shows that no more carbon dioxide is being lost. This means that the reaction has ended.

This graph shows the rate of reaction between copper carbonate and hydrochloric acid. You can use a graph like this to measure and compare the rates of reaction at different times during the reaction. You can use the graph to find out the average volume of carbon dioxide gas given off per second in the period between 10 seconds and 30 seconds.

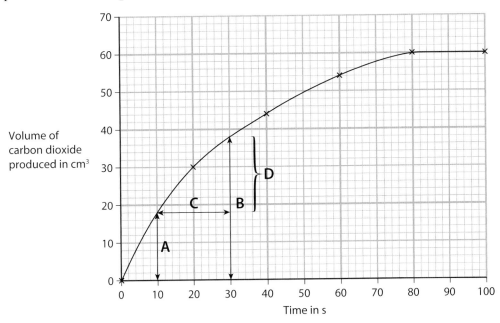

To do this you should draw a line at 10 seconds on the horizontal axis up to where it meets the line of the graph, labelled **A**. Then draw another line at 30 seconds up to the point here it meets the graph, labelled **B**.

Draw line **C** between **A** and **B** as shown.

The distance of **C** represents the time taken, in this case 20 seconds.

The line **D** shows you how much carbon dioxide was produced in this time, in this case 20 cm^3.

If 20 cm^3 of carbon dioxide is produced in 20 seconds. Then on average the rate of reaction over this period of time is 20 cm^3 in 20 seconds or 1 cm^3 per second.

Questions

5   Write the word equation for the reaction between copper carbonate and hydrochloric acid.

6   Use the graph above to find the average rate of reaction between 60 and 80 seconds. How does this rate of reaction compare with the rate between 10 and 30 seconds?

Activity 8.1.1

What makes a good graph?

You will need:

- poster materials and/or access to computers.

Method

1 With a partner, discuss why you may need to plot a graph of your results when you carry out an investigation.

2 Discuss the things that make a good graph; some of the things you might consider are:

- how you know which variable to put on which axis
- what scale to use
- what labels you use
- how the points are plotted
- how you decide to join the points.

3 Make a poster, slide presentation or some other sort of presentation to illustrate how you produce the best possible graphs.

4 Present your poster or presentation to another group or the whole class.

5 Assess the presentations that other groups make to you.

Think like a scientist

Measuring the rate of reaction

In this activity, you are going to measure the rate of reaction between calcium carbonate and hydrochloric acid. You could do this in several different ways. You could do it by measuring the mass of carbon dioxide lost (using a top pan balance, as in the diagram after question 4 earlier in this topic). Or you could collect the carbon dioxide and measure the volume produced either by using a gas syringe (as shown earlier in this topic in Rate of reaction) or by using a trough of water and a measuring cylinder filled with water, as shown here. This is known as **collecting a gas over water**.

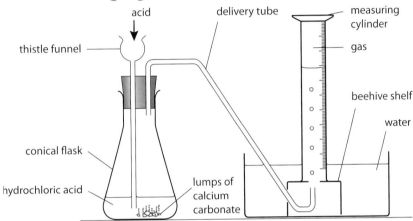

You will need:

You can work out what you will need when you decide which method you will use to measure the rate of reaction.

Answer questions 1–3 before you begin the practical task.

Method

1 Assemble your equipment and put the calcium carbonate in the flask.
2 Add the hydrochloric acid; start the timer and measure the initial mass or volume.
3 After 30 seconds, measure again. Continue to take measurements every 30 seconds until you have three consecutive readings that are the same.

Questions

1 Make a list of the equipment you will need.
2 Write a risk assessment for your investigation.
3 Prepare a table for your results.
4 Plot a graph of your results and describe how the rate of reaction changes over time.
5 What problems did you have when you carried out this reaction?
   How might these have affected your results?
6 How could you improve the reliability of your results?

There are a number of different ways of carrying out the investigation shown on the previous page.
Will the method used have any effect on the accuracy of the results?

Why does the rate of reaction change?

We can use ideas about particle theory to answer this question.

For a chemical reaction to take place, the particles of the reactants involved have to collide with one another with enough energy to react together.

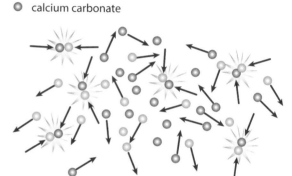

○ hydrochloric acid
◉ calcium carbonate

At the start of the reaction there are a lot of particles that have not reacted. **Collisions** happen frequently. This means that a lot of carbon dioxide is produced in the first 30-second period.

As the particles react, the number of particles that have not reacted gets lower and lower. The chance of two unreacted particles colliding with each other decreases. This means that less carbon dioxide is formed in the later 30-second periods. This means that the rate of reaction is slower.

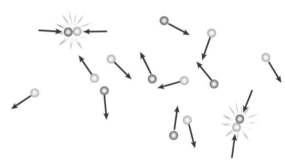

Eventually, all the particles have reacted. There are no more collisions that result in the production of carbon dioxide gas. The reaction has finished.

Fewer particles and less frequent collisions

Summary checklist

- ☐ I know how the rate of reaction changes.
- ☐ I can carry out an investigation safely.
- ☐ I can measure the rate of reaction.
- ☐ I can use graphs to discuss and measure the rate of reaction.
- ☐ I know why the rate of reaction changes.

> 8.2 Surface area and the rate of reaction

In this topic you will:

- investigate the rate of reaction when the surface area of one of the reactants is changed

- carry out an investigation using the reaction between calcium carbonate and dilute hydrochloric acid

- consider how changing the shape of a material can affect the surface area.

Getting started

- Find the surface area of each different face of this book.

- Record the surface area for each face.

- Calculate the total surface area.

- With a partner, arrange your two books so that they are touching and have the least possible total surface area. What is this total surface area?

- Then arrange the books so that they are touching but have the largest possible total surface area. What is this total surface area?

- How does changing the arrangement of the books affect the surface area?

Key words

surface area

The effect of changing the surface area

When you put magnesium ribbon in a Bunsen flame it reacts very quickly, and burns with a bright white flame to form magnesium oxide. However, if you place a large block of magnesium in the Bunsen flame it does not burn. If you place magnesium powder in the Bunsen flame it burns much faster than the ribbon.

Why does this happen?

Think about what is happening as the magnesium reacts with oxygen in the air. Only the magnesium atoms on the surface can make contact with the oxygen and react with it. In the block of magnesium, most of the atoms are inside the block, away from the oxygen. In the magnesium ribbon, more of the atoms are on the surface and react. Magnesium ribbon has a larger total **surface area** than a magnesium block of the same mass. An eqivalent mass of magnesium powder has an even larger total surface area and because it has the most atoms available to react, the reaction is even quicker.

- ● atom at the surface
- ● atom inside

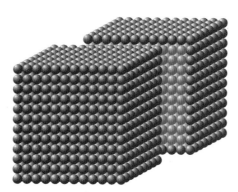

Only the magnesium atoms on the surface of the block can react with oxygen in the air.

In magnesium ribbon, more of the atoms are on the surface and can react with the air.

Small pieces of solids always react faster than larger pieces.

Each time you cut a solid into smaller pieces, you increase the total surface area.

For example, these slices of bread have a total surface area greater than the loaf of bread.

Think like a scientist

Burning iron

You are going to compare what happens when you heat an iron nail, iron wool and iron filings in air. Remember to record your observation for each.

You will need:

- safety glasses, tongs, Bunsen burner, heatproof mat, spatula, iron nail, iron wool, iron filings.

Safety

Wear safety glasses and take care not to touch anything hot.

Method

1   Grip the nail firmly with the tongs and hold it in the flame of a Bunsen burner.

2   Hold the iron wool in tongs and hold it in the flame of a Bunsen burner.

3   Use the end of a spatula to gently sprinkle a few iron filings into a Bunsen flame.

Questions

1   Compare the reactions of these three forms of iron.

2   What effect does increasing the total surface area have on the rate of reaction?

3   Explain the reasons for the change in the rate of reaction.

Activity 8.2.1

Calculating the surface area

You are going to investigate how the surface area changes when you arrange cubes in different ways.

You will need:

- 27 children's construction cubes (all the same size), ruler.

Method: Part 1

Arrange the blocks to form a cube, as shown in the diagram.

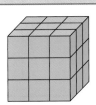

Questions

1   What is the area of one face of one of the small blocks?

2   How many faces of small blocks make up one face of the large cube?

3   What is the area of one face of the large cube?

4   What is the total surface area of the large cube?

Continued

Method: Part 2

Arrange the blocks to form a shape 3 × 9 small blocks, as shown in the diagram.

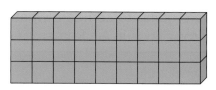

Questions

5   This shape still has 27 blocks. What is the total surface area of this shape?

6   How would this change in shape affect the rate of reaction, if the shapes were zinc metal and they reacted with acid?

Method: Part 3

Separate all the blocks from one another.

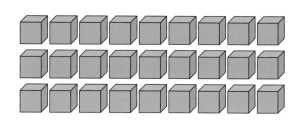

Questions

7   There are still 27 blocks.
    What is the total surface area of all the blocks now they have been separated?

8   How would this change of shape affect the rate of reaction?

9   Explain why a change in surface area changes the rate of reaction.

Think like a scientist

Investigating the effect of surface area on the rate of reaction

In this investigation you will investigate the effect of changing the size of pieces of calcium carbonate (marble chips) in the reaction with hydrochloric acid. You could use any of the methods shown in Topic 8.1.

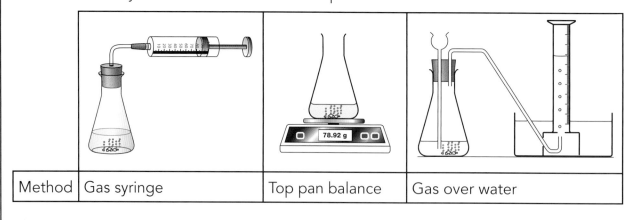

Method	Gas syringe	Top pan balance	Gas over water

Continued

You are going to do the experiment twice, using different sizes of calcium carbonate chips. Whichever method you use, use the same method for the two experiments.

The beaker on the left shows the reaction of small chips of calcium carbonate with hydrochloric acid. The beaker on the right shows the same reaction but with larger calcium carbonate chips.

Answer questions **1–6** before starting the experiment.

Questions

1   Which method will you use?
2   Which reaction do you predict will be the fastest?
3   The size of the pieces of calcium carbonate will be changed, but the total mass of the pieces will be kept the same. Why is it also important to keep the volume, type and concentration of the acid the same?
4   What are the dependent and independent variables?
5   Read through the method and then write a list of the equipment you will need.
6   Construct a results table.

Method

1   Assemble your apparatus
2   Add 5 g of large marble chips to 25 cm^3 of hydrochloric acid in a conical flask.
3   Start the timer and read the volume of gas produced or the mass of the flask and contents every 30 seconds, until you have at least three readings that are the same. Record your results carefully.
4   Repeat, but this time use 5 g of smaller chips.
5   Plot both sets of results on one graph.

Questions

7   Which line on your graph is steeper?
8   Which size of marble chip reacted more quickly?
9   What happens to the rate of reaction as the total surface area of the chips increases?
10 Was your prediction supported by your findings?
11 What do you predict would happen if you repeated the experiment using powdered calcium carbonate?

If you use the same mass of large calcium carbonate chips and small calcium carbonate chips and the same volume and type of acid each time, do you make more carbon dioxide when the reaction is quicker?

Summary checklist

☐ I can safely investigate the rate of reaction when the surface area of one of the reactants is changed.

☐ I can carry out an investigation using the reaction between calcium carbonate and dilute hydrochloric acid.

☐ I know how changing the shape of a material can affect the surface area.

> 8.3 Temperature and the rate of reaction

In this topic you will:

- investigate the effect of temperature on the rate of reaction
- carry out a trial run and preliminary work for the investigation and use the information to improve the investigation method
- select equipment
- plot a graph of results.

Getting started

- Write down what you mean by the phrase 'rate of reaction'.
- Compare your statement with a partner and discuss your answers.
- Discuss how the rate of reaction changes as the reaction progresses and write an explanation of why this happens.
- Be ready to share this with the class.

Key words

precipitate
trial run
preliminary work

Changing the temperature of reactants

If you change the temperature of the reactants in a reaction, the rate of reaction will change.

If you mix hydrochloric acid with a solution of sodium thiosulfate (a salt), the mixture becomes cloudy. This is because sulfur is produced. Sulfur is insoluble in water, so it forms a **precipitate**. The precipitate is opaque – so, when you can no longer see through the solution, you know the sulfur has been formed.

The reaction is good for investigating reaction rates, because you can easily time how long it takes for the sulfur precipitate to be formed.

And by changing the temperature of the solution, you can investigate the effect of temperature on reaction rates.

Think like a scientist

The effect of temperature on the rate of reaction

You are going to measure the rate of reaction between sodium thiosulfate and hydrochloric acid at different temperatures.

There are three parts to this: the trial run, the preliminary work and the investigation.

Part 1: The trial run

First you need to carry out a trial run. A trial run means you will carry out a practice experiment to make sure you can do the experiment safely and effectively. You will then be prepared and be ready to overcome any problems you find.

Safety

Make sure the room is well ventilated, because sulfur dioxide gas will be produced. Place any reacted solutions into a container with some solid sodium hydrogencarbonate for your teacher to remove later. The sodium hydrogencarbonate will react with the sulfur dioxide.

> **You will need:**
> - safety glasses, test tube with stopper, clamp stand, white card with a cross marked on it, timer or stop clock, sodium thiosulfate solution, dilute hydrochloric acid, large beaker containing solid sodium hydrogencarbonate.

Method

1   Place 10 cm^3 of sodium thiosulfate solution in a test tube.

2   Fix the test tube into the clamp stand and arrange the card with the black cross behind it as in the diagram.

3   Add 1 cm^3 hydrochloric acid to the test tube and put the stopper in the tube. Start the timer.

4   Time how long it takes before you can no longer see the cross.

5   When you have finished, place the contents of the test tube in the large beaker containing sodium hydrogencarbonate.

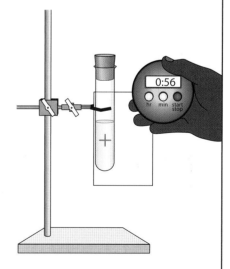

Questions

1   What information did your trial run give you?

2   Will you change the way you carry out your investigation as a result of this trial?

Continued

Part 2: The preliminary work

The next step is to do some **preliminary work** to decide which temperatures you will use. To change the temperature of the sodium thiosulfate solution, warm it in a suitable water bath before adding the acid. Make sure there is a stopper in the tube while it is warming.

Discuss in your group how you will do this preliminary work.

Here are some of the things you will need to consider in your preliminary work:

How large a change in temperature is needed to give a reaction time difference we can measure?

How big a range of temperatures will we use?

Will we start the temperatures at room temperature?

Will we increase the temperature by 5°C or 10°C or 20°C?

Questions

3   What equipment will you need for the preliminary work?
4   Describe what you have decided to do as your preliminary work.
5   How will this help you with your final investigation?
6   What can you do to try to keep your test tube at the same temperature while the reaction is taking place?
7   Write an outline plan for the preliminary work including a results table.
    Once your outline plan has been checked carry out your preliminary work.
8   What did you find out that will help your final investigation?

Part 3: The investigation

Discuss in your group how you will carry out the final investigation using the information you got from the trial run and the preliminary work.

Questions

9   Write a detailed plan for your investigation. You should include a list of equipment you will need and a results table.
    When your plan has been checked by your teacher, carry out your investigation.
10   How did you make sure your investigation was a fair test?
11   Plot a graph of your results.
12   Describe the relationship between the temperature and the rate of reaction.

Looking at typical results

Here is a graph of some typical results for the rate of reaction between marble chips (calcium carbonate) and hydrochloric acid. This was carried out as in the previous topic.

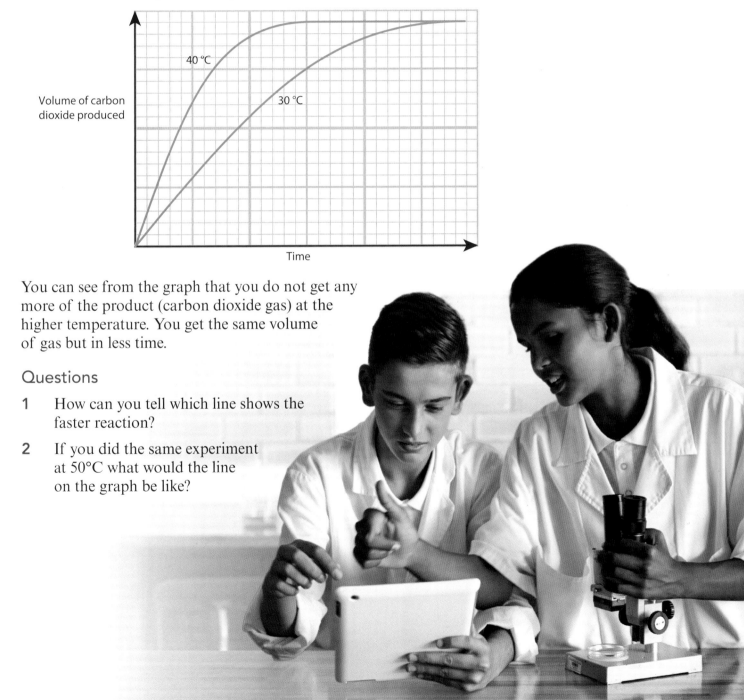

You can see from the graph that you do not get any more of the product (carbon dioxide gas) at the higher temperature. You get the same volume of gas but in less time.

Questions

1   How can you tell which line shows the faster reaction?

2   If you did the same experiment at 50°C what would the line on the graph be like?

Explaining the effect of temperature

Particles move all the time. When the temperature of the reaction is increased, the particles move faster. They collide more often, and with more energy.

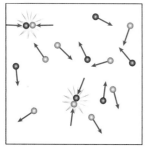
Reaction at 30 °C

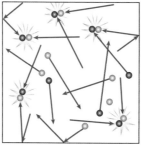
Reaction at 40 °C

The higher the temperature, the faster the rate of reaction.

Summary checklist

- ☐ I can investigate the effect of temperature on the rate of reaction, safely.
- ☐ I can carry out a trial run and preliminary work for an investigation and use the information to improve the investigation method.
- ☐ I can select equipment.
- ☐ I can plot a graph of results.
- ☐ I can explain the effect of temperature on the rate of reaction, using particle theory.

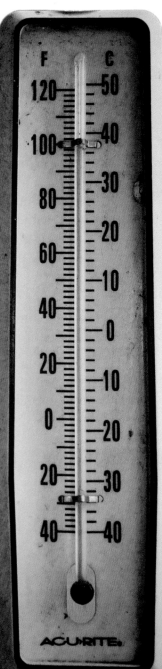

> 8.4 Concentration and the rate of reaction

In this topic you will:

- investigate the effect of concentration on the rate of reaction
- plan an investigation
- explain the effect of changes in concentration on the rate of reaction, using particle theory

Getting started

With a partner, discuss what you think would happen if you carried out an experiment with marble chips (calcium carbonate) using the same mass of chips, all materials at the same temperature but with different concentrations of acid.

Can you explain the reasons behind your ideas?

Be prepared to share your ideas with the class.

Key words

concentration

dilute

In this unit you have investigated different variables and how they affect the rate of reaction. You have also used different methods in your investigations. Now you will investigate the effect of **concentration** on the rate of reaction.

Think like a scientist

Investigating the effect of concentration on the rate of reaction

In this investigation you will change the concentration of the acid used.

Instead of measuring the volume of carbon dioxide produced every 30 seconds, you will use a slightly different method of measuring the rate of reaction.

You will time how long it takes to collect 25 cm³ of carbon dioxide in the measuring cylinder.

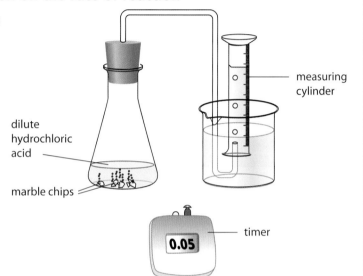

Part 1: Planning the investigation

Discuss in your group how you will carry out this investigation.

- What mass of marble chips will you use?
- Which factors will you keep the same?

Some of the other things you could consider are:
- What volume of acid will you use?
- Which concentrations of acid will you use?
- What are the risks in this investigation?
- What safety precautions should you take?
- What equipment will you need?
  You will need items that are not shown in the diagram.
- Do you need to do a trial run or some preliminary work?
- If so, what do you want to find out?
- Do you need to repeat any of your readings?

Continued

Question

1   Use the results of your group discussion to write a plan for your investigation.

> How does discussing ideas in a group help me to plan a better investigation?

Part 2: Carrying out the investigation

When you have shown your plan to your teacher and had it approved you may carry out the investigation.

Safety

Make sure you follow the safety precautions in your plan.

> **You will need:**
>
> - safety glasses, top pan balance, timer, measuring cylinders (to collect the gas and to measure the volume of acid used), beakers and a marking pen to label the different concentrations of acid, conical flask fitted with a bung and delivery tube, large container for holding the water when collecting the gas over water, marble chips, dilute hydrochloric acid, water.

Method

1   Make up your concentrations of acid. You can do this by diluting the acid you have been given. Make up $50\,cm^3$ each time. Use the table below to help you.

Solution	Acid in cm^3	Water in cm^3	
A	10	40	least concentrated
B	20	30	
C	30	20	↓
D	40	10	
E	50	0	most concentrated

2   Set up the apparatus as shown in the previous diagram.

3   Weigh out the marble chips and place them in the flask.

4   Add the acid and time how long it takes to collect $25\,cm^3$ of carbon dioxide. Record the acid used and the timing.

5   Repeat with different concentrations of acid.

Continued

Questions

2 How did you ensure this was a fair test?

3 How did you ensure the results were reliable?

4 Present your results in a suitable table.

5 Plot a graph of your results.

6 Which concentration of acid gave the fastest results?

7 Describe the pattern in your results.

Typical results

The graph below shows some typical results for the rate of reaction between marble chips and **dilute** hydrochloric acid. These results have been obtained from an experiment in which the volume of carbon dioxide has been measured every 10 seconds. Not like the experiment you have just carried out.

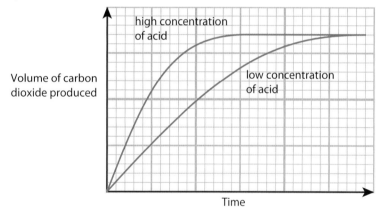

You can see from the graph that you do not get any more product (carbon dioxide gas) at the higher concentration. You get the same volume of gas, but more quickly.

Questions

1 How can you tell which line on the graph shows the faster reaction?

2 If you did the same experiment with an even less concentrated acid what would the line on the graph be like?

Does plotting the results on a graph make it easier to see the pattern?

Explaining the effect of concentration

Once again, we can use particle theory to help explain these results.

The higher the concentration of hydrochloric acid, the more hydrochloric acid particles there are in a given amount of space. This means that there will be more frequent collisions between hydrochloric acid particles and calcium carbonate particles.

○ hydrochloric acid particle

● marble particle

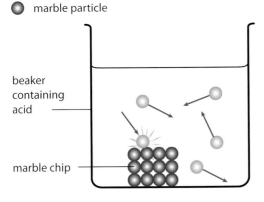

Reaction in dilute acid

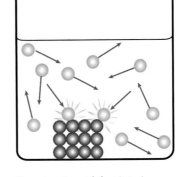

Reaction in acid that is twice as concentrated

Summary checklist

☐ I can plan an investigation.
☐ I can investigate the effect of concentration on the rate of reaction, safely.
☐ I can explain the effect of changes in concentration on the rate of reaction using particle theory.

Project: Gas for sale

In this unit you have looked at various ways to increase the rate of reaction. In this task you are going to imagine that you are manufacturing carbon dioxide gas to sell to the drinks industry. The carbon dioxide puts the 'fizz' into soda. The aim is to make as much soda as possible.

You will use the reaction of marble chips with hydrochloric acid to produce the carbon dioxide gas. You have a 'budget' of $20 and each item you need to use has to be 'paid' for. You can sell the test tubes of carbon dioxide that you produce and the winners are the group that makes the most money. You will have a fixed time in which you can make your product.

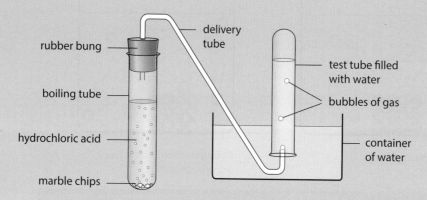

In your group, decide how much equipment you will buy. Use the price list to help you. You can sell your test tubes of carbon dioxide for $5.

Remember that the gas will be tested to check it really is carbon dioxide.

You can use your income to buy more chemicals (and test tubes and bungs) to make more gas.

Your group needs to produce a report that covers how you carried out the task, your profit and how you could improve production of carbon dioxide. Some of the things you could consider including are the list of your purchases and prices and the sales of your product. You could also discuss the practical issues that may result in you not making as much profit as you could have done and how you overcame any of those difficulties. Mention any risk assessment that you made and how you overcame any risks.

A price list is given on the next page.

Continued

Price list

Item	Cost
test tube	50 c
rubber bung	50 c
boiling tube	$1
bung with delivery tube	$1
plastic bowl	$1
5g marble chips	$1
10 cm³ hydrochloric acid	$5
hire of pestle and mortar	$1
heating apparatus	$1
safety glasses	$1

Check your Progress

8.1 The chemical name for marble is calcium carbonate. In the experiment shown below, equal masses of marble lumps, small marble chips and powdered marble were placed into equal volumes of dilute hydrochloric acid.

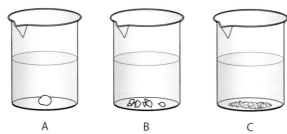

A　　　　　　B　　　　　　C

    a　In which beaker will the reaction be faster?　　　　　　　　　　　　　　　　[1]

    b　Explain why you think this.　　　　　　　　　　　　　　　　　　　　　　[3]

    c　When the reaction between the calcium carbonate and dilute acid occurs, carbon dioxide gas is given off. How would you test for this gas and how would you know that the gas is carbon dioxide?　　[2]

    d　What is the name of the salt formed in this reaction?　　　　　　　　　　[1]

8.2 Arun was investigating the reaction below. He placed 4 g of magnesium ribbon into a beaker of dilute sulfuric acid. He timed how long it took for the magnesium to 'disappear'. It took 45 seconds.

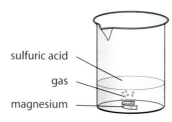

sulfuric acid

gas

magnesium

    a　Write the word equation for the reaction between magnesium and sulfuric acid.　　　　　　　　　　　　　　　　　　　　　　　　　　　[2]

    b　How could he test for the gas given off in this reaction? (Remember to give the result he would get if the test showed that the gas was the one he was testing for.)　　　　　　　　　　　　　　　　　[2]

    c　Which of the following would result in the magnesium ribbon 'disappearing' in less than 45 seconds?

        • warming the acid　　　　　　　　• using 8 g magnesium ribbon

        • stirring the mixture　　　　　　　• adding water to the acid　　　　　[2]

8.3 Zara investigates the rate of reaction between magnesium and dilute hydrochloric acid. She measures how much gas is given off every 30 seconds. The graph shows her results.

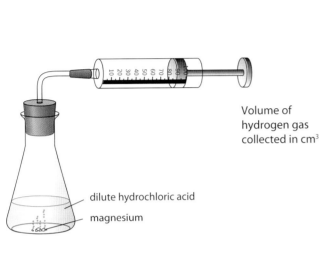

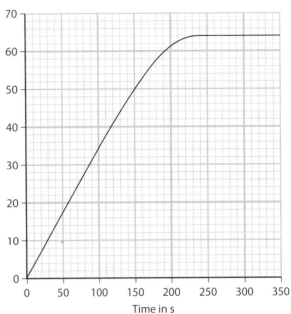

Volume of hydrogen gas collected in cm^3

dilute hydrochloric acid

magnesium

a   How long does it take to collect 30 cm^3 of the gas?   [1]

b   How long does it take for the reaction to finish?   [1]

c   Describe how the rate of reaction changes over the period that the reaction is taking place.   [3]

d   Predict what would happen to the rate of reaction if Zara increased the temperature of the acid.   [1]

e   Explain your answer to part d using particle theory.   [3]

Electricity

> 9.1 Parallel circuits

In this topic you will:

- find out the difference between series and parallel circuits
- find out how current flows in a parallel circuit.

Getting started

Work in pairs to answer these questions.

1   a   Draw a circuit diagram with a cell, a lamp and a buzzer in series (all connected end-to-end).

   b   Name the component used to measure current in circuits.

   c   The current flowing through the lamp is 2 A. What is the current flowing through the buzzer? Assume the lamp and buzzer are both working properly.

   d   What will happen to the lamp if the buzzer breaks?

   e   What will happen to the buzzer if the lamp breaks?

Key words

branches
connected in parallel
connected in series
parallel circuit

Series circuits

The circuits you used at Stage 7 were all series circuits. Series means all the components are connected end-to-end or one after the other. We sometimes say the components are **connected in series**.

In a series circuit, there is only one path for the current to flow. This means the current is the same all the way around a series circuit. In a series circuit, all of the current flowing out of one component flows into the next component.

The circuit in this diagram is a series circuit.

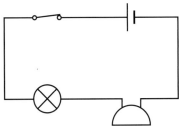

If the switch in this circuit is opened, both the lamp and the buzzer will stop operating. They both stop operating at the same time because the current in the whole circuit stops flowing when the switch is opened.

If we want to operate the lamp and the buzzer separately from the same cell, then we need a parallel circuit.

Parallel circuits

In a **parallel circuit**, there is more than one path for the current to flow.

The paths where the current can flow are called **branches**.

The name parallel comes from the circuit diagram because the branches are drawn using parallel lines. The components in each of the branches are sometimes said to be **connected in parallel**.

Look at the parallel circuit in the diagram to the right. Current from the cell flows to the branch in the circuit. At the branch, the current is divided. If the two lamps are the same, the current will be divided equally between them.

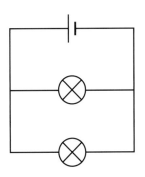

When the current comes to the other side where the branches join again, the current combines (adds together) again.

The parallel circuit in this diagram below has ammeters to show how the current is shared between the branches.

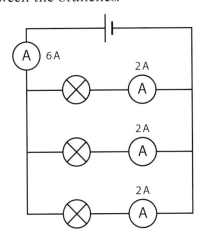

The rule for parallel circuits is:

> the current through the cell is equal to the total of the current in all the branches.

This circuit diagram can be used to summarise the rule for parallel circuits.

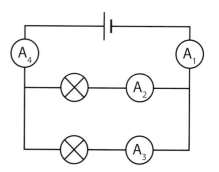

In this first circuit on the right, the readings on ammeters A_1 and A_4 are equal.

The readings on ammeters A_2 and A_3 will add up to the reading on A_1 (and A_4).

This rule still works even when the current in the branches is different.

Look at this second circuit on the right. The circuit has three parallel branches, each with a different current.

The current through the cell is equal to the total of the currents through each of the branches.

So, $1.0\,A + 2.0\,A + 0.5\,A = 3.5\,A$.

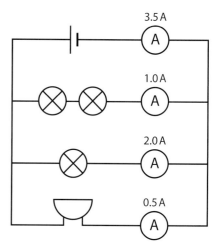

If we know the current through the cell, but do not know the current through one of the branches, we can calculate the missing current. Look at this circuit below. We can calculate the missing current through the buzzer.

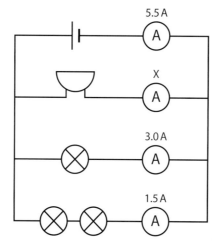

The total current is 5.5 A, so the currents through each of the branches must add up to 5.5 A.

Call the missing current X.

> $X + 3.0 + 1.5 = 5.5$
>
> $X + 4.5 = 5.5$
>
> $X = 5.5 - 4.5$
>
> $X = 1.0$

So, the missing current though the buzzer is 1.0 A.

As with all calculations, do not forget the unit with your answer!

Advantages of parallel circuits

In a parallel circuit, the current through a branch can keep flowing, even if the current stops flowing in the other branches.

This means:

* components in the same circuit can be switched on and off independently

* if a component in one branch stops working, the other branches are not affected.

Look at the parallel circuit in the diagram on the right.

The circuit has two branches. Each branch has a lamp and a switch.

When switch S_1 is closed, then lamp L_1 will light. This will not affect lamp L_2 because L_2 is on a different branch.

When switch S_2 is closed, then lamp L_2 will light. This will not affect lamp L_1 because L_1 is on a different branch.

If both lamps are switched on and lamp L_1 stops working, then lamp L_2 will not be affected.

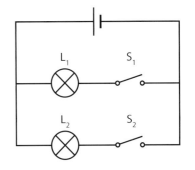

Components in a parallel circuit can be switched on and off separately by having switches on each branch. The components can also be all switched on or off together if the switch is between the cell and the branches.

Look at this second circuit diagram on the right. For any lamp to light in this circuit, switch S_4 must be closed.

Switches S_1, S_2 and S_3 can then be used to control each lamp separately.

If all the lamps are on, then opening S_4 will cause all of the lamps to go off.

If all the lamps are off, but switches S_1, S_2 and S_3 are closed, then closing S_4 will cause all lamps to light together.

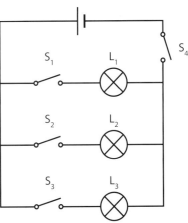

Car headlamps (left) are connected in parallel so they can be switched on and off together. The string of lamps (right) are connected in parallel so, if one lamp fails, the others will still light. The lamps can also be switched on and off together.

Questions

1   Which of these describes the current through the cell in a parallel circuit? Write **one** letter.

   A   The current through the cell is equal to the current in the first branch.

   B   The current through the cell is equal to the current in the last branch.

   C   The current through the cell is the total of the current in each branch.

   D   The current through the cell does not depend on the current in the branches.

2   Which of these are parallel circuits?

   Write the letter or letters that are correct.

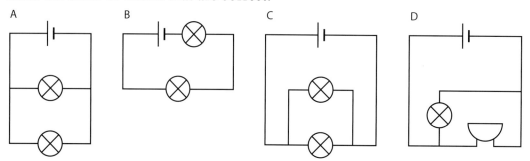

3   A circuit is to be designed with a cell and four identical lamps.

   a   Draw a circuit diagram with

      i   four lamps connected in series with a cell

      ii   four lamps, each connected in parallel with a cell.

   b   Describe **two** advantages of connecting the four lamps in parallel rather than in series.

   c   The four identical lamps are connected in parallel. When all four lamps are working, the current through the cell is 2.0 A. Calculate the current through each lamp.

4   Calculate the missing current, X, in each of these circuits.

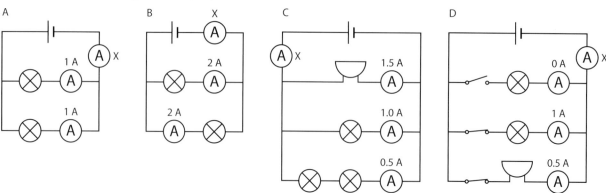

5 Calculate the missing current, X, in each of these circuits.

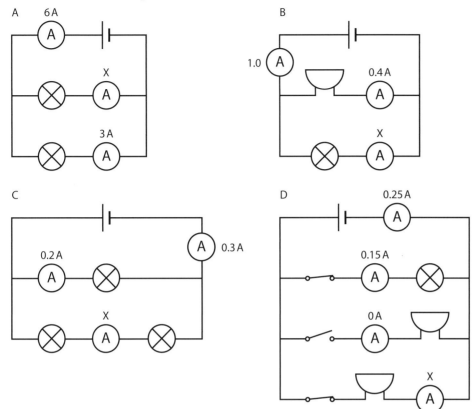

Activity 9.1.1

Measuring current in parallel circuits

In this activity, you will measure the current at various positions in a parallel circuit.

Work in groups of two or three.

You will need:

- three lamps, the correct number of cells to operate one of these lamps, wires, ammeter.

Method

1 Set up a circuit as shown in the first diagram. Do not include the ammeter at this stage.

2 When you are sure that all the lamps are working correctly, you can include the ammeter.

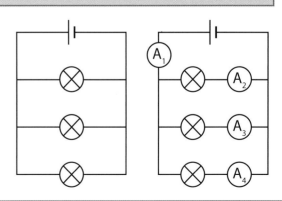

Continued

3   You will put the ammeter into the circuit four times and in a different place each time. These four positions, A_1, A_2, A_3 and A_4, are shown in the second diagram.

4   Measure the current at each position, A_1, A_2, A_3 and A_4.

Questions

1   Record your results in a suitable table.

2   Explain what your results show about current in a parallel circuit.

Think like a scientist

Making predictions about current

In this investigation, you will make predictions about current and then test your predictions.

Work in groups of two or three.

You will need:

- three lamps, one buzzer, other electrical components (optional), the correct number of cells to operate these components, wires, ammeter.

Method

1   Set up a circuit as shown in the first diagram.

2   When you know the circuit is working correctly, put the ammeter in the position shown in the second diagram.

3   Remove the ammeter and put it in the position shown in the third diagram.

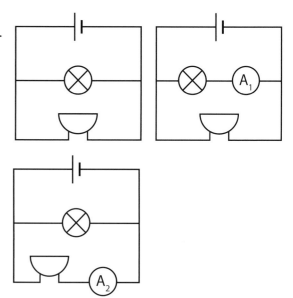

Continued

Questions

1   Record the currents A_1 and A_2 that you measured.

2   Use your values of A_1 and A_2 to predict the current flowing through the cell. Call this current A_3.

3   Check your prediction by putting the ammeter in the position shown in the next diagram.

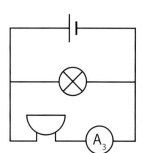

4   Build other parallel circuits and measure the current in each of the branches. Use these currents to predict the current through the cell. Check your prediction each time.

5   Draw circuit diagrams for each circuit you build, and label the ammeters.

6   Build some other parallel circuits.
    This time measure the current through the cell and all but one of the branches.
    Use these currents to predict the current through the other branch.
    Check your prediction each time.

7   Draw circuit diagrams for each circuit you build, and label the ammeters.

Peer assessment

For each of these statements, decide on how confident you are.
Give yourself 5 if you are very confident and 1 if you are not confident at all.

I know:

- how to build parallel circuits from circuit diagrams
- how to measure the current at different positions in a parallel circuit
- how to correctly predict a missing current value in a parallel circuit.

Summary checklist

- ☐ I know how current divides in a parallel circuit
- ☐ I can calculate missing current values in parallel circuits.
- ☐ I can measure the current in a parallel circuit.
- ☐ I can describe the advantages of parallel circuits compared to series circuits for some applications.

> 9.2 Current and voltage in parallel circuits

In this topic you will:

- compare current and voltage in series and parallel circuits
- describe the effects of adding cells and lamps on current and voltage in circuits.

Getting started

Work in pairs to discuss answers to these questions.

1 Name the particles that flow inside wires when current flows.

2 What happens to the speed of these particles as current increases.

3 State the unit of current.

Key words

battery
mains
rating
supply
voltage
voltmeter
volts

What is voltage?

Voltage is linked to the electrical energy in a circuit. Voltage is measured in units called volts. The symbol for **volts** is V.

Voltage is related to the electrical energy supplied to a circuit by the cell, battery or power supply. Voltage is linked to energy, but it is not the same as energy.

Most cells supply 1.5 V. A **battery** is two or more cells connected in series. Batteries commonly supply 6 V, 9 V or 12 V. Each of the cells or batteries in this picture has a different voltage.

The sockets found on the walls of buildings supply a **mains** voltage. Mains in this context means an electrical supply that comes from a power station or generator of some kind. In most countries the mains voltage is between 220 and 240 V. In some countries, the mains voltage is 110 or 120 V. The next picture shows some mains sockets from different countries.

Sometimes, we refer to the source of energy in a circuit as the **supply**. The supply could be a cell, a battery, a power supply or the mains.

This diagram shows circuit symbols for a battery made from two cells, a battery made from many cells, and a 240 V mains supply.

Voltage is also linked to the energy changed by components in a circuit. For example, lamps change electrical energy into light and thermal energy. Most components have a voltage **rating**.

The lamps used in schools for electrical experiments are often rated at 3 V or 6 V. The rating tells us the maximum voltage that can be used.

Measuring voltage

Voltage is measured using a **voltmeter**.

This picture shows a digital voltmeter, an analogue voltmeter and the circuit symbol for a voltmeter.

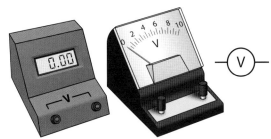

A voltmeter is connected in a different way to an ammeter.

An ammeter measures the current flowing through a component, so the ammeter is connected in series with the component.

The voltmeter measures the energy difference either side of a component, so the voltmeter is connected in **parallel** with the **component**.

Look at the drawing of the circuit and circuit diagram. The ammeter is connected in series with the lamp and the voltmeter is connected in parallel with the lamp.

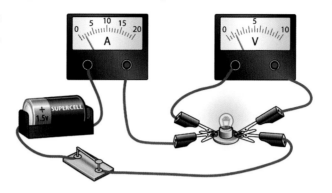

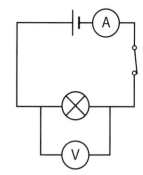

Voltage in a series circuit

Energy is always conserved, so the energy changed by the components in a circuit must be equal to the energy supplied by the cell, battery or power supply.

That means the voltages across each component in a series circuit must add up to the voltage of the supply.

Look at the circuit in this diagram. All three lamps are identical. They change the same quantity of energy, so have the same voltage. The voltage across all the lamps adds up to the voltage from the battery.

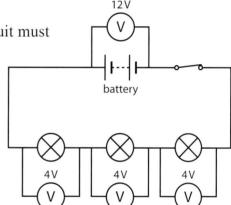

Look at this next circuit, where the components are not the same.

In this circuit, the lamp is changing more energy than the buzzer, so the voltage across the lamp is higher than the buzzer. The voltages across the lamp and buzzer add up to the voltage of the battery.

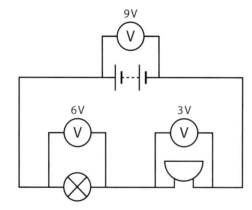

The voltages across all the components in a series circuit add up to the voltage of the supply.

We discovered at Stage 7 that the current is the same all the way around a series circuit. This is because the circuit has no branches and the current can only flow in one path. The voltage in a series circuit can be different across different components.

Adding more components in a series circuit

The voltage from the supply in a series circuit is shared between each of the components. That means adding components such as lamps or buzzers will cause each component to get a smaller share of the voltage.

Compare these two series circuits. Both have the same type of battery and both have identical lamps.

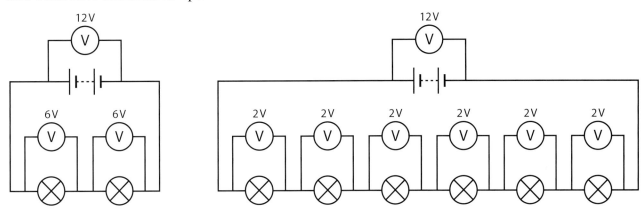

Adding more components in a series circuit will decrease the current. As components are added, it becomes more difficult for the power supply to push the electrons around the circuit.

Compare these two series circuits. The one with more components has a smaller current.

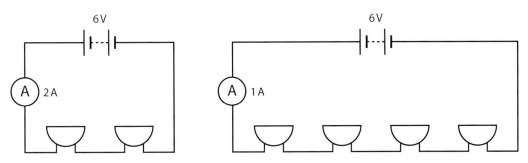

Adding more cells in a series circuit increases the voltage of the supply.

One 1.5 V cell gives a supply voltage of 1.5 V.

Two 1.5 V cells gives a supply voltage of $2 \times 1.5 \text{ V} = 3 \text{ V}$.

A 12 V battery contains eight cells each of 1.5 V making $8 \times 1.5 \text{ V} = 12 \text{ V}$.

Increasing the number of cells in the same series circuit will:

- increase the current in the circuit
- increase the voltage across each component.

Voltage in a parallel circuit

Look carefully at the drawing of a parallel circuit.

Lamp 1 is connected directly across the terminals of the 1.5 V cell. The voltage across lamp 1 is 1.5 V.

If you follow the wires from lamp 2, you can get to the terminals of the cell *without* going through lamp 1. That means we can think of lamp 2 also being connected directly across the terminals of the cell. That means the voltage across lamp 2 is also 1.5 V.

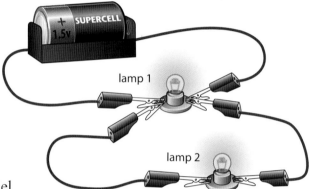

The voltages across each of the branches of a parallel circuit are equal to the voltage of the supply.

Look at these circuit diagrams.

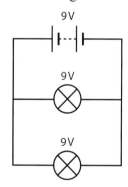 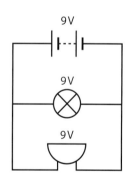

The voltage of the battery in both circuits is 9 V.

In the left circuit, the voltage across each lamp is also 9 V.

Look at the right circuit and you will see that the voltage across the branches of a parallel circuit is the same whether or not the components are the same. The lamp and the buzzer are different, but the voltage across the branches is still the same (9 V).

Topic 9.1 explained that the current can be different in the branches of a parallel circuit. This is because the current can flow in different paths. The voltage in all branches of a parallel circuit is the same.

Adding more components in a parallel circuit

Adding more branches to a parallel circuit gives more paths for the current to flow through. The more paths there are for current to flow through, the easier it becomes. That means the current though the cell increases.

Compare these two parallel circuits. Each has the same type of battery and the lamps are identical.

Adding more components to any one branch of a parallel circuit will decrease the current in that branch. Remember that the voltage across any branch will be the same, so adding more components in the branch makes it harder for current to flow in that branch.

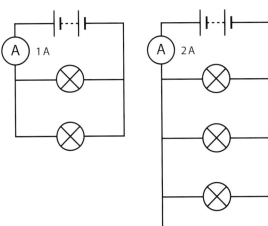

Adding cells to a parallel circuit increases the supply voltage so it also:

- increases the voltage across each branch
- increases the current through the cell
- increases the current through each branch.

Questions

1 Copy and complete the sentences using words from the list.

> **series   parallel   current   voltage**

An ammeter is used to measure the .... through a component.

An ammeter should be connected in .... with the component.

A voltmeter is used to measure the .... across a component.

A voltmeter should be connected in .... with the component.

2 Sofia wants to measure the current through a lamp and the voltage across the lamp.

Which of these shows the correct way to do this? Write **one** letter.

A
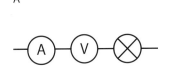

B
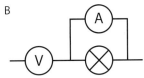

C
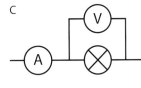

D
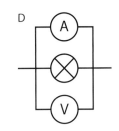

3 A school classroom has six identical lamps. Each of the lamps is connected in parallel across a 220 V mains supply, as shown in the diagram.

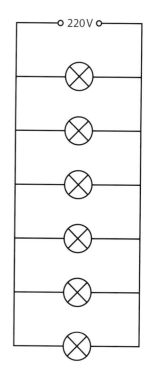

    a State the voltage across one of the lamps in the diagram.

    b The classroom has one light switch. The light switch is used to switch all of the lamps on or off together. Copy the diagram and include the switch in the correct position.

    c The current from the mains supply to all six lamps is 2.4 A.

        i Calculate the current through one of the lamps.

        ii Two more lamps, identical to the other six, are added, each in a new separate branch of the parallel circuit.

        State what will happen to the total current from the mains supply when the new lamps are added.

4 Marcus has a box containing ten identical lamps rated at 2.0 V. He also has a 12 V battery.

    a Explain why Marcus cannot connect these lamps, each individually in parallel across the battery.

    b Marcus connects the lamps in series with the 12 V battery.

        i Calculate the number of these lamps that can be connected in series to operate properly.

        ii Draw the circuit diagram for these lamps connected in series with the battery.

        iii Add a voltmeter to your circuit diagram to show how the voltage across **one** lamp could be measured.

5 Zara has a series circuit with a 9 V battery, a lamp and a buzzer as shown in the diagram.

The voltage across the lamp L_1 is 2 V.

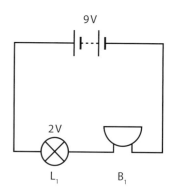

    a Calculate the voltage across the buzzer, B_1.

    b Zara adds another lamp, L_2, in series with the other components.

        i State what happens to the voltage across L_1 when the new lamp is added.

        ii State what happens to the current in the circuit when the new lamp is added.

6 Arun has a series circuit with a 6 V battery, two identical buzzers and two identical lamps.

The voltage across one buzzer is 1 V.

a Calculate the voltage across one lamp.

b Arun adds another 6 V battery in series with the first battery. All the components continue to work properly.

    i State the voltage across one of the buzzers when the second battery is added.

    ii State the effect on the current in the circuit of adding the second battery.

Activity 9.2.1

Measuring voltage in a series circuit

In this activity, you will measure the voltage across different components in a series circuit.

> **You will need:**
>
> - power supply, battery or cells, voltmeter, two or three lamps, another component – such as a buzzer, switch, wires, connectors.

Safety

Do not exceed the voltage rating for any component. Your teacher will show you how many of each component to connect. Switch off before adding or removing any components.

Always ask your teacher before connecting any new component into your circuit.

Method

1 Set up a series circuit as shown in the diagram.

2 Connect the voltmeter across the battery. Measure and record this voltage. Do not worry if the voltmeter reading is not the same as the value printed on the battery or the setting of the power supply. Use your voltage measurement.

3 Connect the voltmeter separately across each of the components. Measure and record these voltages.

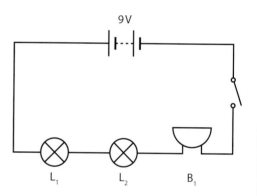

Questions

1 Draw the circuit diagram that you used. Label each of the components, for example, L_1 and L_2 for two lamps.

2 Draw the circuit diagram again and include the voltmeter in position across one of the components to show how voltage is measured.

3 Draw a suitable table for your voltage measurements and write the results into the table.

4 Explain what your results show about voltages in series circuits.

5 If you have time and access to other components, you could make other series circuits. Can you confirm that a similar trend in results can be observed in these?

Think like a scientist

Measuring current in a parallel circuit

In this investigation, you will investigate how the current through a battery depends on the number of identical branches in a parallel circuit.

You will need:
- four or six identical lamps, battery or suitable power supply to light up to six lamps in parallel, switch, ammeter, leads, connectors.

Method

1 Set up the circuit as shown in the first diagram.

2 Measure and record the current with one lamp.

3 Add another lamp in parallel with the first lamp as shown in the second diagram.

4 Measure and record the current with two lamps.

5 Continue adding lamps in parallel, one at a time. Do not change the position of the ammeter. Measure and record the current through the battery each time.

6 Repeat each measurement two further times. Decide whether any more repeats are needed.

7 Calculate the average result for each set of measurements.

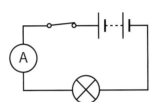
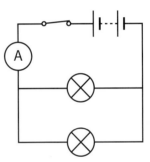

Questions

1 Record your results in a table.

2 Plot a line graph of your results. Put the number of lamps on the x-axis and the current on the y-axis. Draw the most appropriate line.

3 a Describe the trend in the results.

   b What happens to the current when the number of lamps in parallel doubles?

   c Explain this trend. Use ideas about how current flows around a circuit.

4 Use your results to predict the current through the battery if you had eight lamps in parallel.

Summary checklist

☐ I can measure current and voltage in series and parallel circuits.

☐ I know how adding more cells or more lamps affects current and voltage in series circuits.

☐ I know how adding more cells or more lamps affects current and voltage in parallel circuits.

> 9.3 Resistance

In this topic you will:

- discover how resistance affects current in a circuit
- calculate resistance from voltage and current.

Getting started

1. Describe how current flows in a conductor.
2. Describe the difference between a conductor and an insulator in terms of current flow.
3. What does the word resistance mean in everyday language?

Key words

filament
ohms
Ohm's law
resistor
resistance

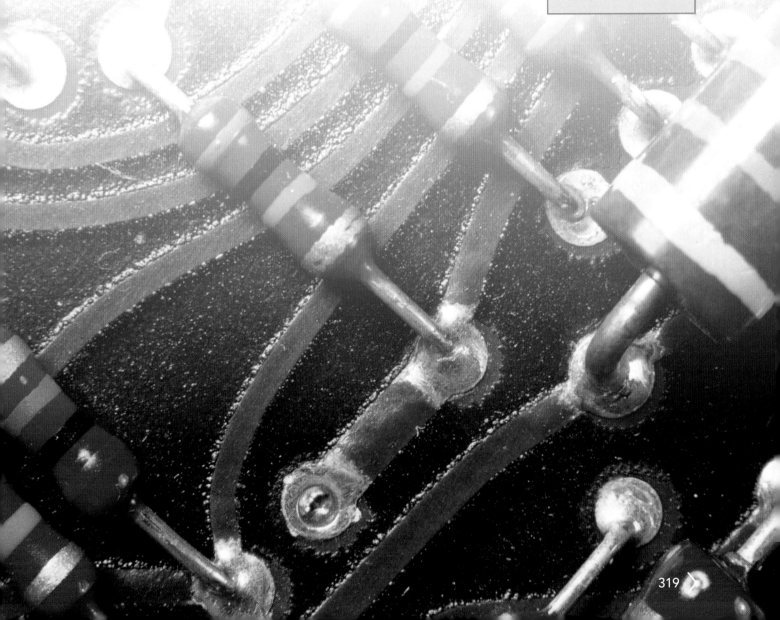

Resistance

Resistance is a measure of how easy or difficult it is for electrons to move though a material.

Conductors, such as copper, have very low resistance.

Insulators, such as most plastics, have very high resistance.

Resistance is measured in units called **ohms**. Ohms have the symbol Ω which is the Greek letter omega.

A 100 m length of copper wire, for example, can have a resistance of 0.5–1.0 Ω.

A 1 cm length of some plastics have a resistance of over a 1 000 000 000 000 Ω.

Resistance slows the flow of electrons, so lowers current.

Copper wire is designed to have very low resistance so the wires in a circuit affect the current as little as possible.

The resistance of insulators – such as the plastic around this copper wire – is so high that they do not allow current to flow at all under most circumstances.

Some conductors are designed to have a high resistance. Inside some lamps, there is a small wire called a **filament**. The filament has a high resistance. When current flows through the filament, thermal energy is transferred. There is so much thermal energy that the filament glows and emits light.

As resistance makes it difficult for current to flow:

the greater the resistance in a circuit, the smaller the current in the circuit.

Ohm's law

Georg Simon Ohm was a scientist who studied resistance. Ohm discovered there was a link between voltage, current and resistance in wires. The link between voltage, current and resistance applies to many electrical components and not only to wires.

Ohm's law states that:

voltage = current × resistance

These are often given letter symbols:

V = voltage, in volts

I = current, in amps

R = resistance, in ohms.

The letter I is used for current because in the French language, current was originally called *intensité du courant*.

So, we can write Ohm's law as:

$V = I \times R$ or just $V = IR$

We can put Ohm's law into a formula triangle like this:

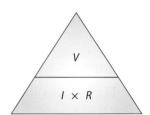

Worked example

Question

A current of 2 A flows through a buzzer. The voltage across the buzzer is 10 V.

Calculate the resistance of the buzzer.

Answer

Using Ohm's law, the equation can be rearranged to

$$R = \frac{V}{I}$$

$V = 10$ and $I = 2$, so

$$R = \frac{10}{2}$$

$$= 5\,\Omega$$

Resistors

A **resistor** is a type of electrical component designed to have a known resistance.

The picture shows some resistors.

Many resistors, such as those in the picture, have coloured bands. The colours form a code to show the resistance value in ohms.

This is the circuit symbol for a resistor:

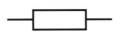

The value of the resistor is usually written with the circuit symbol. When the value of the resistor is not important, or when you have to calculate the value, the letter R is usually written beside the symbol.

Questions

1 Copy and complete the sentences using words from the list.

Each word can be used once, more than once or not at all.

low   high   easy   difficult

Copper wires have a very .... resistance.

That makes it very .... for current to flow in copper wires.

A resistor of 10 000 Ω has a .... resistance.

2 **a** Write the unit of resistance.

b Write the equation for Ohm's law.

c State what the letter I represents in the equation for Ohm's law.

3 Calculate the values of these resistors. Show your working and give the unit with each answer.

a Resistor R_1: The voltage across R_1 is 6 V and the current through R_1 is 3 A.

b Resistor R_2: The voltage across R_2 is 9 V and the current through R_2 is 2 A.

c Resistor R_3: The voltage across R_3 is 1.5 V and the current through R_3 is 0.5 A.

4 The diagrams in this question show parts of circuits.

a This circuit contains a 6 Ω resistor.
The current through the resistor is 2 A.

Calculate the voltage across this resistor.
Show your working and give the unit with your answer.

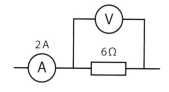

b This circuit contains a 100 Ω resistor.
The voltage across the resistor is 12 V.

Calculate the current through this resistor.
Show your working and give the unit with your answer.

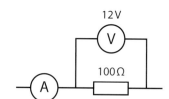

Activity 9.3.1

Working out resistance

In this activity, you will work out the resistance of different components.

Work in groups of two or three.

> You will need:
> - cell or battery, range of different components (such as a lamp, a buzzer and a resistor), ammeter, voltmeter, switch, wires, connectors.

Safety

Ask your teacher to check your circuits. Switch off before changing components.

Method

1 Connect each component in turn to the cell or battery.

2 Measure the current through the component and the voltage across the component.

Questions

1 Draw a circuit diagram to show how this is done for one of your components.

2 Record your voltage and current results for each component in a table.

3 a Use the results to calculate the resistance of each component. Show your working.

   b Add another column to the table for the resistance values. Remember to include the unit in the column header.

4 State which of your components had

   a the highest resistance

   b the lowest resistance.

Think like a scientist

Current and voltage in a resistor

In this investigation, you will investigate how the current through a resistor depends on the voltage across the resistor.

You will need:

- minimum of four 1.5 V cells, resistor of about 10 Ω, ammeter, voltmeter, switch, wires, connectors.

Method

1   Set up the circuit with one cell as shown in the diagram.

2   Measure and record the current and voltage with one cell.

3   Add another cell in series with the first.

4   Measure and record the current and voltage with two cells.

5   Repeat with three, then four cells.

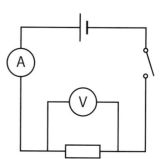

Questions

1   Record your results in a table.

2   Plot a line graph of your results. Put voltage on the x-axis and current on the y-axis. Draw the most appropriate line.

3   a   Describe the trend in the results.

    b   Explain why the current changes in the way that you observe.

4   Sketch how the graph would be different if the experiment were repeated with

    a   a resistor with a higher resistance

    b   a resistor with a lower resistance.

If you have time, you could repeat this experiment with another resistor to test your prediction.

Summary checklist

☐   I know how resistance affects current in a circuit.

☐   I know the equation linking voltage, current and resistance (Ohm's law).

☐   I can use Ohm's law to calculate resistance from voltage and current.

> 9.4 Practical circuits

In this topic you will:

- draw circuit diagrams that include symbols for cells, switches, resistors, variable resistors, ammeters, voltmeters, lamps and buzzers
- make circuits that include some or all of these components.

Getting started

Work in pairs.

1   Draw the circuit symbol for each of these: cell, switch, resistor, ammeter, voltmeter, lamp and buzzer.

2   Beside each circuit symbol, write the function of each component.

3   Describe, in words or with a diagram, how to connect

   a   a voltmeter to measure the voltage across a lamp

   b   an ammeter to measure the current through a resistor.

Key words

dimmer
fixed resistor
variable resistor
volume

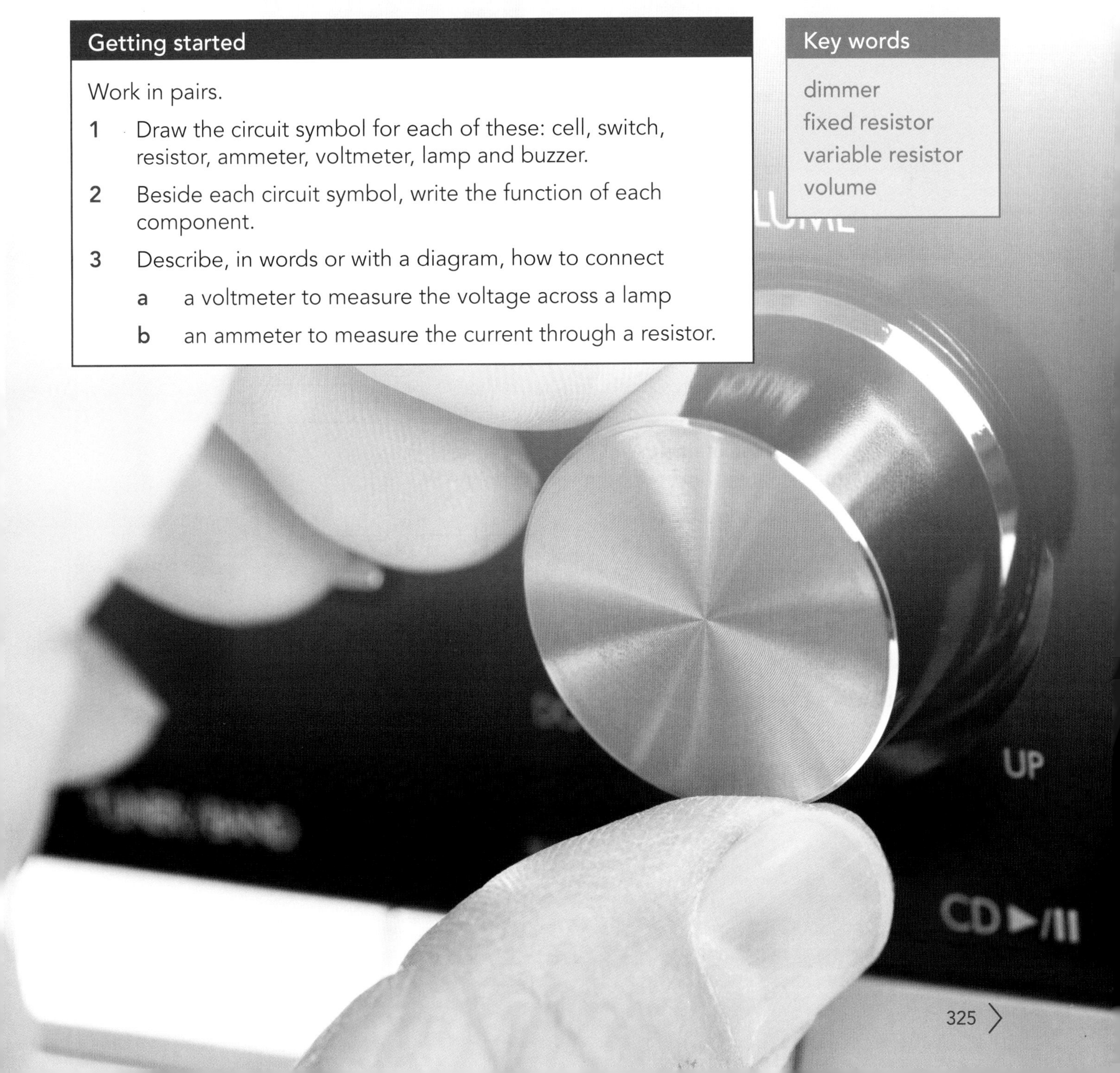

Variable resistors

In many circuits, it is useful to be able to change the resistance. For example, in a **dimmer** switch for a lamp, or in the **volume** control of a music player. In this case, the word volume means loudness of sound.

The component that is used to change resistance is called a **variable resistor**.

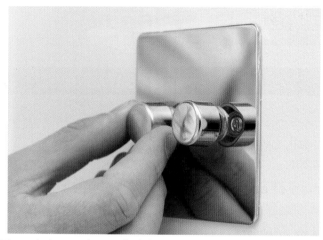

These light switches (called dimmer switches) contain variable resistors that can be turned to control the brightness of lamps in a room.

Sliding controls at the bottom of this sound recording equipment are variable resistors for adjusting volume.

The circuit symbol for a variable resistor is similar to that for a **fixed resistor**, but with an arrow through the symbol.

The term fixed resistor is sometimes used for the type of resistors you learnt about in Topic 9.3, to avoid confusion with variable resistors.

This diagram shows how a variable resistor is used to control the brightness of a lamp.

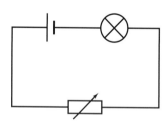

As the resistance of the variable resistor is increased, the current in the circuit decreases. A smaller current flowing through the lamp makes the lamp dimmer.

As the resistance of the variable resistor is decreased, the current in the circuit increases. A larger current flowing through the lamp makes the lamp brighter.

Everyday circuits

Electric circuits are used in many homes, schools, cars, bicycles, phones, music systems, watches, computers and lots more things that we use every day.

Scientists are always designing new circuits, many of which make life easier for us. Here we will look at some examples.

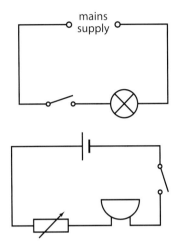

When opening the door of a refrigerator (fridge), a light comes on inside. The circuit for this is shown in the diagram.

The switch is opened and closed by the movement of the fridge door. When the door is open, the switch is closed and when the door is closed, the switch is open.

Some equipment is fitted with buzzer to make a warning sound if something is done incorrectly. Often, the loudness of the sound can be adjusted. This circuit shows how this is done.

Some cars have a buzzer that makes a sound when the driver opens the door while the headlamps are switched on. The door of the car controls the switch for the buzzer, but the buzzer should only operate when the headlamps are on.

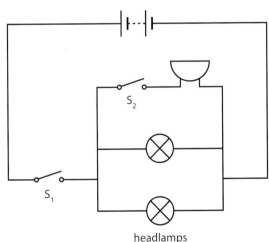

headlamps

The headlamps are connected in parallel, so they can be switched on and off together. The buzzer is part of the same branch of the parallel circuit, as shown in the diagram.

Switch S_1 controls the headlamps. Switch S_2 is controlled by the door. When the door is open, the switch is closed and when the door is closed, the switch is open. Current cannot flow to switch S_2 unless switch S_1 for the headlamps is closed. That means a buzzer will sound when you open the door while the headlamps are on.

Equipment that uses 12 V batteries include cars, trucks and some boats. These batteries need to be recharged from time to time. Sometimes, a battery voltage indicator is fitted so the voltage of the battery can be measured.

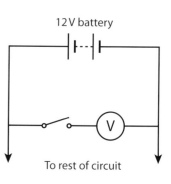

12 V battery

To rest of circuit

The circuit diagram shows how a switch can be used to display the battery voltage. A voltmeter is connected in parallel across the battery, and a switch is included in this branch of the parallel circuit.

Sometimes a lamp with a low voltage rating is required in a circuit with a battery of higher voltage. For example, a 6 V lamp can be operated using a 12 V battery. Resistors are used to produce different voltages. If two resistors of equal resistance are connected in series with a battery, then the battery voltage will be shared equally across each resistor. A 6 V lamp can then be safely connected in parallel with one of the resistors, as shown. The lamp will receive a 6 V supply and work properly.

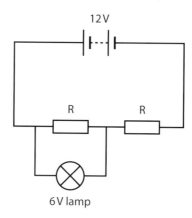

12 V

R   R

6 V lamp

Questions

1   Draw the circuit symbol for

    a   a fixed resistor

    b   a variable resistor.

2   Look at the circuit diagram.

    What can this circuit be used for? Write **one** letter.

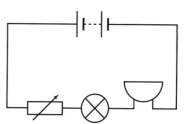

    A   Changing the loudness of the buzzer, keeping the brightness of the lamp constant.

    B   Changing the brightness of the lamp, keeping the sound from the buzzer constant.

    C   Changing the loudness of the buzzer and brightness of the lamp at the same time.

    D   Changing the loudness of the buzzer and brightness of the lamp separately.

3   A circuit will use one cell and two lamps.

    One switch must turn both lamps on and off at the same time.
    The brightness of each lamp must be controlled separately.
    Draw a circuit diagram for this circuit.

4   A circuit has two cells, a lamp and a buzzer in series.

   a   Draw a circuit diagram to show how the current through the buzzer and the voltage across the buzzer could be measured at the same time.

   b   Draw **one** circuit diagram to show how:
   •   the lamp and the buzzer can be switched on and off separately
   •   the brightness of the lamp can be changed without affecting the sound from the buzzer.

Think like a scientist

Designing and building circuits

In this activity, you will draw circuit diagrams and then build the circuits.

Work in pairs.

You will need:
•   cells, lamps, buzzers, variable resistor, voltmeter, ammeter, selection of fixed resistors, wires, connectors.

Method

1   Write a risk assessment for building electric circuits.
2   Draw circuit diagrams for the following circuits.

Circuit 1	Circuit 2
• two lamps can be switched on and off separately • the current through one of the lamps can be measured	• two lamps can be switched on and off together using one switch • the brightness of one of the lamps can be varied
Circuit 3	**Circuit 4**
• a fixed resistor and a variable resistor in series • the voltage across the variable resistor can be measured	• one lamp can be switched on and off • a buzzer can only be switched on at the same time the lamp is on • the brightness of the lamp can be varied without affecting the sound from the buzzer

3   Ask your teacher to check your risk assessment and circuit diagrams, and then build each of the circuits.

Continued

Questions

1   Did all your circuits work as you expected? Describe any observations that you did not expect.

2   Describe any improvements you could make to your circuits. You can suggest the use of different equipment. You should describe this equipment, rather than suggesting 'better' equipment.

Summary checklist

☐ I can draw the circuit symbol for a variable resistor.

☐ I know how variable resistors are used in circuits.

☐ I can compare circuit diagrams that contain cells, switches, fixed resistors, variable resistors, ammeters, voltmeters, lamps and buzzers.

☐ I can build circuits that contain cells, switches, fixed resistors, variable resistors, ammeters, voltmeters, lamps and buzzers.

Project: Circuits for schools and houses

Background

In schools and houses that have electricity, many things work from the same electricity supply. This supply is usually a mains supply from a power station or a generator.

Your task

You will make a model of a school or a house.

You will use cells, a battery or a power supply as an analogy for the mains supply.

Next, you will design a circuit to operate lamps and other electrical equipment in the building.

Remember that lamps in each room must be switched on and off separately.

Include other equipment. For example, a school may have a buzzer that sounds at the start and end of lessons. A house or school may have an alarm that makes a sound when an outside door is opened. There will also be an electricity meter that shows how much electrical current is flowing at any time. There may also be an emergency switch that turns off the electricity to all the equipment at once.

Include anything else that you have the equipment to make.

Work in pairs.

Your pair will need:

- cardboard boxes to make the rooms
- scissors to cut the boxes
- glue or adhesive tape to join the boxes
- cells, battery or power supply
- switches
- lamps
- buzzers
- ammeter
- other components
- wires and connectors.

By the end of the project you should be able to:

- demonstrate how all the equipment in the school or house works
- show one fully labelled circuit diagram for all the equipment.

Check your progress

9.1 These circuits show identical lamps connected in parallel.
The readings on some of the ammeters are given.

a

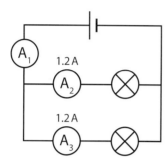

Calculate the reading on ammeter A_1 [1]

b

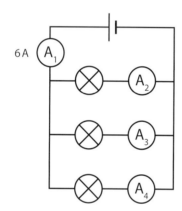

    i   Calculate the reading on ammeter A_4. [1]

    ii   Write an equation linking the readings on all four ammeters in this circuit. [1]

9.2 A circuit has a lamp and a resistor in series.

Describe how to connect:

    a   an ammeter to measure the current through both components [1]

    b   a voltmeter to measure the voltage across the resistor. [1]

9.3 A circuit has two identical lamps in series.
Describe the effect of adding another identical lamp in series:

    a   on the brightness of the lamps [1]

    b   on the current in the circuit [1]

    c   on the voltage across one of the lamps. [1]

9.4 A circuit has a resistor in series with an ammeter and a cell.

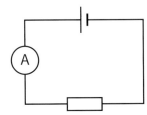

State the effect on the current through the cell when making these changes separately:

a   adding another cell in series with the first cell   [1]

b   adding another resistor in parallel with the first resistor.   [1]

9.5 a   Write an equation to calculate resistance from voltage and current.   [1]

b   State the unit of resistance.   [1]

9.6 This circuit contains a resistor, an ammeter and a voltmeter.

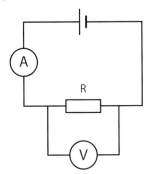

In each of these questions, show your working and give the unit with your answer.

Calculate:

a   the value of R when the voltage is 12 V and the current is 2 A   [3]

b   the reading on the voltmeter when the current is 0.5 A and R is 18 Ω   [3]

c   the reading on the ammeter when the voltage is 6 V and R is 4 Ω   [3]

9.7 Look at the circuit diagram.

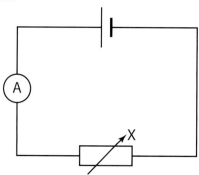

a   Name the component labelled **X**.   [1]

b   Explain what happens to the reading on the ammeter when the value of X
    is increased.   [2]

9.8 Look at the four circuit diagrams, A–D.

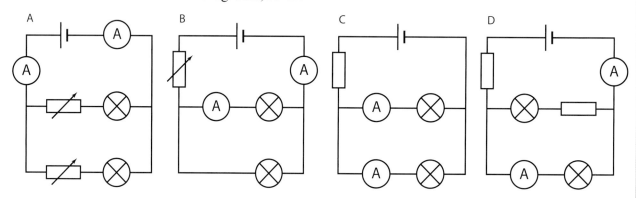

a   Which **two** circuits have two ammeters that show the same current?   [2]

b   Which circuit can control the brightness of two lamps by adjusting one
    component?   [1]

c   Which circuit can control the brightness of two lamps separately?   [1]

9.9 Draw a single circuit diagram for a circuit where:

  • two lamps and a buzzer can each be switched on and off separately

  • the current through one lamp can be measured

  • the brightness of the other lamp can be changed.   [4]

> Science Skills

Working with equations

In science, we often use equations to show how two or more quantities are related. You need to be able to use equations. Sometimes you will have to rearrange an equation before you can calculate the quantity you are interested in.

Here is an equation from Topic 3.1:

$$\text{density} = \frac{\text{mass}}{\text{volume}}$$

This equation tells us how we can calculate the density of a substance. We need to know two quantities:

- the mass of a sample of the substance
- the volume of the sample.

Then we calculate the density of the substance by dividing mass by volume.

Remembering an equation

You may be able to memorise an equation simply by repeating it to yourself. It may be easier if you change the names of the quantities into letters or other symbols, like this:

$$\text{density} = \frac{\text{mass}}{\text{volume}}$$

$$D = \frac{m}{V}$$

Another way is to think about the meaning of the quantity. Density tells us how to compare two materials – which is heavier, when their volumes are the same? So we compare the masses of $1\,cm^3$ or $1\,m^3$.

An alternative is to think about units. The unit of density is g/cm^3, or kg/m^3. This should remind you to divide the mass (in g or kg) by the volume (in cm^3 or m^3).

Rearranging an equation

The equation above, for density, has density as its subject (the quantity on its own, on the left). But sometimes, we might want to calculate one of the other quantities. For example:

The density of mercury = $13.5\,g/cm^3$. What is the mass of $4\,cm^3$ of mercury?

We need to rearrange the equation to make mass m its subject. To do this, multiply both sides by volume V:

$$D \times V = m$$

So

$$m = D \times V$$
$$= 13.5 \times 4$$
$$= 54\,g$$

It can help if you think about units. We want to know the mass (in g). We can find this if we multiply the density (in g/cm³) by the volume (in cm³).

$$m = 13.5\,\text{g/cm}^3 \times 4\,\text{cm}^3$$

$$= 54.0\,\text{g}$$

(The cm³ units cancel out.)

Notice how calculations should be set out, with only one equals sign on each line. If you do this, you should make fewer mistakes!

Another method is to use a 'formula triangle'. The three quantities in the equation are put into a triangle, as shown. Mass m is at the top.

To find the equation which has volume V as its subject, cover the V in the triangle.

You will see that this leaves $\frac{m}{D}$

$$\text{volume} = \frac{\text{mass}}{\text{density}}$$

$$V = \frac{m}{D}$$

It is better to rearrange the equation before you put the numbers in.

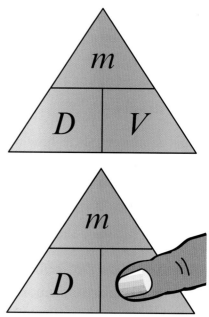

Question

1 The diagram below shows the formula triangle for pressure.

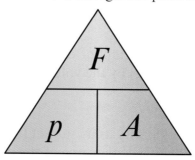

    a Use the pressure formula triangle to find the equation with area A as its subject.

    b Calculate the force on an area of $3\,\text{m}^2$ when a pressure of $50\,\text{N/m}^2$ acts on it.

2 Here is the equation for the moment of a force:

    moment = force × distance from pivot

    a Rearrange the equation to make force the subject.

    b Calculate the force which must be applied at a distance of $10\,\text{m}$ from a pivot to give a moment of $500\,\text{N\,m}$.

Why is planning so important?

Careful planning of an investigation is important to make sure the investigation does what it is supposed to.

One example where planning was not done properly was a space mission in 1998. The Mars Climate Orbiter was a 640 kg space probe with no people on board, and it looked similar to the one in the picture. The mission was intended to investigate the climate on Mars.

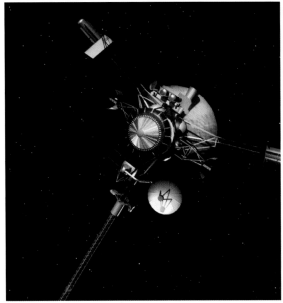

The probe was launched from Earth in 1998 and arrived at the planet Mars in 1999. It was planned to orbit Mars and collect results about the climate. Results would be transmitted back to scientists on Earth.

Soon after going into orbit around Mars, the probe crashed and was destroyed before any results had been collected.

What happened?

An enquiry discovered that the two teams of scientists who designed the probe had not carried out their planning together. One group used standard international scientific (SI) units, such as newtons and metres. The other group had used American units, such as pounds and feet. The calculations from the computer that controlled the probe gave quantities in SI units, but the engine took these as being in American units! That meant the force produced by the engine was less than a quarter of what it was supposed to be.

In 1999, the cost of this mission was almost 330 million US dollars – a very expensive mistake!

An investigation that 'failed' – but won a Nobel Prize

In the year 1887, people already knew that the Earth travels at almost 110 000 km/h around the Sun. They also knew that light travels very fast.

In 1887, an American scientist called Michelson made a prediction: light would seem to travel faster in the opposite direction to Earth's movement, and slower in the same direction. This is similar to throwing an object out of a moving car. If you throw the object backwards, it will seem to go away from you faster than if you throw it forward. Note that this is an analogy and you should never throw anything out of a moving car!

Michelson worked with a colleague called Morley and designed an investigation to test his prediction, using a light ray and some mirrors to reflect the ray.

The picture shows Michelson checking some of the equipment.

The investigation was repeated many times but each time, the results failed to support the prediction. The results showed that the speed of light was the same in all directions.

However, rather than being a true failure, these results were the first to show that the speed of light is constant in air. This 'failed' investigation won Michelson a Nobel Prize in physics.

This example shows that significant discoveries can be made even when the results are unexpected. It is how we make the conclusions from the results that is important.

> Glossary and index

concentration	A measure of how many particles of a substance are in a fixed volume of a solution.	292
conduction	Method of thermal energy transfer where more vigorously vibrating particles cause neighbouring particles to vibrate by colliding; conduction works best where particles are close together in solids and liquids.	120
connected in parallel	Components that are attached across each other, so that the terminals of one component are connected to the terminals of the other.	301
connected in series	Components that are joined so that all the current flowing out of one component flows into the next.	301
conserved	In this context, conserved means the total quantity of something is kept the same.	107
continental coasts	The outlines of the continents that form the boundary between land and sea or ocean.	235
convection	Method of thermal energy transfer where more vigorously vibrating particles cause expansion and decrease in density in a liquid or gas; the less dense material then rises because it floats, setting up a convection current.	122
convection current	Method by which all of a liquid or gas becomes heated through convection; particles flow through the material due to differences in density.	122
covalent bond	A link formed when atoms share electrons to form a molecule.	68
created	To be made from nothing or from something different.	107
crucible	A piece of laboratory equipment; a container that is heated directly at high temperatures.	199
crystallisation	The process of turning into crystals.	184
crystallise	To form crystals.	189
density	Property of an object or material, calculated as $\text{density} = \dfrac{\text{mass}}{\text{volume}}$ and usually has the units g/cm^3 or kg/m^3.	85
destroyed	Cease to exist	108
dimmer	In circuits, a control used to adjust the brightness of a lamp, usually a variable resistor.	326
dilute	Adding water to a solution dilutes it; there are fewer particles of the solute in a fixed volume of the solution.	294
displacement reaction	A reaction in which a more reactive metal 'pushes out' a less reactive one from a compound.	172
DNA	A chemical made up of long molecules with a shape like a twisted ladder.	246

radiation	Method of thermal energy transfer that uses waves and does not depend on particles; occurs through a vacuum, through gases and through transparent solids.	123
random	Not predictable or not following any pattern.	131
rate of reaction	How quickly or slowly a reaction happens.	272
rating	The maximum current or voltage that can be safely used without damaging a component.	309
reactivity	How quickly or slowly a chemical reacts.	169
reactivity series	A list of metals in order of how reactive they are; the most reactive are at the top of the list and the least reactive at the bottom.	169
regular	Of a three-dimensional shape, such as a cube or cuboid, having a volume that can be calculated using a simple equation.	86
reinforce	In this context, where interference results in an increase in amplitude.	218
renal	To do with kidneys.	156
resistance	In an electrical circuit, anything that tends to slow the flow of current.	320
resistant	Of bacteria, able to survive in the presence of an antibiotic.	263
resistor	An electrical component designed to have a known resisistance.	321
root hairs	Specialised cells on the outer surface of a root, which absorb water and mineral ions from the soil.	143
salt	A compound formed when a metal reacts with an acid, for example, magnesium chloride.	180
sex chromosomes	Chromosomes that determine the sex of an organism; in humans, a female has two X chromosomes, while a male has one X chromosome and one Y chromosome.	250
sex inheritance	The way in which X and Y chromosomes are inherited.	251
slush	Partly-melted snow.	35
solid	In this context, an object that has no space filled with air on the inside.	85
southern hemisphere	The part of the Earth that is south of the equator.	230
sperm cell	A male gamete that can swim actively.	248
stable	Firmly fixed.	61
stellar nurseries	Places within some nebulae where stars are formed.	230
stomata	Small holes in the epidermis of a leaf, which allow gases to diffuse into and out of the leaf (the singular is stoma).	18
sulfate	A salt that is made from sulfuric acid.	180

Acknowledgements

The authors and publishers acknowledge the following sources of copyright material and are grateful for the permissions granted. While every effort has been made, it has not always been possible to identify the sources of all the material used, or to trace all copyright holders. If any omissions are brought to our notice, we will be happy to include the appropriate acknowledgements on reprinting.

Thanks to the following for permission to reproduce images:

Cover Stephan Geist/EyeEm/GI; Inside **Unit 1** Tim Graham/GI; Nigel Cattlin/SPL; Ashley Cooper/GI; Ger Bosma/GI; Eduard Muzhevskyi/Science Photo Library/GI; Gokhanilgaz/GI; Feifei Cui-Paoluzzo/GI; Ed Reschke/GI; NoDerog/GI; Pixelfusion3d/GI; Nigel Cattlin/SPL; Nigel Cattlin/Alamy Stock Photo; Henry Arden/GI; Iain Sarjeant/GI; Oscar Porras González/GI; Halim Qomarudin/GI; Doug Armand/GI; Mrs/GI; Cavan Images/GI; Ithinksky/GI; Martina Cattadori/GI; Webguzs/GI; A.Martin UW photography/GI; Samir Hussein/GI; Chris Butler/SPL; Elen11/GI; Mike Agliolo/GI; Michael Godek/GI; Andrzej Wojcicki/GI; Guillem Sartorio/Bloomberg/GI; Rehman Asad/GI; Stefan Mokrzecki/GI; Mantaphoto/GI; Kenneth Canning/GI; Leonello Calvetti/GI; KTSDesign/Science Photo Library/GI; **Unit 2** KTSDesign/Science Photo Library/GI; Giphotostock/GI; KTSDesign/Science Photo Library/GI; Robert Brook/Science Photo Library/GI; Alfred Pasieka/GI; Taylor Hill/GI; MariusFM77/GI; Steven Puetzer/GI; Historic Images/Alamy Stock Photo; Kryssia Campos/GI; J A Steadman/GI; Science & Society Picture Library/GI; Steve Horrell/SPL/GI; **Unit 3** Jaap-Willem/GI; Lawrence Manning/GI; Suleyman Orcun Guler/GI; Johner Images/GI; Laranik/GI; Steve Clancy Photography/GI; Walter Zerla/GI; Andrii Afanasiev/GI; Alexey Sizov/GI; Frank Rothe/GI; Puneet Vikram Singh, Nature & Concept photographer/GI; AndyL/GI; Westend61/GI; Muhammad Fathi Khalid/GI; Chris Hellier/GI; Scanrail/GI; Jacobs Stock Photography Ltd/GI; JazzIRT/GI; Ollo/GI; Delta Images/GI; Anke Wittkowski/GI; Seseg Zhigzhitova/GI; Wanwisa Hernandez/GI; Golfbress/GI; Ghady Gebrayel/GI; Neustockimages/GI; AleksandarNakic/GI; RapidEye/GI; Art at its best!/GI; DieterMeyrl/GI; Georgeclerk/GI; Damian Gillie/Construction Photography/Avalon/GI; Marc Volk/GI; Artisteer/GI; Bambu Productions/GI; Megapress/Alamy Stock Photo; Kajonsak Intarapong/Alamy Stock Photo; Visoot Uthairam/GI; Raimund Linke/GI; Image by Chris Winsor/GI; **Unit 4** Power and Syred/SPL; Dr David Furness, Keele University/SPL; SPL; Joost Lagerweij/GI; Nigel Cattlin/Alamy Stock Photo; Marina Tomic/GI; Magicmine/GI; Sebastian Kaulitzki/Science Photo Library/GI; Pedre/GI; Ydl/GI; Chris Tobin/GI; Tony Craddock/SPL; Hiraman/GI; Ariel Skelley/GI; Philpell/GI; **Unit 5** DeAgostini/GI; Astrid & Hanns-Frieder Michler/SPL; Jon Helgason/Alamy Stock Photo; Hailshadow/GI; Sciencephotos/Alamy Stock Photo (x2); 35007/GI; Lowefoto/Alamy Stock Photo; Ute Grabowsky/Photothek/GI (x2); Vladj55/GI; Ido Meirovich/GI; Enrico Spanu/Reda&Co/Universal Images Group/GI; Jeff Overs/BBC news & current affairs/GI; Dean Mouhtaropoulos/GI; Andy Buchanan/GI; Bartosz Hadyniak/GI; Pictures Ltd/Corbis/GI; Geogphotos/Alamy; Charles D.Winters/SPL; Karl Gaff/SPL; Charles D.Winters/SPL; Geoff Jones; Martyn F.Chillmaid/SPL; PM Images/GI; Prisma/UIG/GI; Guido Mieth/GI; **Unit 6** Steven Puetzer/GI; Wladimir Bulgar/GI; Runstudio/GI; Chris Clor/GI; Imagenavi/GI; Knape/GI; Nattapong Wongloungud/GI; Jonathan Knowles/GI; Dave G Kelly/GI; CristiNistor/GI; Parameter/GI; Stocktrek Images/GI (x2); Jasmin Merdan/GI; Sololos/GI; K.Muller/GI; Anton Winter/GI; Stocktrek Images/GI; NASA; NASA/GI; Dominik Eckelt/GI; Emil Von Maltitz/GI; Daderot on Wikimedia CC0; Stocktrek Images/GI; Universal History Archive/Universal Images Group/GI; **Unit 7** Mehau Kulyk/Science Photo Library/GI; Pr.G Gimenez-Martin/SPL; Power and Syred/SPL; Olympia Valla/EyeEm/GI; Dianne Avery photography/GI; Mehau Kulyk/SPL; Bsip/GI; CNRI/Science Photo Library/GI; Dennis Kunkel Microscopy/SPL (x2); SPL; John Scott/GI; Cynoclub/GI; Geoff Jones; Momo Productions/GI; Fotosearch/GI; George Pachantouris/GI; Images from BarbAnna/GI; John Lund/GI; Scott Tilley/GI; Ian_Redding/GI; Seppfriedhuber/GI; Universal History Archive/UIG/GI; Cavan Images/GI; Martin Fletcher/GI; **Unit 8** Thomas Koehler/Photothek/GI; Hudiemm/GI; Mikroman6/GI; Portishead1/GI; SPL; Martyn F.Chillmaid/SPL; Arthur Dries/GI; Martyn F.Chillmaid/SPL; Sciencephotos/Alamy Stock Photo; Klaus Vedfelt/GI; Brandy Arivett/GI; Karl Gaff/SPL; SPL; Alenaohneva/